T0212896

Lecture Notes in Computer Science 14066

Founding Editors

Gerhard Goos
Juris Hartmanis

The series Lecture Notes in Computer Science (LNCS), including its subseries Lecture Notes in Artificial Intelligence (LNAI) and Lecture Notes in Bioinformatics (LNBI), has established itself as a medium for the publication of new developments in computer science and information technology research, teaching, and education.

LNCS enjoys close cooperation with the computer science R & D community, the series counts many renowned academics among its volume editors and paper authors, and collaborates with prestigious societies. Its mission is to serve this international community by providing an invaluable service, mainly focused on the publication of conference and workshop proceedings and postproceedings. LNCS commenced publication in 1973.

Virgile Prevosto · Cristina Seceleanu
Editors

Tests and Proofs

17th International Conference, TAP 2023
Leicester, UK, July 18–19, 2023
Proceedings

 Springer

Editors
Virgile Prevosto ⓘ
Université Paris-Saclay, CEA, Institut List,
DILS/LSL
Gif-sur-Yvette Cedex, France

Cristina Seceleanu ⓘ
Mälardalen University
Västerås, Sweden

ISSN 0302-9743   ISSN 1611-3349 (electronic)
Lecture Notes in Computer Science
ISBN 978-3-031-38827-9   ISBN 978-3-031-38828-6 (eBook)
https://doi.org/10.1007/978-3-031-38828-6

Preface

It is a pleasure for us to introduce the articles that have been presented at the 17th International Conference on Tests and Proofs (TAP). TAP 2023 took place in Leicester (UK), in July 2023, as part of STAF 2023, a federation of conferences on Software Technologies, Applications and Foundations, which included two more conferences besides TAP: ICGT (International Conference on Graph Transformation), and ECMFA (European Conference on Modelling Foundations and Applications).

TAP 2023 featured two invited talks. One was given by Kim G. Larsen, Ålborg University, Denmark, on symbolic, statistical and randomized verification algorithms in UPPAAL, and was shared with STAF. The other one was given by Mattias Ulbrich, Karlsruhe Institute of Technology, Germany, on the KeY verification platform. This volume includes 10 papers that were presented in the research track, out of which 8 were regular papers and 2 were short papers reporting on more experimental results, and 2 extended abstracts of the invited talks. In total TAP 2023 had 15 submissions, including 1 submitted abstract that was withdrawn before a full submission was made. Each submission was reviewed by at least three persons. 9 papers were readily accepted at the end of the reviewing phase, and 1 paper was conditionally accepted and subsequently successfully shepherded towards full acceptance. Out of the 10 accepted papers, 8 are regular research papers of 16 pages, 1 is a tool paper of 8 pages, and 1 is a short paper of 6 pages. All papers were reviewed following a single-blind review process conducted by TAP's 2023 Program Committee and external sub-reviewers.

We thank all the authors for their work and their interest in TAP 2023, as well as the PC members and sub-reviewers for their very thorough reviews and insightful remarks that have greatly helped to improve the quality of the papers that are presented in this volume. We also extend our thanks to the STAF steering committee for all their support in preparing the conference, as well as to the local organizers at University of Leicester.

July 2023

Virgile Prevosto
Cristina Seceleanu

Organization

STAF General Chair

Reiko Heckel   University of Leicester, UK

Program Committee Chairs

Virgile Prevosto	Université Paris Saclay, CEA-List, France
Cristina Seceleanu	Mälardalen University, Sweden

Steering Committee

Bernhardt K. Aichernig	TU Graz, Austria
Jasmin Blanchette	Vrije Universiteit Amsterdam, The Netherlands
Achim D. Brucker	University of Sheffield, UK
Catherine Dubois (Chair)	ENSIIE, France
Martin Gogolla	University of Bremen, Germany
Nikolai Kosmatov	Thales, France
Burkhart Wolff	Université Paris-Saclay, France

Program Committee

Peter Backeman	Mälardalen University, Sweden
Einar Broch Johnsen	University of Oslo, Norway
Eduard Paul Enoiu	Mälardalen University, Sweden
Carlo A. Furia	Università della Svizzera italiana, Switzerland
Dilian Gurov	KTH Royal Institute of Technology, Sweden
Falk Howar	TU Dortmund University, Germany
Marieke Huisman	University of Twente, The Netherlands
Reiner Hähnle	Technical University of Darmstadt, Germany
Joost-Pieter Katoen	RWTH Aachen University, Germany
Konstantin Korovin	University of Manchester, UK
Laura Kovacs	Vienna University of Technology, Austria
Florian Lorber	Aalborg University, Denmark
Brian Nielsen	Aalborg University, Denmark

Jakob Nordström	University of Copenhagen, Denmark and Lund University, Sweden
Patrizio Pelliccione	Gran Sasso Science Institute, Italy
Luigia Petre	Åbo Akademi University, Finland
Sahar Tahvili	Ericsson AB, Sweden
Neil Walkinshaw	University of Sheffield, UK
Heike Wehrheim	University of Oldenburg, Germany

Additional Reviewers

Jesper Amilon
Richard Bubel
Jan Haltermann
Christian Lidström
Fedor Shmarov

Invited Talks

Symbolic, Statistical and Randomized Engines in UPPAAL

Kim Guldstrand Larsen

Department of Computer Science, Aalborg University, Denmark

1 Introduction

The modelling formalism underlying UPPAAL (www.uppaal.org) [1] is that of timed automata [25], with the tool providing support for model checking of hard real-time properties. Since the introduction of the tool in 1995, significant effort has been put into development and implementation of efficient datastructures and algorithmic methods for the analysis of timed automata. By now these methods have resulted in symbolic, statistical and randomized engines as will be indicated in the rest of this abstract.

Besides development of the verification engine, significant effort has over the years been put on the graphical interface of the tool (e.g. [4]), and on the modelling side the introduction of user-defined, structured datatypes and procedures has undoubtedly made the tool significantly more usable.

2 UPPAAL Branches

Since the introduction of UPPAAL in 1995 a number of branches has emerged extending and redirecting the original modeling formalism and symbolic verification engine in different directions:

UPPAAL CORA was introduced in 2001. Motivated by the need for addressing (optimal) usage of resource, the extension of priced timed automata was introduced [5] (independently) demonstrating decidability of cost-optimal reachability. Soon after efficient priced extension of the symbolic zone datastructures was implemented in the branch Uppaal Cora, which combined with a symbolic A* algorithm providing a new generic tool for cost-optimal planning competetive to traditional OR methods such as Mixed-Integer Linear Programming [22].

UPPAAL TIGA released in 2005, allows for control strategies to be synthesized from timed games, i.e. two-player games played on a timed automata [3, 8]. The branch implements an efficient symbolic on-the-fly algorithm for synthesizing winning strategies for reachability, safety as well as Büchi objectives and taking possible partial observability into account [9].

UPPAAL Ecdar was introduced in 2010 in order to support a scalable methodology for compositional development and stepwise refinenemet of real-time systems [14, 15]. The Uppaal Ecdar branch uses heavily the Uppaal Tiga engine to solve various games that arise in the computing the various composition operators and refinements.

UPPAAL SMC introduced in 2011 allows for performance evaluation of the much richer formalism of stochastic hybrid automata [12, 13] and has been widely applied to analysis of a variety of case studies ranging from biological examples, COVID-19, schedulability for mixed-critical systems, evaluation of controllers for energy-aware buildings as well as performance evaluation of a variety of wireless communication protocols.

UPPAAL Stratego from 2014 [10, 11] is the most recent branch of the Uppaal tool suite that combines symbolic synthesis with reinforcement learning to construct safe and near-optimal strategies for Timed and Hybrid Markov Decision Processes (TMDP, HMDP). The engine of the branch combines the symbolic methods from the UPPAAL TIGA branch with the statistical method from UPPAAL SMC (for reinforcement learning). The branch has by now been succesfully applied to a number of industrial cases convering floor heating, heat-pumps, trafic lights, storm detention ponds, and swarms of robots.

3 Symbolic, Statistical and Randomized Engines

The algorithm methods used in branches of UPPAAL span *symbolic* and *statistical* engines. Most recently complementing *randomized* methods have been developed and integrated into the engines of the various branches of UPPAAL as part of the PhD thesis by Andrej Kiviriga [19]. The three types of engines may be characterized as follows:

Symbolic engines are complete and exhaustive and is the basis for proving that safety properties hold of a given timed automata, or that a there exist a truly winning strategin in a given timed game. Datastructures (e.g. DBM [23], CDDs [6]) for symbolic representation of state-spaces that is ameneable to efficient manipulations during exploration of the given timed automata model. Still there is the problem of state-space explosion.

Statisical engines equip the TA formalism with a stochastic semantics refining the non-deterministic delays and discrete transitions – often in accordance with known or observed frequencies of a the modelled system. This allows probabilities of properties to be estimated with confidence intervals using a number of random concrete simulations. Now the challenges become how to limit the number of concrete runs needed to make an estimation with a certain confidence (e.g.techniques such as importance sampling [16] and splitting [24]) and how to efficiently generate single runs (e.g. dependency analysis of components of the network model).

Randomized engines are quite similar to statistical ones in that they are based on randomly generated concrete runs of the model. However, in contrast to SMC where the stochastic semantics of the model underlies the random generation, in randomized model checking the exploration algorithm itself is subject to randomization and may favor edge-cases in order to increase the likelyhood of revealing (possibly low-probability) erronoeous behaviours. Also, in contrast to the statiscal engine – which is required to generate several random runs of the given stochastic model in order to estimate the probability of a given property – generation of random runs of the randomized engine may stop once a failing run has been found.

Now symbolic, statistical and randomized methods has been combined in different ways in the different branches of UPPAAL including the following:

– Randomized methods has proven an efficient method for detection of safety violations of TA [21] or to falsify refinements between TAs [18]. Due to the simple explicit-state nature of the method, it excels at quick falsification of models (or refinements) and can greatly improve the efficiency of a model-based development process: using lightweight randomized methods early in the development for the discovery of bugs, followed by expensive symbolic verification only at the very end.
– PTA allow for generic modelling of resource-consumption problems for systems with real-time constraints. Optimal schedules for allocation of resources may here be recast as optimal reachability problems. Explicit-state randomization of PTA has been used as the basis for adapting Monte Carlo Tree Search to PTA optimal reachability proboems improving significantly the performance of existing symbolic optimal reachability engines for PTAs [17].
– Falsification testing is a popular method for efficiently identifying inputs that witness the violation of a given specifications. The generated counterexamples are used to locate and explain faults and debug the system. However, in a given environment not all counterexamples have the same value. On one hand, faults resulting from common system usage are more likely to happen in practice than faults triggered by esoteric inputs. On the other hand, some faults can have more severe consequences than others. Together, the probability and the severity of a fault determine its impact, an important aspect that is neglected by the existing falsification testing techniques. We have proposed a new falsification testing methodology [20] that is aware of the system's expected usage and the underlying risks associated to different faulty behaviors. Given a user profile in the form of a STA, an associated risk model, an executable black-box implementation of the system and its formalized requirements, we provide a test generation method that (1) uses efficient randomized methods to generate multiple violating traces, and (2) estimates the probability and the severity using statistical methods, and hence the impact of each counterexample, thus providing their ranking to the engineer.
– UPPAAL Stratego combines symbolic and statistical (learning) methods for constructing safe and near-optimal control synthesis for Timed and Hybrid Markov Decision Processes. One way of obtaining safety of the learned controller is to use a shield (before or after the learning), which is correct by design. However, obtaining a shield for hybrid environments is itself intractable. We propose the construction of a shield using the so-called barbaric method, where an approximate finite representation of an underlying partition-based two-player safety game is extracted via randomly picked samples of the true transition function [7]. While hard safety guarantees are out of reach, strong statistical safety guarantees may be experimentally demonstrated.

4 Input and Output to UPPAAL

Whereas the undertlying algorithms of the various branches of UPPAAL are absolutely vital, we believe that another key to the success of the tool has been the significant effort that has been put into the GUI of the tool over the years. Currently effort is being made towards a hierarchical modelling formalism, where first prototypes are being obtained using model transformations to the existing non-hierarchical formalism. Here a main challenge is how to translate e.g. counter-examples found in the in the transform model back to the hierarchical model.

Some of the results provided by UPPAAL are significantly more complex than mere yes/no answers and the way they are communicated to the user requires great care:

- Counter examples are crucial feedback from a (failing) model checking query. Chellenges that has been address is how to provide short and concrete counter examples – even for failing liveness properties.
- The result of statistical queries are often best illustrated using distributions over properties of state-spaces. A challenge is how to best use the graphical interface for communicating this to the user.
- The result of synthesis or learning queries are strategies, i.e. essentially maps from the state-space of a (game of decision) model to one (or more) controllable actions. For symbolic synthesis these strategies are represented symbolically using BDDs/CDDs whereas strategies obtained from reinforcement learning are reprsented as decision trees. In both case it is in several case crucial that the control strategy is understandable to the domain engineer. A ongoing challenge is thus how to reduce the graphical representatons of strategies with out loosing safety and (to much) optimality [2].

References

1. Alur, R., Dill, D.: Automata for modeling real-time systems. In: Paterson, M.S. (eds.) ICALP 1990. LNCS, vol. 443, pp. 322–335. Springer, Heidelberg (1990). https://doi.org/10.1007/BFb0032042
2. Ashok, P., Křetínský, J., Larsen, K.G., Le Coënt, A., Taankvist, J.H., Weininger, M.: SOS: safe, optimal and small strategies for hybrid Markov decision processes. In: Parker, D., Wolf, V. (eds.) QEST 2019. LNCS, vol. 11785, pp. 147–164. Springer, Cham (2019). https://doi.org/10.1007/978-3-030-30281-8_9
3. Behrmann, G., Cougnard, A., David, A., Fleury, E., Larsen, K.G., Lime, D.: UPPAAL-Tiga: time for playing games! In: Damm, W., Hermanns, H. (eds.) CAV 2007. LNCS, vol. 4590, pp. 121–125. Springer, Heidelberg (2007). https://doi.org/10.1007/978-3-540-73368-3_14
4. Behrmann, G., David, A., Larsen, K.G., Pettersson, P., Yi, W.: Developing UPPAAL over 15 years. Softw. Pract. Exp. **41**(2), 133–142 (2011). https://doi.org/10.1002/spe.1006
5. Behrmann, G., et al.: Minimum-cost reachability for priced time automata. In: Di Benedetto, M.D., Sangiovanni-Vincentelli, A. (eds.) HSCC 2001. LNCS, vol. 2034, pp. 147–161. Springer, Heidelberg (2001). https://doi.org/10.1007/3-540-45351-2_15

6. Behrmann, G., Larsen, K.G., Pearson, J., Weise, C., Yi, W.: Efficient timed reachability analysis using clock difference diagrams. In: Halbwachs, N., Peled, D. (eds.) CAV 1999. LNCS, vol 1633, pp. 341–353. Springer, Heidelberg (1999). https://doi.org/10.1007/3-540-48683-6_30

7. Brorholt, A.H., Jensen, P.G., Larsen, K.G., Lorber, F., Schilling, C.: Shielded reinforcement learning for hybrid systems (2023)

8. Cassez, F., David, A., Fleury, E., Larsen, K.G., Lime, D.: Efficient on-the-fly algorithms for the analysis of timed games. In: Abadi, M., de Alfaro, L. (eds.) CONCUR 2005. LNCS, vol. 3653, pp. 66–80 (2005). Springer, Heidelberg. https://doi.org/10.1007/11539452_9

9. Cassez, F., David, A., Larsen, K.G., Lime, D., Raskin, J.F.: Timed control with observation based and stuttering invariant strategies. In: Namjoshi, K.S., Yoneda, T., Higashino, T., Okamura, Y. (eds.) ATVA 2007. LNCS, vol. 4762, pp. 192–206. Springer, Heidelberg (2007). https://doi.org/10.1007/978-3-540-75596-8_15

10. David, A., et al.: On time with minimal expected cost! In: Cassez, F., Raskin, J.F. (eds.) ATVA 2014. LNCS, vol. 8837, pp. 129–145. Springer, Cham (2014). https://doi.org/10.1007/978-3-319-11936-6_10

11. David, A., Jensen, P.G., Larsen, K.G., Mikučionis, M., Taankvist, J.H.: UPPAAL STRATEGO. In: Baier, C., Tinelli, C. (eds.) TACAS 2015. LNCS, vol. 9035, pp. 206–211. Springer, Heidelberg (2015). https://doi.org/10.1007/978-3-662-46681-0_16

12. David, A., Larsen, K.G., Legay, A., Mikucionis, M., Poulsen, D.B.: Uppaal SMC tutorial. STTT 17(4), 397–415 (2015). https://doi.org/10.1007/s10009-014-0361-y

13. David, A., Larsen, K.G., Legay, A., Mikučionis, M., Wang, Z.: Time for statistical model checking of real-time systems. In: Gopalakrishnan, G., Qadeer, S. (eds.) CAV 2011. LNCS, vol. 6806, pp. 349–355. Springer, Heidelberg (2011). https://doi.org/10.1007/978-3-642-22110-1_27

14. David, A., Larsen, K.G., Legay, A., Nyman, U., Wasowski, A.: Timed I/O automata: a complete specification theory for real-time systems. In: Johansson, K.H., Yi, W. (eds.) Proceedings of the 13th ACM International Conference on Hybrid Systems: Computation and Control, HSCC 2010, Stockholm, Sweden, 12–15 April 2010, pp. 91–100. ACM (2010). https://doi.org/10.1145/1755952.1755967

15. David, A., Larsen, K.G., Legay, A., Nyman, U., Wąsowski, A.: ECDAR: an environment for compositional design and analysis of real time systems. In: Bouajjani, A., Chin, WN. (eds.) ATVA 2010. LNCS, vol. 6252, pp. 365–370 (2010). Springer, Heidelberg. https://doi.org/10.1007/978-3-642-15643-4_29

16. Jegourel, C., Larsen, K.G., Legay, A., Mikučionis, M., Poulsen, D.B., Sedwards, S.: Importance sampling for stochastic timed automata. In: Fränzle, M., Kapur, D., Zhan, N. (eds.) SETTA 2016. LNCS, vol. 9984, pp. 163–178. Springer, Cham (2016). https://doi.org/10.1007/978-3-319-47677-3_11

17. Jensen, P.G., Kiviriga, A., Guldstrand Larsen, K., Nyman, U., Mijačika, A., Høiriis Mortensen, J.: Monte Carlo Tree search for priced timed automata. In: Ábrahám, E., Paolieri, M. (eds.) QEST 2022. LNCS, vol. 13479, pp. 381–398. Springer, Cham (2022). https://doi.org/10.1007/978-3-031-16336-4_19

18. Kiviriga, A., Larsen, K.G., Nyman, U.: Randomized refinement checking of timed I/O automata. In: Pang, J., Zhang, L. (eds.) SETTA 2020. LNCS, vol. 12153, pp. 70–88. Springer, Cham. https://doi.org/10.1007/978-3-030-62822-2_5

19. Kiviriga, A.: Efficient Model Checking Techniques: The Power of Randomness. Ph.D. thesis, Aalborg University (2023)

20. Kiviriga, A., Larsen, K.G., Nickovic, D., Nyman, U.: Usage- and risk-aware falsification testing for cyber-physical systems (2023)

21. Kiviriga, A., Larsen, K.G., Nyman, U.: Randomized reachability analysis in UPPAAL: fast error detection in timed systems. Int. J. Softw. Tools Technol. Transf. **24**(6), 1025–1042 (2022). https://doi.org/10.1007/s10009-022-00681-z

22. Larsen, K., et al.: As cheap as possible: efficient cost-optimal reachability for priced timed automata. In: Berry, G., Comon, H., Finkel, A. (eds.) CAV 2001. LNCS, vol. 2102, pp. 493–505. Springer, Heidelberg (2001). https://doi.org/10.1007/3-540-44585-4_47

23. Larsen, K.G., Larsson, F., Pettersson, P., Yi, W.: Efficient verification of real-time systems: compact data structure and state-space reduction. In: Proceedings of the 18th IEEE Real-Time Systems Symposium (RTSS 1997), 3–5 December 1997, San Francisco, CA, USA, pp. 14–24. IEEE Computer Society (1997). https://doi.org/10.1109/REAL.1997.641265

24. Larsen, K.G., Legay, A., Mikučionis, M., Poulsen, D.B.: Importance splitting in UPPAAL. In: Margaria, T., Steffen, B. (eds.) ISoLA 2022. LNCS, vol. 13703, pp. 433–447. Springer, Cham (2022). https://doi.org/10.1007/978-3-031-19759-8_26

25. Larsen, K.G., Pettersson, P., Yi, W.: UPPAAL in a nutshell. Int. J. Softw. Tools Technol. Transf. **1**(1–2), 134–152 (1997). https://doi.org/10.1007/s100090050010

KeY: A Verification Platform for Java

Mattias Ulbrich

Karlsruhe Institute of Technology, Karlruhe, Germany

In recent years and decades, the research community has unleashed a diverse variety of approaches to formally assess and establish the correctness of programs at source code level. How to bring together the results of these different verification techniques profitably is still an active research area [10].

In this talk, I will present how the verification ecosystem surrounding the KeY tool [1] allows one to combine a number of successful approaches. At its core, KeY is a deductive verification engine for the formal analysis of Java programs annotated with formal specifications written in the Java Modeling Language JML [13]. It employs a dynamic logic calculus for Java driven by symbolic execution. We will learn about the working principles of this verification method and see how it was used to prove (or disprove) the correctness of relevant real-world Java components, for instance from the JDK [5, 6, 8, 9].

Deductive verification is a versatile and powerful tool to ensure the correctness of programs. However, it is also quite costly since the verifying person has to provide (potentially extensive) auxiliary specifications or user interaction that guide the prover machinery to successfully find a closed proof.

I am happy to present the *Karlsruhe Java Verification Suite (KaJaVe)* [11]: we enriched the KeY prover infrastructure by a number of approaches that leverage other verification principles such that they can be used in combination with the deductive verifier. In my talk, I will present the following players from KaJaVe:

Bounded Model Checking. The bounded model checker JJBMC [4] can be used to analyse JML annotated Java sources up to a predefined unwinding depth, thus turning the question of program correctness from an undecidable unbounded (possibly infinite) problem into a decidable question on finite data structures. This is particularly helpful for a number of scenarios: 1) If programs contain bounded loops, this may alleviate the need for loop specifications, in particular loop invariants; 2) bounded model checking may serve as a first formal analysis of a method that allows us to gain trust in our specifications before submitting them to the more costly deductive verification engine.

Property Type Systems. It is not easy to apply deductive verification on larger scales. While KeY verifies methods of a Java class individually (modularly), and thus, in theory, scales to arbitrary code sizes, the need for prover guidance makes it still difficult to fully verify larger code bases. Type systems, on the other hand, scale very well and easily allow one to cover tens of thousands of lines of code that can be checked within seconds. We have designed a type system that interacts with JML specifications and allows us to specify properties as types and to thus propagate them throughout the program without the need for a heavyweight specification engine [12]. The verification engine is still needed to verify that properties are established initially, but at fewer places, and it may in return also rely on the properties obtained from type annotations. This technique allows one to cover programs with formal guarantees that would otherwise not be accessible to formal treatment (like code for graphical user interfaces).

Quantitative Analysis. Sometimes, it may happen that a proof for a method cannot be closed. Usually this is a very bad moment for the person conducting the deductive verification: unlike in testing where every additional test case adds to the confidence one gains about the system under test, a deductive proof with a single open proof goal is as good as no proof at all. To improve this situation, we devised a technique that allows us to draw conclusions from unfinished proofs [3]. Since KeY relies on symbolic execution, open proof goals can be connected to paths through the program, which allows us to dynamically identify when an unproved situation is hit during runtime. By employing statistically chosen samples or monitoring at runtime, it is thus possible to predict statistically how often a method runs into an unproved execution. Finally, at a venue such as Tests and Proofs, it is worth mentioning KeY's capabilities to generate helpful test cases from failed proof attempts [2, 7].

When combining different verification techniques that make heterogeneous assumptions about the source code under test, there are a number of pitfalls to be aware of. We will discuss challenges with a common JML and Java syntax and semantics within KaJaVe and the benefits of a method-modular approach.

References

1. Ahrendt, W., Beckert, B., Bubel, R., Hähnle, R., Schmitt, P.H., Ulbrich, M. (eds.): Deductive Software Verification - The KeY Book: From Theory to Practice. LNCS, vol. 10001. Springer, Cham (2016). https://doi.org/10.1007/978-3-319-49812-6
2. Beckert, B., Gladisch, C., Tyszberowicz, S., Yehudai, A.: KeYGenU: combining verification-based and capture and replay techniques for regression unit testing. Int. J. Syst. Assur. Eng. Manage. **2**(2), 97–113 (2011). https://doi.org/10.1007/s13198-011-0068-3
3. Beckert, B., Herda, M., Kobischke, S., Ulbrich, M.: Towards a notion of coverage for incomplete program-correctness proofs. In: Margaria, T., Steffen, B. (eds.) ISoLA 2018. LNCS, vol. 11245, pp. 53–63. Springer, Cham (2018). https://doi.org/10.1007/978-3-030-03421-4_4
4. Beckert, B., Kirsten, M., Klamroth, J., Ulbrich, M.: Modular verification of JML contracts using bounded model checking. In: Margaria, T., Steffen, B. (eds.) ISoLA 2020. LNCS, vol. 12476, pp. 60–80. Springer, Cham (2020). https://doi.org/10.1007/978-3-030-61362-4_4
5. Beckert, B., Schiffl, J., Schmitt, P.H., Ulbrich, M.: Proving JDK's dual pivot quicksort correct. In: Paskevich, A., Wies, T. (eds.) VSTTE 2017. LNCS, vol. 10712, pp 35–48. Springer, Cham (2017). https://doi.org/10.1007/978-3-319-72308-2_3
6. Boer, M.D., Gouw, S.D., Klamroth, J., Jung, C., Ulbrich, M., Weigl, A.: Formal specification and verification of JDK's identity hash map implementation. In: ter Beek, M.H., Monahan, R. (eds.) IFM 2022. LNCS, vol. 13274, pp. 45–62. Springer, Cham (2022). https://doi.org/10.1007/978-3-031-07727-2_4

7. Engel, C., Hähnle, R.: Generating unit tests from formal proofs. In: Gurevich, Y., Meyer, B. (eds.) TAP 2007. LNCS, vol. 4454, pp 169–188. Springer, Heidelberg (2007). https://doi.org/10.1007/978-3-540-73770-4_10

8. de Gouw, S., Rot, J., de Boer, F.S., Bubel, R., Hähnle, R.: OpenJDK's Java.utils.Collection.sort() is broken: the good, the bad and the worst case. In: Kroening, D., Păsăreanu, C. (eds.) CAV 2015. LNCS, vol. 9206, pp. 273–289. Springer, Cham (2015). https://doi.org/10.1007/978-3-319-21690-4_16

9. Hiep, H.D.A., Maathuis, O., Bian, J., de Boer, F.S., van Eekelen, M., de Gouw, S.: Verifying OpenJDK's LinkedList using KeY. In: Biere, A., Parker, D. (eds.) TACAS 2020. LNCS, vol. 12079, pp. 217–234. Springer, Cham (2020). https://doi.org/10.1007/978-3-030-45237-7_13

10. Huisman, M., Monti, R., Ulbrich, M., Weigl, A.: The VerifyThis collaborative long term challenge. In: Ahrendt, W., Beckert, B., Bubel, R., Hähnle, R., Ulbrich, M. (eds.) Deductive Software verification: future perspectives. LNCS, vol. 12345, pp. 246–260. Springer, Cham (2020). https://doi.org/10.1007/978-3-030-64354-6_10

11. Klamroth, J., Lanzinger, F., Pfeifer, W., Ulbrich, M.: The Karlsruhe Java verification suite. In: Ahrendt, W., Beckert, B., Bubel, R., Johnsen, E.B. (eds.) The Logic of Software. A Tasting Menu of Formal Methods. LNCS, vol. 13360, pp. 290–312. Springer, Cham (2022). https://doi.org/10.1007/978-3-031-08166-8_14

12. Lanzinger, F., Weigl, A., Ulbrich, M., Dietl, W.: Scalability and precision by combining expressive type systems and deductive verification. Proc. ACM Program. Lang. **5**(OOPSLA) (2021). Article no: 143. https://doi.org/10.1145/3485520

13. Leavens, G.T., et al.: JML Reference Manual, May 2013. http://www.eecs.ucf.edu/leavens/JML//refman/jmlrefman.pdf, revision 2344

Contents

Low-Level Code Verification

BIRD: A Binary Intermediate Representation for Formally Verified
Decompilation of X86-64 Binaries 3
  Daniel Engel, Freek Verbeek, and Binoy Ravindran

Low-Level Reachability Analysis Based on Formal Logic 21
  Nico Naus, Freek Verbeek, Marc Schoolderman, and Binoy Ravindran

Testing a Formally Verified Compiler 40
  David Monniaux, Léo Gourdin, Sylvain Boulmé, and Olivier Lebeltel

Formal Models

Certified Logic-Based Explainable AI – The Case of Monotonic Classifiers 51
  Aurélie Hurault and Joao Marques-Silva

Context Specification Language for Formally Verifying Consent Properties
on Models and Code 68
  Myriam Clouet, Thibaud Antignac, Mathilde Arnaud, and Julien Signoles

Model-Based Test Generation

Proving Properties of Operation Contracts with Test Scenarios 97
  Martin Gogolla and Lars Hamann

Testing Languages with a Languages-as-Databases Approach 108
  Matteo Cimini

Symbolic Observation Graph-Based Generation of Test Paths 127
  *Kais Klai, Mohamed Taha Bennani, Jaime Arias, Jörg Desel,
  and Hanen Ochi*

Abstraction and Refinement

Slow Down, Move Over: A Case Study in Formal Verification, Refinement,
and Testing of the Responsibility-Sensitive Safety Model for Self-Driving
Cars 149
  Megan Strauss and Stefan Mitsch

Abstract Interpretation of Recursive Logic Definitions for Efficient
Runtime Assertion Checking 168
    Thibaut Benajmin and Julien Signoles

Author Index 187

Low-Level Code Verification

BIRD: A Binary Intermediate Representation for Formally Verified Decompilation of X86-64 Binaries

Daniel Engel[1]([✉]) [iD], Freek Verbeek[1,2] [iD], and Binoy Ravindran[2] [iD]

[1] Open University, 6419 AT Heerlen, The Netherlands
{daniel.engel,freek.verbeek}@ou.nl
[2] Virginia Tech, Blacksburg, VA 24061, USA

Abstract. We present *BIRD: A Binary Intermediate Representation for formally verified Decompilation of x86-64 binaries*. BIRD is a generic language capable of representing a binary program at various stages of decompilation. Decompilation can consist of various small translation passes, each raising the abstraction level from assembly to source code. Where most decompilation frameworks do not guarantee that their translations preserve the program's operational semantics or even provide any formal semantics, translation passes built on top of BIRD must prove their output to be bisimilar to their input. This work presents the mathematical machinery needed to define BIRD. Moreover, it provides two instantiations - one representing x86-64 assembly, and one where registers have been replaced by variables—as well as a formally proven correct translation pass between them. This translation serves both as a practical first step in trustworthy decompilation as well as a proof of concept that semantic preserving translations of low-level programs are feasible. The entire effort has been formalized in the Coq theorem prover. As such, it does not only provide a mathematical formalism but can also be exported as executable code to be used in a decompiler. We envision BIRD to be used to define provably correct binary-level analyses and program transformations.

Keywords: Formal Methods · Decompilation · Static Analysis

1 Introduction

Verification of software on the binary level has numerous advantages: the trusted code base (TCB) is reduced [13], and applicability is widened to software where source code is not available. The latter may occur in the context of legacy systems, third-party proprietary software, or software that was (partially) hand-written in assembly. However, binary-level verification is notoriously difficult: at this low level of abstraction, there are no variables, no structured control flow, no typing information, no a priori function boundaries, etc. Methods typically are either interactive or tailored towards specific low-level properties. Mostly,

V. Prevosto and C. Seceleanu (Eds.): TAP 2023, LNCS 14066, pp. 3–20, 2023.
https://doi.org/10.1007/978-3-031-38828-6_1

binary-level verification consists of static analysis tools that are based on heuristics, rather than based on a formal foundation.

Hypothetically, if one could decompile binaries to high-level code then a large body of research in formal methods at the source code level becomes directly applicable. This would require a formally proven *sound* decompiler: a decompiler whose output is shown to be semantically equivalent to the original binary. Even for the big players in this field [11,18,21,23], decompilation is considered to be more of an art form than an exact science. Typically, decompilers do not produce a semantically equivalent program and a human-in-the-loop is needed to interpret the decompiler's hints to do reverse engineering based on experience [4, 5,25].

We argue for the need for formally verified decompilation. Such an approach should consist of numerous small *translation steps* that each lift the program to a representation with a higher level of abstraction. Each such step should be accompanied by a mathematical proof of correctness that shows the step to be semantics-preserving.

In this paper, we present *BIRD*: a Binary Intermediate Representation for formally verified Decompilation. It serves as the data structure on which provably semantics-preserving translations on the level of assembly programs can be implemented. BIRD is a generic, optionally SSA-based language that can represent an x86-64 program at various stages of decompilation. The concept of *storage cells* abstracts over registers and their aliasing behavior, and variables that have strong non-aliasing semantics. *Annotations* can be used to augment storage cells with additional information that may be needed for them to operate correctly. An annotation can carry low-level information like the original bit-pattern or higher-level data like typing information. Lastly, *labels* can be multi-byte values as in the original binary or more abstract identifiers like in assembly dialects such as relocatable Netwide Assembler (NASM). Figure 1 (which is elaborated in Sect. 5) shows how BIRD can be used as an intermediate representation (IR) during decompilation. Each of the rectangular boxes contains a representation of the original binary; each of the arrows constitutes a translation step. BIRD is sufficiently generic to model all these representations. It requires – by construction – all translation steps to be semantics-preserving.

We then show two example instantiations for BIRD: 1. the original x86-64 assembly as found in the binary after disassembly (storage cells are registers, no annotations are needed), and 2. the *early BIRD* language in which registers are replaced by variables. In Fig. 1, the contributions of this paper are marked in bold. We aim to provide both an IR allowing translation steps in decompilation to be tackled in a formal and semantics-preserving fashion, as well as a practical first step toward formally proven correct decompilation.

All definitions are implemented in the Coq theorem prover [6]. With this formal approach, the TCB shrinks to our definitions of the semantics of assembly and the core of Coq itself. The Coq code[1] can be exported to Haskell, making the translation executable [17].

---

[1] Made available here: https://doi.org/10.5281/zenodo.7928215.

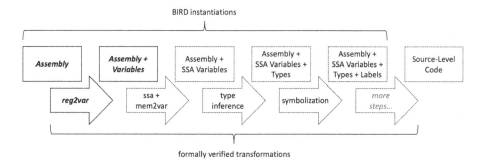

Fig. 1. Overview of an example micro-step decompiler using BIRD

2   Related Work

While not directly applicable to the tasks of decompilation, the Static Single Assignment (SSA) form [7] IRs used in modern compilers have served as inspiration for the design of BIRD. One of the most popular such IRs is the *LLVM IR* [14] which is used in real-world compilers such as *clang*. LLVM is implemented in C++ and does not focus on formally proven transformations, but work by Zakowski et al. formalizes an executable semantics for a subset of the IR in Coq [26]. The Multi-Level Intermediate Representation (MLIR) [15] aims to support different requirements in a unified framework. Similar to BIRD Instantiation, MLIR supports user-defined dialects. As such MLIR is very extensible, but giving formal semantics to it is difficult. The *CompCert* project [16] investigates compilation of C code in a formally proven correct way. Our work mirrors their graph structure for SSA RTL [1] in that the nodes are instructions that are annotated by phi-nodes.

In the field of decompilation, most work focuses on retrieving an approximation of a high-level program that may produce the input binary. *Ghidra* [18] is a large scale reverse engineering suite developed by NSA's Research Directorate. It offers support for a wide variety of assembly dialects which it translates into high P-Code and then into C. Recent work by Naus et al. [19] provides formal semantics for an augmented version of P-Code and shows that the current version cannot be given an executable semantics. Ghidra is fundamentally unable to produce an output of which it can be formally proven that it preserves the semantics of the input program. The *Binary Analysis Platform* (BAP) [2] aims to decompile binaries in order to analyze them. Similar to our work, it transforms assembly code into an intermediate language on which state-of-the-art program analyses can be executed. Currently, x86, ARM, MIPS and PowerPC are supported by BAP. As noted by the authors, the lifting process cannot be proven correct as "the semantics of the x86 ISA is not formally defined". Instead, the authors aim to catch bugs through randomized testing. The Interactive Disassembler (IDA) [11] is a disassembler for a large variety of executable formats, including MS-DOS, EXE, ELF, etc. It lifts these binaries into assembly-level programs, but with additional plugins, C code can be generated [9]. No formal argument is given on why this C code represents the same program as the original binary. *Binary Ninja* [23] is another reverse-engineering platform which lifts a range of assembly dialects into several internal IR to analyze them and produce decompiled code. Similarly to the other large decompilation tools, no formal semantics are defined for these languages and as such, no soundness can be proven.

Recent work in the field aims at guaranteeing that the decompiled output is recompilable and semantically equivalent to the input. Schulte et al. [22] use an evolutionary search through a large database of "big code" to arrive at a high-level program. This output can then be recompiled to measure how many bytes are equivalent with the input. The authors report that on a test bed of 19 programs, 10 could be decompiled by this technique to full byte equivalence, the remaining programs matched to $> 80\%$. *Phoenix* [3] uses a more conventional approach based on semantics preserving structural analysis to arrive at an output whose control flow graph (CFG) is provably equivalent to the input's CFG. However, no formal criteria are defined on what constitutes a "semantics preserving" analysis, nor are there formal arguments on why their transformations are correct.

Dasgupta et al. [8] provide formal semantics for more than 774 different x86 instructions. It is implemented in the $\mathbb{K}$ framework to define a correct-by-construction deductive verifier. As such, it can be used to analyze assembly programs directly and perform provable correct transformations on these programs. It cannot represent a higher-level language than x86, thus transformations that lift the abstraction (such as variable recovery) are not possible within this framework. Kennedy et al. [12] provide formal semantics for a subset of x86 in the Coq theorem prover. They define macros to write higher-level assembly-like code directly inside Coq and assemble it into bytes. Parts of this translation are proven to be correct. This formalization also focuses on having x86 as the highest level language and thus cannot support higher abstractions. However, due to being formalized within Coq, its value types serve as a practical foundation on which BIRD is built.

3   Formalization

All the mathematical structures presented in this section are implemented in the Coq theorem prover. For the sake of simplicity, we will not distinguish between the different universes of Coq's type theory and use $\mathbb{T}$ to mean a type of any level and $\mathbb{P}$ to mean the type of propositions. Relations of type $R : T_1 \to \ldots \to T_n \to \mathbb{P}$ use the set-theoretical notation $R \subseteq T_1 \times \ldots \times T_n$. We make use of Coq's standard library and write $\mathbb{B}$ for booleans, $\mathbb{N}$ for natural numbers, $\mathbb{L}(T)$ for lists of T and $\mathbb{O}(T)$ for optionals of T. The `Some` constructor of optionals is left implicit and $\emptyset$ is the empty element of monoids like lists and optionals. We also use the *bits* library [12] which defines the primitive type for `bytes` (8 tuple of $\mathbb{B}$) together with its operations. We do not use *bits'* bigger types (16,

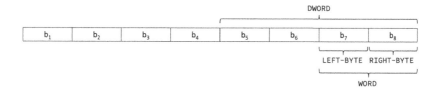

Fig. 2. Word parts of a full QWORD

32, 64 tuple of $\mathbb{B}$) as they are inconvenient for byte-granular operations. Instead, we define $\mathbb{V}_n$ as n tuples of **bytes**. The type $\mathbb{S} :=$ BYTE | WORD | DWORD | QWORD contains the valid sizes for values (1, 2, 4, 8 bytes respectively). Word parts $\mathbb{WP} :=$ QWORD | DWORD | WORD | RIGHT-BYTE | LEFT-BYTE correspond to the parts on which a register can be accessed (Figure 2 visualizes these access patterns).

3.1 Generic BIRD

All definitions for the generic IR *BIRD* are polymorphic in the types

- *Storage cells* ($\mathcal{C}$) which serve as the primitive objects into which values can be written. They are themselves writable and they form the basis for addresses.
- *Cell annotations* ($\mathcal{A}$) which express additional information for the cells such as read/write patterns or data types.
- *Labels* ($\mathcal{L}$) which are the locations at which data and instructions can be found. We require labels to be isomorphic to $\mathbb{V}_8$ so that their values can be stored in memory and pointer arithmetic can be performed.

Additionally, the semantics requires functions over storage cells and their state (Γ, to be defined later) to be provided to describe how they are accessed.

- A function of type $PartFunc := (\mathcal{C} \times \mathcal{A}) \to \mathbb{WP}$ to assign each annotated cell a word part to describe how they are narrowed and widened by reads and writes.
- A function of type $ReadFunc := \Gamma \to \mathcal{C} \to \mathbb{V}_8$ to describe how a raw cell is read from its state.
- A function of type $WriteFunc := \Gamma \to \mathcal{C} \to \mathbb{V}_8 \to \Gamma$ to describe how a raw cell is written into its state.

Definition 1 (BIRD). *A binary intermediate representation for decompilation (BIRD) is a tuple of these generic elements.*

$$bird := \langle \mathcal{C} : \mathbb{T}, \mathcal{A} : \mathbb{T}, \mathcal{L} : \mathbb{T}, p : PartFunc, r : ReadFunc, w : WriteFunc \rangle$$

For all of the following elements, we define shorthand instantiations. For example, given a BIRD $ir = \langle \mathcal{C}, \mathcal{A}, \mathcal{L}, p, r, w \rangle$, the type of programs in ir is defined $Prog(ir) := Prog(\mathcal{C}, \mathcal{A}, \mathcal{L})$.

Syntax. BIRD programs are organized in overapproximating CFGs over instructions. The edges represent possible transitions from one instruction to another. The nodes in the graph are generic labels. Each label is assigned an instruction and any number of phi-assignments.

Instructions ($Instr(ls)$) are dependently typed in their program's labels ls. We categorize instructions into plain operations (OP), stack operations (PUSH, POP), and control flow operations (JMP, CALL, RET). Plain operations contain an opcode (Op), a number of sources ($\vec{Src}$) to read from, a number of destinations ($\vec{Dst}$) to write to, and optionally a successor label ($\in ls$). The successor label points to the next instruction to be executed, if no successor label is given, the instruction terminates the program. The stack operations contain the source to be pushed onto the stack or the destination into which the stack top is popped. They also contain a pair of cells to read the current and write the updated stack pointer value. The jump instruction contains a condition ($Cond$) deciding whether to jump to one of the true labels ($ls_\top$) or to the false label ($l_\perp$, the next instruction in the assembly), and a source from which the jump target is read. Similar to the jump, the call contains a return label (l_r) which is pushed on the stack and a number of possible callee labels (ls_c) and a source from which the call target is read. Like the stack instructions, both the call and the return contain a pair of cells to update the stack pointer. The return contains a list of possible return labels (ls_r). A phi-instruction (Φ) consists of exactly one destination *cell* to which it writes and any number of *sources* from which one is read.

Sources (Src) are either an immediate qword value, a cell from which some bytes are read, an expression over cells for which the value is computed, an address from which some bytes are read from memory or the current value of the instruction pointer. Destination (Dst) are only cells or addresses. Expressions ($Expr$) are formed over cells, qword offsets, cell scalings ($\in \{1, 2, 4, 8\}$) and arithmetic operations thereof. All elements of an expression are optional and can be left empty. Addresses ($Addr$) are expressions together with a size describing the number of bytes to be read. Absolute addresses ($AbsAddr$) are labels and as such are isomorphic to qwords.

A dependently typed mapping from all labels of a program to their instructions is called code ($Code_{Instr}$), the dependent mapping to the phi instructions is called phi-code ($Code_\Phi$). The type of nodes ($Node(p)$) describes all labels that are in a program p and similar to (phi-)codes, it is indexed by the labels. A program ($Prog$) is a tuple of labels and the (phi-)code for the (phi-)instructions of these labels, and an entry label at which program execution starts. Figure 3 summarizes this syntax.

Notably, programs are not organized in functions to form a call graph, they only contain instructions to form a control flow graph. At this level of representation, function boundaries have not yet been established and a RET is not guaranteed to return to its caller. As a consequence, exploits such as return-oriented programming are expressable in this format.

Program	$Prog$	$::= \langle ls : \mathbb{L}(\mathcal{L}), entry \in ls,$
		$\quad Code_{\Phi}(ls), Code_{Instr}(ls)\rangle$
Node in program	$Node(p)$	$::= \langle l : \mathcal{L} \mid l \in p.ls\rangle$
Instruction	$Code_{Instr}(ls)$	$::= \langle l : \mathcal{L} \mid l \in ls\rangle \to Instr(ls)$
mapping	$Code_{\Phi}(ls)$	$::= \langle l : \mathcal{L} \mid l \in ls\rangle \to \Phi$
Instructions	$Instr(ls)$	$::= \mid \mathtt{OP}\langle Op, \vec{Src}, \vec{Dst}, l \in ls \cup \{\emptyset\}\rangle$ — plain ops
		$\mid \mathtt{PUSH}\langle Src, \langle \mathcal{C}, \mathcal{C}\rangle, l \in ls\rangle$ — stack ops
		$\mid \mathtt{POP}\langle Dst, \langle \mathcal{C}, \mathcal{C}\rangle, l \in ls\rangle$
		$\mid \mathtt{JMP}\langle Cond, Src, l_{\perp} \in ls, ls_{\top} \subseteq ls\rangle$ — cf ops
		$\mid \mathtt{CALL}\langle Src, \langle \mathcal{C}, \mathcal{C}\rangle, l_r \in ls, ls_c \subseteq ls\rangle$
		$\mid \mathtt{RET}\langle \langle \mathcal{C}, \mathcal{C}\rangle, ls_r \subseteq ls\rangle$
Operation	Op	$::= \mathtt{MOV} \mid \mathtt{ADD} \mid \mathtt{CMP} \mid \ldots \mid \mathtt{XCHG}$
codes	$Cond$	$::= \mathtt{JMP} \mid \mathtt{JZ} \mid \mathtt{JNZ} \mid \ldots \mid \mathtt{JC}$
Phi node	Φ	$::= \mathbb{L}(Dst \text{ '='} \mathbb{L}(Src))$
Operands	Src	$::= Addr \mid \mathcal{C} \times \mathcal{A} \mid Expr \mid \mathbb{V}_8 \mid \mathtt{rip} \pm \mathbb{V}_8$
	Dst	$::= Addr \mid \mathcal{C} \times \mathcal{A}$
Addresses	$Addr$	$::= \mathbb{S} \text{ '- PTR'} \text{ '['} Expr \text{ ']'}$
	$Expr$	$::= \mathcal{C} \pm (1|2|4|8) * \mathcal{C} \pm AbsAddr$

Fig. 3. Syntax definitions for the generic BIRD language. Everything is polymorphic in $\mathcal{C}$, $\mathcal{A}$ and $\mathcal{L}$.

Semantics. Figure 4 describes the formal semantics of BIRD. Before these can be explained, we first introduce the constituents used to define these semantics: *reading*, *writing* and *denotations*. Reading and writing from the state requires evaluation of the expressions used in operands of instructions, and up-/downcasting of values. We thus first define these.

Definition 2 (Up-Downcast). *A qword* $q : \mathbb{V}_8$ *can be downcasted to any* $\mathbb{V}_n$ *with a word part* p *by extracting the correct bytes (notation* $\Downarrow_p b$*). For example,* $\Downarrow_{\text{LEFT-BYTE}} \langle b_1, \ldots, b_8\rangle = b_7$. *Symmetrically, the upcasting operator (notation* $\Uparrow_p b$*) transforms a* $\mathbb{V}_n$ *to a* $\mathbb{V}_8$ *by filling all other bytes with 0. For example,* $\Uparrow_{\text{WORD}} \langle b_1, b_2\rangle = \langle 0, 0, 0, 0, 0, 0, b_1, b_2\rangle$.

Definition 3 (Update). *Given a word part* $p : \mathbb{WP}$, *an old value* $o : \mathbb{V}_8$ *and a new value* $n : \mathbb{V}_8$, *the update (notation* $o \otimes_p n$*) computes an updated* $\mathbb{V}_8$ *value. Intuitively, this corresponds to the writing behavior of x86 registers.*

$$\langle o_1, \ldots, o_8\rangle \otimes_{\text{LEFT-BYTE}} \langle n_1, \ldots, n_8\rangle := \langle o_1, o_2, o_3, o_4, o_5, o_6, n_7, o_8\rangle$$
$$\langle o_1, \ldots, o_8\rangle \otimes_{\text{RIGHT-BYTE}} \langle n_1, \ldots, n_8\rangle := \langle o_1, o_2, o_3, o_4, o_5, o_6, o_7, n_8\rangle$$
$$\langle o_1, \ldots, o_8\rangle \otimes_{\text{WORD}} \langle n_1, \ldots, n_8\rangle := \langle o_1, o_2, o_3, o_4, n_5, n_6, n_7, n_8\rangle$$
$$\langle o_1, \ldots, o_8\rangle \otimes_{\text{DWORD}} \langle n_1, \ldots, n_8\rangle := \langle 0, 0, 0, 0, n_5, n_6, n_7, n_8\rangle$$
$$\langle o_1, \ldots, o_8\rangle \otimes_{\text{QWORD}} \langle n_1, \ldots, n_8\rangle := \langle n_1, n_2, n_3, n_4, n_5, n_6, n_7, n_8\rangle$$

Definition 4 (Denotation). *The denotation for the operators* Op *is given by a* computation *for the actual value (or multiple computations for instruction like* $\mathtt{XCHG}$*), and an* effect *for the change to the flags. Given an* $op : Op$, *the denotation (notation* $[\![op]\!]$*) returns these two functions. For example, the computation of* the **add** instruction computes the sum of both values, ignoring the carry flag. The side effect writes the carry bit into **CF** and populates **ZF**.

$$[\![\ ADD\ ]\!] \ :=\ \langle\ \lambda v_1, v_2 \quad \mapsto v_1 + v_2, \qquad\qquad \textit{— computation}$$
$$\lambda v_1, v_2, \sigma \mapsto let\ \langle sum, carry \rangle := v_1 + v_2 \qquad \textit{— side effect}$$
$$in\ \sigma[CF \leftarrow carry][ZF \leftarrow sum = 0]\ \rangle$$

For a condition $c : Cond$, the denotation returns a predicate. For example, the predicate for **JMP** is always true, the one for **JZ** returns the **ZF**.

$$[\![\ JMP\ ]\!] := \lambda\sigma \mapsto true \qquad\qquad [\![\ JZ\ ]\!] := \lambda\sigma \mapsto \sigma[ZF]$$

Definition 5 (State). *The semantics of BIRD programs is given over states* (Σ). *States consist of a state for cells* (Γ), *a state for the memory* (Θ), *a state for flags* (Ξ) *and the label of the next instruction to be executed* $(\boldsymbol{rip})$. *The cell-state maps each cell to a qword value where individual bytes can be extracted using the cell's word part, the memory-state maps each absolute address to one byte, bigger regions can be read and written to by multiple read and write applications, the flags-state maps the flags* (**ZF**, **OF**, ...) *to one bit.*

$$\Sigma := \langle \Gamma, \Theta, \Xi, \boldsymbol{rip} : \mathcal{L} \rangle \quad \Gamma := \mathcal{C} \to \mathbb{V}_8 \quad \Theta := AbsAddr \to \mathbb{V}_1 \quad \Xi := Flag \to \mathbb{B}$$

For a full state $\sigma = \langle \gamma, \theta, \xi, \boldsymbol{rip} \rangle : \Sigma$, reading takes a $s : Src$ and returns the correct $\mathbb{V}_n$ for the source by dispatching to a substate.

$$\sigma[s] := \begin{cases} v & \textit{if s is an immediate } v \\ e|_{\mathrm{read}(\gamma)} & \textit{if s is an expression } e \\ \langle b_0, \cdots, b_{s-1} \rangle & \textit{if s is an address } \langle s, e \rangle,\ b_i = \gamma(e|_{\mathrm{read}(\gamma)} + i) \\ \Downarrow_{\mathrm{part}(c,a)} (\mathrm{read}(\gamma, c)) & \textit{if s is an annotated cell } \langle c, a \rangle \\ \boldsymbol{rip} + d & \textit{if s is a rip relative } \boldsymbol{rip} + d \end{cases}$$

Writing is defined similarly, but cells are updated based on their old value

$$\sigma[d \leftarrow v] := \begin{cases} \langle \gamma, \theta', \xi, \boldsymbol{rip} \rangle & \textit{if s is an address } \langle s, e \rangle \\ & \textit{where } \theta' = \theta[e|_{\mathrm{read}(\gamma)+i} \mapsto v_i], i \in \{0, .., 7\} \\ \langle \gamma', \theta, \xi, \boldsymbol{rip} \rangle & \textit{if s is an annotated cell } \langle c, a \rangle \\ & \textit{where } \gamma' = \mathrm{write}(\gamma, c, v') \\ & \textit{and } v' = \sigma[\langle c, a \rangle] \otimes_{\mathrm{part}(c,a)} (\Uparrow_{\mathrm{part}(c,a)} v) \end{cases}$$

Here, the expression evaluation $(e|_f)$ takes an expression e and a cell evaluation function $f : \mathcal{C} \to \mathbb{V}_8$ to compute the value of e.

$$[b \pm s * i \pm d]|_f := f(b) \pm s \cdot f(i) \pm d$$

The semantics for executing nodes in a program is given by a small step relation $p \vdash \langle \sigma, k \rangle \Rightarrow \langle \sigma', k' \rangle \subseteq Prog \times Node(p) \times \Sigma \times \mathbb{O}(Node(p)) \times \Sigma$ which describes executing node k in state σ to arrive in state σ' where k' needs to be executed next. The execution of the phi instructions is given by the relation $p \vdash \sigma\ \Phi_k^{k'}\ \sigma' \subseteq$ $Prog \times \Sigma \times \Sigma \times Node(p) \times Node(p)$ which assigns the phi's nth source to its destination if k is the nth predecessor of k'. Figure 4 shows the rules for these relations. The transitive closure has one case for terminal and one for nonterminal nodes. The nonterminal rule implements the transitivity and is interleaved with the execution of the phi instructions. For two nodes s and k where k is the nth predecessor of s, the phi rule executes all phi assignments by evaluating to their nth source. An OP instruction is executed by first running the operation's main effect and then the side effect to populate the flags. If the instruction has no successor labels, program execution halts. Depending on the evaluation of a JMP's condition, it jumps to the next instruction $k_\perp$ or one of its jump targets $ks_\top$. A PUSH first writes its target into the memory at the current stack pointer value s_{sp} and then sets the new stack pointer d_{sp} to the old value minus the size of the target. A POP does the opposite by first incrementing the stack pointer and then writing the value read from memory to its target. A CALL essentially pushes the label of the next instruction onto the stack and then jumps to its target. Similarly, a RET pops the label of the next instruction from the stack and then jumps to it.

Definition 6 (Program semantics). *The semantics of a whole program is given by the transitive closure of the entry node's small step semantics.*

$$p \vdash \sigma_1 \Downarrow \sigma_2 := p \vdash \langle \sigma_1, p.entry \rangle \Rightarrow^* \langle \sigma_2, \emptyset \rangle$$

Translation. A translation is a function between programs of two BIRDs together with a semi-decider on program equivalence. When this semi-decider returns true then the input and output of the translation must be bisimilar. A translation step then returns the translated program if it is bisimilar to the input program or nothing if no bisimilarity could be proven.

Definition 7 (Bisimulation). *Given two BIRDs ir_1, ir_2 and two programs $p_1 : Prog(ir_1), p_2 : Prog(ir_2)$, the programs are considered bisimilar $(p_1 \sim p_2)$ if there exists a relation $R \subseteq \Sigma(ir_1) \times \Sigma(ir_2)$ such that R and R^{-1} are simulations. R is a simulation, if for every $\langle \sigma_1, \sigma_2 \rangle \in R$ and $\sigma_1' : \Sigma(ir_1)$*

$$p_1 \vdash \sigma_1 \Downarrow \sigma_1' \implies \exists \sigma_2', p_2 \vdash \sigma_2 \Downarrow \sigma_2' \wedge R(\sigma_1', \sigma_2')$$

Definition 8 (Translation). *Given two birds ir_1, ir_2, we define translations and translation steps*

$$\text{translation} := \langle \tau : Prog(ir_1) \rightarrow Prog(ir_2), (\equiv) \subseteq Prog(ir_1) \times Prog(ir_2) \rangle$$
$$\text{translation-step}(\langle \tau, \equiv \rangle) := \lambda p \mapsto\ \text{if } p \equiv \tau(p) \text{ then } \tau(p) \text{ else } \emptyset$$

where translations *have the requirement*

$$\forall p, p \equiv \tau(p) \implies p \sim \tau(p)$$

The composition of two steps $step_1, step_2$ is defined as the monadic bind.

$$step_1 \circ step_2 := \lambda p \mapsto\ \text{if } step_1(p) = p' \text{ then } step_2(p') \text{ else } \emptyset$$

$$\text{TERMINAL}\frac{p \vdash \langle \sigma_1, k \rangle \Rightarrow \langle \sigma_2, \emptyset \rangle}{p \vdash \langle \sigma_1, k \rangle \Rightarrow^* \langle \sigma_2, \emptyset \rangle}$$

$$\text{NONTERMINAL}\frac{\begin{array}{c} p \vdash \langle \sigma_1, k_1 \rangle \Rightarrow \langle \sigma_2, k_2 \rangle \\ p \vdash \sigma_2 \; \Phi^{k_3}_{k_2} \; \sigma_3 \\ p \vdash \langle \sigma_3, k_3 \rangle \Rightarrow^* \langle \sigma_4, k_4 \rangle \end{array}}{p \vdash \langle \sigma_1, k_1 \rangle \Rightarrow^* \langle \sigma_4, k_4 \rangle}$$

$$\text{PHI}\frac{\text{is-pred}_n(k,s) \quad phi = \text{phi}(s)}{p \vdash \sigma_1 \; \Phi^s_k \; \sigma_2} \qquad \sigma_2 = \text{run-phis}(n, phi, \sigma_1)}{p \vdash \sigma_1 \; \Phi^s_k \; \sigma_2}$$

$$\text{run-phis}(n, ps, \sigma) := \\ \text{foldr}(\text{run-phi}(n), \sigma, ps) \\ \text{run-phi}(n, \langle d, s \rangle, \sigma) := \\ \sigma[\langle d, \text{QWORD} \rangle \leftarrow \sigma[\langle s_n, \text{QWORD} \rangle]]$$

$$\text{OP}\frac{\begin{array}{c} \text{instr}(k_1) = \text{OP}(op, \vec{s}, \vec{d}, k_2) \\ \sigma_2 = \sigma_1[\text{rip} \leftarrow k_2] \quad \langle \vec{f}, e \rangle = [\![op]\!] \\ \sigma_3 = \sigma_2[\vec{d} \leftarrow \vec{f}(\sigma_2[\vec{s}])] \\ \sigma_4 = e(\sigma_3[\vec{s}], \sigma_3) \end{array}}{p \vdash \langle \sigma_1, k_1 \rangle \Rightarrow \langle \sigma_4, k_2 \rangle}$$

$$\text{JUMP}\frac{\begin{array}{c} \text{instr}(k_1) = \text{JMP}(c, s, k_\perp, ks_\top) \\ \sigma_2 = \sigma_1[\text{rip} \leftarrow k_\perp] \quad f = [\![c]\!] \\ f(\sigma_2) \implies k_2 \in ks_\top \wedge k_2 = \sigma_2[s] \\ \neg f(\sigma_2) \implies k_2 = k_\perp \end{array}}{p \vdash \langle \sigma_1, k_1 \rangle \Rightarrow \langle \sigma_2, k_2 \rangle}$$

$$\text{PUSH}\frac{\begin{array}{c} \text{instr}(k_1) = \text{PUSH}(s, s_{sp}, d_{sp}, k_2) \\ v = \sigma_2[s] \quad n = \text{size}(s) \quad \sigma_1[d_{sp}] \geq s \\ \sigma_2 = \sigma_1[\text{rip} \leftarrow k_2] \\ \sigma_3 = \sigma_2[n\text{-PTR}[s_{sp}] \leftarrow v] \\ \sigma_4 = \sigma_3[d_{sp} \leftarrow \sigma_3[s_{sp}] - n] \end{array}}{p \vdash \langle \sigma_1, k_1 \rangle \Rightarrow \langle \sigma_4, k_2 \rangle}$$

$$\text{POP}\frac{\begin{array}{c} \text{instr}(k_1) = \text{POP}(d, s_{sp}, d_{sp}, k_2) \\ v = \sigma_3[n\text{-PTR}[s_{sp}]] \quad n = \text{size}(d) \\ \sigma_2 = \sigma_1[\text{rip} \leftarrow k_2] \\ \sigma_3 = \sigma_2[d_{sp} \leftarrow \sigma_2[s_{sp}] + n] \\ \sigma_4 = \sigma_3[d \leftarrow v] \end{array}}{p \vdash \langle \sigma_1, k_1 \rangle \Rightarrow \langle \sigma_4, k_2 \rangle}$$

$$\text{CALL}\frac{\begin{array}{c} \text{instr}(k_1) = \text{CALL}(d, s_{sp}, d_{sp}, k_r, ks) \\ \sigma_1[s_{sp}] \geq 8 \quad k_2 = \sigma_2[d] \quad k_2 \in ks \\ \sigma_2 = \sigma_1[\text{rip} \leftarrow k_r] \\ \sigma_3 = \sigma_2[\text{QWORD-PTR}[s_{sp}] \leftarrow k_2] \\ \sigma_4 = \sigma_3[d_{sp} \leftarrow \sigma_3[s_{sp}] - 8] \end{array}}{p \vdash \langle \sigma_1, k_1 \rangle \Rightarrow \langle \sigma_4, k_2 \rangle}$$

$$\text{RET}\frac{\begin{array}{c} \text{instr}(k_1) = \text{RET}(s_{sp}, d_{sp}, ks) \\ k_2 = \sigma_1[\text{QWORD-PTR}[s_{sp}]] \quad k_2 \in ks \\ \sigma_2 = \sigma_1[\text{rip} \leftarrow k_2] \\ \sigma_3 = \sigma_2[d_{sp} \leftarrow \sigma_2[s_{sp}] + 8] \end{array}}{p \vdash \langle \sigma_1, k_1 \rangle \Rightarrow \langle \sigma_3, k_2 \rangle}$$

Fig. 4. Formal semantics for BIRD programs. From top to bottom: The transitive closure for (phi-)instruction semantics, the phi semantics, and the small step semantics for instructions.

Note that if a translation step returns the translation of an input program then the translation is bisimilar to the input. This, combined with transitivity of bisimulation, ensures that if the composition of two steps returns the translation of an input program then the composed translation is bisimilar to the input.

3.2   Instantiation 1: X86

For X86 assembly, the storage cells are registers and no annotations (a.k.a the unit tuple) are needed. Reading and writing is implemented with the aliasing semantics of registers.

Definition 9 (Register). *Registers are the general-purpose registers* $Reg:: = $ $\boldsymbol{rax} \mid \boldsymbol{eax} \mid \ldots \mid \boldsymbol{r15b}$. *A register's word part is given as follows*

$$\text{part}_{reg}(\boldsymbol{rax},\_) := \text{QWORD} \quad \text{part}_{reg}(\boldsymbol{eax},\_) := \text{DWORD} \quad \text{part}_{reg}(\boldsymbol{ax},\_) := \text{WORD}$$

$$\text{part}_{reg}(\boldsymbol{al},\_) := \text{RIGHT-BYTE} \quad \text{part}_{reg}(\boldsymbol{ah},\_) := \text{LEFT-BYTE} \quad \ldots$$

Definition 10 (Register read, write). *Given a register state* $\gamma : Reg \to \mathbb{V}_8$ *and a register* $r : Reg$, *reading is the function application*

$$\text{read}_{reg}(\gamma, r) := \gamma(r)$$

and writing is the aliasing function update

$$\text{write}_{reg}(\gamma, r, v) := \text{W}_{regs}(\gamma, \text{aliases}(r), v)$$
$$\text{W}_{regs}(\gamma, rs, v) := \text{fold}((\lambda\gamma', r \mapsto \gamma'[r \mapsto v]), \gamma, rs)$$
$$\text{aliases}(\boldsymbol{rax}) := [\boldsymbol{rax}, \boldsymbol{eax}, \boldsymbol{ax}, \boldsymbol{al}, \boldsymbol{ah}], \quad \ldots$$

Definition 11 (Well formed X86 state). *A register state* $\gamma : Reg \to \mathbb{V}_8$ *is* well formed *if all aliasing registers contain the same* $\mathbb{V}_8$ *value.*

$$\text{wf}(\gamma) := \forall r_1 r_2, \text{aliases}(r_1) = \text{aliases}(r_2) \implies \gamma(r_1) = \gamma(r_2)$$

Definition 12 (X86 BIRD). *The X86 language is the IR with registers, no annotations, absolute addresses as labels and the aforementioned aliasing semantics for registers.*

$$X86 := \langle Reg, \langle\rangle, AbsAddr, \text{part}_{reg}, \text{read}_{reg}, \text{write}_{reg}\rangle$$

3.3 Instantiation 2: Early BIRD

For the Early BIRD language, the storage cells are mutable variables and the annotations are the word parts corresponding to the word parts of the registers from which the variable originates. Reading and writing have no aliasing semantics.

Definition 13 (Mutable Variable). *A* mutable variable *is a string identifier* $Var := \boldsymbol{string}$. *Its word part is determined entirely by its annotation*

$$\text{part}_{var}(\_, a) := a$$

Definition 14 (Variable read, write). *Given a variable state* $\gamma : Var \to \mathbb{V}_8$ *and a variable* $var : Var$, *reading is again the function update and writing is the non-aliasing function update*

$$\text{read}_{var}(\gamma, var) := \gamma(var) \quad \text{write}_{var}(\gamma, var, v) := \gamma[var \mapsto v]$$

Definition 15 (Early BIRD). *The Early BIRD language is the IR with variables, word parts as annotations, absolute addresses as labels and the aforementioned non aliasing semantics for variables*

$$EarlyBIRD := \langle Var, \mathbb{WP}, AbsAddr, \text{part}_{var}, \text{read}_{var}, \text{write}_{var}\rangle$$

```
1  MOV R8D, EDI              1  MOV R8(dword), DI(dword)
2  LEA RAX, [R8 - 1]         2  LEA AX(qword), [R8 - 1]
3  INC R8B                   3  INC R8(right byte)
```

(a) Original X86 code   (b) Corresponding Early BIRD code

Fig. 5. Example of the `reg2var` translation.

4   X86 to Early BIRD

In this section, we define the translation `reg2var` where the function τ is overloaded for all syntactical elements. We then define a congruence relation $\cong$ between X86 states and Early BIRD states and extend τ to also translate states. These two definitions serve as the bisimulation relation and the method to compute new related states needed for Definition 7. Based on these definitions, we show that τ always produces bisimilar states, thus the semi-decider on program equivalence is the constant `true` function. Figure 5 shows an example X86 program together with its `reg2var` transformation.

Definition 16. *For (annotated) registers, τ returns (annotated) cells. All aliasing registers are mapped to the same variable*

$$\tau(\mathbf{rax}) := \text{``}AX\text{''} \quad \tau(\mathbf{eax}) := \text{``}AX\text{''} \quad \ldots \quad \tau(\mathbf{r15w}) := \text{``}15\text{''} \quad \tau(\mathbf{r15b}) := \text{``}15\text{''}$$

and the resulting variables annotation is the word part of the registers

$$\tau(\langle r : Reg, a : \mathbf{unit}\rangle) := \langle \tau(r), \text{part}_{reg}(r, a)\rangle$$

Sources are translated by translating the contained data, all other syntactical elements work similarly.

$$\tau(s) := \begin{cases} v & \text{if } s \text{ is an immediate } v \\ \tau(e) & \text{if } s \text{ is an expression } e \\ \langle s, \tau(e)\rangle & \text{if } s \text{ is an address } \langle s, e\rangle \\ \tau(\langle r, a\rangle) & \text{if } s \text{ is an annotated register } \langle r, a\rangle \\ \mathbf{rip} + d & \text{if } s \text{ is an rip relative } \mathbf{rip} + d \end{cases}$$

All nodes that appear in a program $p : Prog(X86)$ also appear in the program $\tau(p)$ because τ does not change the control flow structure, only the instructions. As such, we can implicitly cast any node from $Node(p)$ to $Node(\tau(p))$. In particular, the statements $p \vdash \langle \sigma_1, k\rangle \Rightarrow \langle \sigma_1', k'\rangle$ and $\tau(p) \vdash \langle \sigma_2, k\rangle \Rightarrow \langle \sigma_2', k'\rangle$ have meaningful semantics.

Definition 17 (Reg2Var congruence). *The relation $\cong$ between a X86 state σ_1 and an Early BIRD state σ_2 requires the memory, flags and $\mathbf{rip}$ of both states to be identical. For the cells, the values of all registers must match their translated counterparts.*

$$\sigma_1 \cong \sigma_2 := \forall(a : AbsAddr), \sigma_1[a] = \sigma_2[a] \qquad \wedge \forall(f : Flag), \sigma_1[f] = \sigma_2[f]$$
$$\wedge \forall(c : Reg \times \textbf{\textit{unit}}), \sigma_1[c] = \sigma_2[\tau(c)] \wedge \sigma_1[\textbf{\textit{rip}}] = \sigma_2[\textbf{\textit{rip}}]$$

This will be the bisimulation relation R for Definition 7.

Definition 18. *The translation for states $\tau : \Sigma(X86) \to \Sigma(EarlyBIRD)$ keeps memory, flags and **rip** unchanged and evaluates all variables by forwarding to the corresponding register.*

$$\tau(\langle \gamma, \theta, \xi, \textbf{\textit{rip}} \rangle) := \langle\langle \gamma', \theta, \xi, \textbf{\textit{rip}} \rangle\rangle$$
$$\gamma' := \lambda(v : Var) \mapsto \gamma(r), \text{ where } \tau(r) = v$$

For the rest of the section, we can assume such an r with $\tau(r) = v$ to exist as all variables in this transformation originate from registers. This will be the state σ_2' for Definition 7.

To show bisimilarity between any program p and its translation $\tau(p)$, we first need to show that state congruence preserves all values. First, we show that registers and their translation have the same value (Lemma 1), that expressions and their translation evaluate to the same value (Lemma 2) and that reading from a source is the same as reading from its translation (Lemma 3). We then show that writing preserves congruence (Lemma 4). Based on these, we show that executing (phi-)instructions preserves the small-step semantics (Lemmas 5,6 and 7), and extend this to the transitive closure (Lemma 8). Finally, we show that the semantics of the entire program is preserved (Corollary 1) and thus, $\cong$ is a bisimulation (Theorem 1). For the rest of the section, we always assume X86-states to be well-formed.

Lemma 1. *Given two states σ_1, σ_2, for all registers r and annotations a*

$$\sigma_1 \cong \sigma_2 \implies \sigma_1[\langle r, a \rangle] = \sigma_2[\tau(\langle r, a \rangle)]$$

Proof 1. Unfolding the definitions, we need to show $\Downarrow_{\mathrm{part}(r,a)} \gamma_1(r) = \Downarrow_{\tau(\langle r,a \rangle)} \gamma_2(\tau(r))$. By definition, $\mathrm{part}(r, a)$ and $\tau(\langle r, a \rangle)$ are equal. By a case analysis on r, we need to show cases such as $\gamma_1(\textbf{EAX}) = \gamma_2(\text{``}AX\text{''})$. This is true by the assumption $\sigma_1 \cong \sigma_2$. □

Lemma 2. *Given two states γ_1, γ_2, for all expressions $e = [d \pm b \pm s * i]$*

$$\gamma_1 \cong \gamma_2 \implies e|_{\mathrm{read}(\gamma_1)} = \tau(e)|_{\mathrm{read}(\gamma_2)}$$

Proof 2. Unfolding the definition of expression evaluation, we need to show $d \pm \gamma_1[b] \pm s \cdot \gamma_1[i] = d \pm \gamma_2[\tau(b)] \pm s \cdot \gamma_2[\tau(i)]$. By Lemma 1, we have $\gamma_1[b] = \gamma_2[\tau(b)]$ and $\gamma_1[i] = \gamma_2[\tau(i)]$. □

Lemma 3. *Given two states σ_1, σ_2, for all sources s*

$$\sigma_1 \cong \sigma_2 \implies \sigma_1[s] = \sigma_2[\tau(s)]$$

Proof 3. Case analysis over s. For an immediate v, $\tau(s) = v$ and $\forall \sigma, \sigma[v] = v$. For an expression e, Lemma 2 shows that evaluation of e and $\tau(e)$ yield the same result. For an address $\langle s, e \rangle$, s stays the same and the evaluation of e and $\tau(e)$ are equal. Reading from $\langle s, e \rangle$ in σ_1 and $\tau(\langle s, e \rangle)$ in σ_2 is the same by $\sigma_1 \cong \sigma_2$. For an annotated register $\langle r, a \rangle$, Lemma 1 shows the goal. For a **rip** *relative* **rip** $+ d$, *equality follows from $\sigma_1 \cong \sigma_2$.* ☐

Lemma 4. *Given two states σ_1, σ_2, for all destinations d and values v*

$$\sigma_1 \cong \sigma_2 \implies \sigma_1[d \leftarrow v] \cong \sigma_2[\tau(d) \leftarrow v]$$

Proof 4. Case analysis over d. For an annotated register $\langle r, a \rangle$, we only need to consider the cell state parts as all other state parts are unchanged by the write. We need to show $\text{write}_{reg}(\gamma_1, r, a, v) = \text{write}_{var}(\gamma_2, \tau(\langle r, a \rangle), \tau(r), v)$. By Lemma 1 we know that the old values of r in γ_1 and $\tau(r)$ in γ_2 are equivalent, thus updating with v results in the same value. Again, by Lemma 1, we know that reading from r and $\tau(r)$ after writing results in the same value. For an address $\langle s, e \rangle$, we only need to consider the memory state part. By Lemma 2, we know that e and $\tau(e)$ evaluate to the same value, thus the same memory update is performed. Also by Lemma 2, Reading after the the memory update yields the same value. ☐

Lemma 5. *Given two states σ_1, σ_2, a list of source registers s, a destination register d and a natural number n, we have*

$$\sigma_1 \cong \sigma_2 \implies \text{run−phi}(n, \langle d, s \rangle, \sigma_1) \cong \text{run−phi}(n, \tau\langle d, s \rangle, \sigma_2)$$

Unfolding the definitions, we need to show

$$\sigma_1[d \leftarrow \sigma[\langle s_n, \text{QWORD} \rangle]] \cong \sigma_2[\tau(d) \leftarrow \sigma[\langle \text{map}(\tau, s)_n, \text{QWORD} \rangle]]$$

By Lemma 3, we know that $\sigma_1[\langle s_n, \text{QWORD} \rangle]$ and $\sigma_2[\langle \text{map}(\tau, s)_n, \text{QWORD} \rangle]$ evaluate to the same $v : \mathbb{V}_8$. The remaining $\sigma_1[d \leftarrow v] \cong \sigma_2[\tau(d) \leftarrow v]$ follows from Lemma 4. ☐

Lemma 6. *Given a program $p : Prog(X86)$, two nodes in the program k_1, k_2, two states σ_1, σ_1', a state σ_2, and $\sigma_2' := \tau(\sigma_1')$, we have*

$$\sigma_1 \cong \sigma_2 \wedge p \vdash \sigma_1 \; \Phi_{k_1}^{k_2} \; \sigma_1' \implies \tau(p) \vdash \sigma_2 \; \Phi_{k_1}^{k_2} \; \sigma_2'$$

Proof 5. Inversion on the phi step relation. We have an n, such that $\text{is−pred}_n(k_1, k_2)$ and $\sigma_1' = \text{run−phis}(n, \text{phi}(k_2), \sigma_1)$. We show $\sigma_2' = \text{run−phis}(n, \tau(\text{phi}(k_2)), \sigma_2)$ by an induction on $\text{phi}(k_2)$ and application of Lemma 5. ☐

Lemma 7. *Given a program $p : Prog(X86)$, two nodes in the program k_1, k_2, two states σ_1, σ_1', a state σ_2, and $\sigma_2' := \tau(\sigma_1')$, we have*

$$\sigma_1 \cong \sigma_2 \wedge p \vdash \langle k_1, \sigma_1 \rangle \Rightarrow \langle k_2, \sigma_1' \rangle \implies \tau(p) \vdash \langle k_1, \sigma_2 \rangle \Rightarrow \langle k_2, \sigma_2' \rangle$$

Proof 6. We show the OP *rule as an example. All other rules are similar. Doing an inversion, we get 1. p, $\text{instr}(k_1) = OP(op, \vec{s}, \vec{d}, k_2)$, 2. $\sigma_a = \sigma_1[\boldsymbol{rip} \leftarrow k_2]$, 3. $\langle \vec{f}, e \rangle = [\![op]\!]$, 4. $\sigma_b = \sigma_a[\vec{d} \leftarrow \vec{f}(\sigma_a[\vec{s}])]$ and 5. $\sigma'_1 = e(\sigma_b[\vec{s}], \sigma_b)$. We need to show:*

- $\sigma_a \cong \sigma'_a$ *where $\sigma'_a = \sigma_2[\boldsymbol{rip} \leftarrow k_2]$. Follows by definition of writing to $\boldsymbol{rip}$.*
- $\sigma_b \cong \sigma'_b$ *where $\sigma'_b = \sigma'_a[\tau(\vec{d}) \leftarrow \vec{f}(\sigma'_a[\tau(\vec{s})])]$. Follows from Lemmas 3 and 4.*
- $\sigma_1 \cong \sigma'_2$ *where $\sigma'_2 = e(\sigma'_b[\tau(\vec{s})])$. Follows from Lemmas 3 and 4.*

$\square$

Lemma 8. *Given a program $p : Prog(X86)$, two nodes in the program k_1, k_2, two states σ_1, σ'_1 a state σ_2, and $\sigma'_2 := \tau(\sigma'_1)$, we have*

$$\sigma_1 \cong \sigma_2 \wedge p \vdash \langle k_1, \sigma_1 \rangle \Rightarrow^* \langle k_2, \sigma'_1 \rangle \implies \tau(p) \vdash \langle k_1, \sigma_2 \rangle \Rightarrow^* \langle k_2, \sigma'_2 \rangle$$

Proof 7. Induction over $p \vdash \langle k_1, k_2 \rangle \Rightarrow^* \langle \sigma_1, \sigma'_1 \rangle$ with σ_2 generalized. The TERMI-NAL *base case follows by Lemma 7 and the* NONTERMINAL *inductive case follows from Lemmas 6, 7 and the induction hypothesis.* $\square$

Corollary 1. *Given a program $p : Prog(X86)$ and the states $\sigma_1, \sigma'_1, \sigma_2$ and $\sigma'_2 := \tau(\sigma'_1)$, we have*

$$\sigma_1 \cong \sigma_2 \wedge p \vdash \sigma_1 \Downarrow \sigma'_1 \implies \sigma'_1 \cong \sigma'_2 \wedge \tau(p) \vdash \sigma_2 \Downarrow \sigma'_2$$

Proof 8. $\sigma'_1 \cong \sigma'_2$ follows by definition of τ, the rest by Definition 6 and Lemma 8. $\square$

Theorem 1. *Given a program $p : Prog(X86)$, we have $p \sim \tau(p)$*

Proof 9. We need to provide a relation $R \subseteq \Sigma(X86) \times \Sigma(EarlyBIRD)$, such that both R and R^{-1} are simulations. We choose $R := (\cong)$.

$$\forall \langle \sigma_1, \sigma_2 \rangle \in (\cong), \forall \sigma'_1, p \vdash \sigma_1 \Downarrow \sigma_2 \implies \exists \sigma'_2, \sigma_2 \cong \sigma'_2 \wedge \tau(p) \vdash \sigma_2 \Downarrow \sigma'_2$$

We provide $\sigma'_2 := \tau(\sigma'_1)$, the remaining

$$\sigma_1 \cong \sigma_2 \wedge p \vdash \sigma_1 \Downarrow \sigma'_1 \implies \sigma'_1 \cong \tau(\sigma'_1) \wedge \tau(p) \vdash \sigma_2 \Downarrow \tau(\sigma'_1)$$

is exactly Corollary 1. The case for $(\cong)^{-1}$ is similar. $\square$

The first step in the translation chain (Fig. 1) is the `reg2var` step between the $X86$ and the $EarlyBIRD$ languages. Its translation is implemented by the τ function defined in this section. By Theorem 1, this translation step always produces an $EarlyBIRD$ program whose semantics are equivalent to the semantics of the original $X86$ program. Thus, the semi-decider for program equivalence between input and output of the τ function is the constant `true` function. By Definition 8, we obtain a provably correct translation step.

5   Conclusion

In this paper, we presented the mathematical framework *BIRD* to describe low-level programs in a generic assembly language, translations between different instantiations of that language, and the soundness criteria thereof. We presented two example instantiations: X86 and Early BIRD with their full formal semantics, and showed a translation step to replace the registers of the former with mutable variables of the latter and proofed soundness of this translation.

As such, BIRD is the first of its kind as it allows decompilation to be performed in an exact and provably correct way that requires no human intervention. Opposed to most of the competing platforms, it does not aim to produce human-readable code and instead produces machine analyzable code.

For usage in a real-world decompiler, the limited set of instructions presented in this paper can be extended by leveraging work such as [8, 10, 12, 24]. By implementing the language definition and transformation in Coq, we are able to use its language extraction feature to produce around 500 lines of Haskell code to be used in our internal x86-64 decompilation suite.

Apart from the `reg2var` translation that was introduced here, we see three more steps as the immediate future work that can directly build upon BIRD. Figure 1 shows a hypothetical compiler that uses these steps to leverage the low-level assembly into fully typed, SSA-based programs.

ssa, mem2var SSA-form programs are often used by static analysis tools to better reason about mutable variables. In its current state, an Early BIRD program still uses mutable variables, but the generic definition supports the definition of immutable SSA variables too. Notably, phi nodes with their semantics based on incoming edges are defined as part of Fig. 4. The register-based variables can already be SSA transformed, but there still remain memory accesses that make statically analyzing an assembly program hard. We argue that these memory accesses need to be replaced by SSA variables wherever possible.

symbolization The Early BIRD language uses $\mathbb{V}_8$ values as the labels for all instructions. As such, they can be the result of computations to implement indirect jumps. If one was to reorder instructions in the program, or insert new ones, these $\mathbb{V}_8$ labels would no longer match and indirect jumps would break. A symbolization step can introduce more abstract, position-independent labels. This would allow for semantics preserving, *structure altering* translations.

type inference The registers modeled so far (and thus the variables) are based on 1,2,4 and 8 byte integers. There is no information yet on signedness of values or whether or not they form more complex compound data structures, but such information can be used to guide program analyses [20]. An extension of the current framework may see the introduction of floating point instructions and SIMD registers.

Acknowledgements. This work is supported by the Defense Advanced Research Projects Agency (DARPA) and Naval Information Warfare Center Pacific (NIWC Pacific) under Contract No. N66001-21-C-4028.

References

1. Barthe, G., Demange, D., Pichardie, D.: A formally verified SSA-based middle-end: Static single assignment meets compcert. In: Proceedings of the 21st European Conference on Programming Languages and Systems. p. 47–66. ESOP'12, Springer-Verlag, Berlin, Heidelberg (2012). https://doi.org/10.1007/978-3-642-28869-2_3
2. Brumley, D., Jager, I., Avgerinos, T., Schwartz, E.J.: BAP: A binary analysis platform. In: Gopalakrishnan, G., Qadeer, S. (eds.) Computer Aided Verification. pp. 463–469. Springer, Berlin Heidelberg, Berlin, Heidelberg (2011). 0.1007/978-3-642-22110-1_37
3. Brumley, D., Lee, J., Schwartz, E.J., Woo, M.: Native x86 decompilation using semantics-preserving structural analysis and iterative control-flow structuring. In: USENIX Security Symposium (2013)
4. Burk, K., Pagani, F., Kruegel, C., Vigna, G.: Decomperson: How humans decompile and what we can learn from it. In: 31st USENIX Security Symposium (USENIX Security 22), pp. 2765–2782. USENIX Association, Boston, MA (Aug 2022) https://www.usenix.org/conference/usenixsecurity22/presentation/burk
5. Canzanese, R., Oyer, M., Mancoridis, S., Kam, M.: A survey of reverse engineering tools for the 32-bit microsoft windows environment (01 2005)
6. Coq Development Team: The coq proof assistant. https://coq.inria.fr/ Accessed 12 May 2023
7. Cytron, R., Ferrante, J., Rosen, B.K., Wegman, M.N., Zadeck, F.K.: Efficiently computing static single assignment form and the control dependence graph. ACM Trans. Program. Lang. Syst. **13**(4), 451–490 (oct 1991). https://doi.org/10.1145/115372.115320
8. Dasgupta, S., Park, D., Kasampalis, T., Adve, V.S., Roşu, G.: A complete formal semantics of x86–64 user-level instruction set architecture. In: Proceedings of the 40th ACM SIGPLAN Conference on Programming Language Design and Implementation, pp. 1133–1148. PLDI 2019, Association for Computing Machinery, New York, NY, USA (2019). https://doi.org/10.1145/3314221.3314601
9. Eagle, C.: The IDA Pro Book: The Unofficial Guide to the World's Most Popular Disassembler. IT Pro, No Starch Press (2008). https://books.google.de/books?id=BoFaZ1dB1H0C
10. Hamlen, K.W., Fisher, D., Lundquist, G.R.: Source-free machine-checked validation of native code in coq. In: Proceedings of the 3rd ACM Workshop on Forming an Ecosystem Around Software Transformation, pp. 25–30. FEAST'19, Association for Computing Machinery, New York, NY, USA (2019). https://doi.org/10.1145/3338502.3359759
11. Hex Rays: Ida pro. https://hex-rays.com/ida-pro/ Accessed 12 May 2023
12. Kennedy, A., Benton, N., Jensen, J.B., Dagand, P.E.: Coq: The world's best macro assembler? In: Proceedings of the 15th Symposium on Principles and Practice of Declarative Programming, pp. 13–24. PPDP '13, Association for Computing Machinery, New York, NY, USA (2013). https://doi.org/10.1145/2505879.2505897

13. Kumar, R., Mullen, E., Tatlock, Z., Myreen, M.O.: Software verification with ITPs should use binary code extraction to reduce the TCB. In: Avigad, J., Mahboubi, A. (eds.) Interactive Theorem Proving, pp. 362–369. Springer International Publishing, Cham (2018). https://doi.org/10.1007/978-3-319-94821-8_21

14. Lattner, C., Adve, V.: LLVM: a compilation framework for lifelong program analysis & transformation. In: International Symposium on Code Generation and Optimization, 2004. CGO 2004, pp. 75–86 (2004). https://doi.org/10.1109/CGO.2004.1281665

15. Lattner, C., et al.: MLIR: Scaling compiler infrastructure for domain specific computation. In: 2021 IEEE/ACM International Symposium on Code Generation and Optimization (CGO), pp. 2–14 (2021). https://doi.org/10.1109/CGO51591.2021.9370308

16. Leroy, X.: Formal verification of a realistic compiler. Commun. ACM **52**(7), 107–115 (2009). https://doi.org/10.1145/1538788.1538814, http://xavierleroy.org/publi/compcert-CACM.pdf

17. Letouzey, P.: Extraction in coq: An overview. In: Beckmann, A., Dimitracopoulos, C., Löwe, B. (eds.) Logic and Theory of Algorithms. pp. 359–369. Springer, Berlin Heidelberg, Berlin, Heidelberg (2008). https://doi.org/10.1007/978-3-540-69407-6_39

18. N. S. Agency: Ghidra. https://ghidra-sre.org/Accessed 12 May 2023

19. Naus, N., Verbeek, F., Ravindran, B.: A formal semantics for P-Code. In: 14th International Conference on Verified Software: Theories, Tools, and Experiments (2022). https://doi.org/10.1007/978-3-031-25803-9_7

20. Palsberg, J.: Type-based analysis and applications. In: ACM SIGPLAN/SIGSOFT Workshop on Program Analysis for Software Tools and Engineering (07 2001). https://doi.org/10.1145/379605.379635

21. PNF Software: Jeb decompiler. https://www.pnfsoftware.com/ Accessed 12 May 2023

22. Schulte, E., Ruchti, J., Noonan, M., Ciarletta, D., Loginov, A.: Evolving exact decompilation. In: Shoshitaishvili, Y., Wang, R.F. (eds.) Workshop on Binary Analysis Research. San Diego, CA, USA (Feb 18–21 2018). https://doi.org/10.14722/bar.2018.23008, https://www.ndss-symposium.org/ndss2018/bar-workshop-programme/

23. Vector 35 Inc.: Binary ninja. https://binary.ninja/ Accessed 12 May 2023

24. Verbeek, F., Bharadwaj, A., Bockenek, J., Roessle, I., Weerwag, T., Ravindran, B.: X86 instruction semantics and basic block symbolic execution. Archive of Formal Proofs (Oct 2021). https://isa-afp.org/entries/X86_Semantics.html, Formal proof development

25. Yakdan, K., Dechand, S., Gerhards-Padilla, E., Smith, M.: Helping johnny to analyze malware: A usability-optimized decompiler and malware analysis user study. In: 2016 IEEE Symposium on Security and Privacy (SP), pp. 158–177. IEEE Computer Society, Los Alamitos, CA, USA (May 2016). https://doi.org/10.1109/SP.2016.18

26. Zakowski, Y., Beck, C., Yoon, I., Zaichuk, I., Zaliva, V., Zdancewic, S.: Modular, compositional, and executable formal semantics for LLVM IR. Proc. ACM Program. Lang. 5(ICFP) (Aug 2021). https://doi.org/10.1145/3473572

Low-Level Reachability Analysis Based on Formal Logic

Nico Naus[1,2(✉)] , Freek Verbeek[1,2] , Marc Schoolderman[3] ,
and Binoy Ravindran[1]

[1] Virginia Tech, Blacksburg, VA, USA
{niconaus,freek,binoy}@vt.edu
[2] Open University, Heerlen, The Netherlands
{nico.naus,fvb}@ou.nl
[3] Radboud University Nijmegen, Nijmegen, The Netherlands
m.schoolderman@cs.ru.nl

Abstract. Reachability is an important problem in program analysis. Automatically being able to show that – and how – a certain state is reachable, can be used to detect bugs and vulnerabilities. Various research has focused on formalizing a program logic that connects preconditions to post-conditions in the context of reachability analysis, e.g., must+, Lisbon Triples, and Outcome Logic. Outcome Logic and its variants can be seen as an adaptation of Hoare Logic and Incorrectness Logic. In this paper, we aim to study 1.) how such a formal reachability logic can be used for automated precondition generation, and 2.) how it can be used to reason over low-level assembly code. Automated precondition generation for reachability logic enables us to find inputs that provably trigger an assertion (i.e., a post-condition). Motivation for focusing on low-level code is that low-level code accurately describes actual program behavior, can be targeted in cases where source code is unavailable, and allows reasoning over low-level properties like return pointer integrity. An implementation has been developed, and the entire system is proven to be sound and complete (the latter only in the absence of unresolved indirections) in the Isabelle/HOL theorem prover. Initial results are obtained on litmus tests and case studies. The results expose limitations: traversal may not terminate, and more scalability would require a compositional approach. However, the results show as well that precondition generation based on low-level reachability logic allows exposing bugs in low-level code.

Keywords: Formal verification · Formal Methods · Reachability analysis

1 Introduction

Reachability is an important problem in program analysis. Being able to automatically show that a certain state is reachable allows us to detect bugs and vulnerabilities in code. Currently most reachability analysis approaches target high-level code [7,22,27]. However, high-level code is still an abstraction over the actual program behavior. The actual execution is defined by the assembly code produced by compilation. It is at this level where we can fully reason over properties such as memory safety and return pointer integrity, which are the major cause of software vulnerabilities [23]. For example, an out-of-bounds memory write not prevented by memory unsafe languages such as C can overwrite the return address stored on the stack, before a function returns. Other vulnerabilities and exploitation techniques such as return-oriented-programming (ROP) are also only detectable at the lowest level [5]. An ROP attack is executed by chaining together instructions already present in memory, to perform arbitrary operations. In addition, reasoning over low-level code opens up the ability to reason over reachability in programs where source code is unavailable.

Reasoning over low-level code also has its drawbacks. For starters, memory is not structured, and treated as an array-like structure. As a result, a write or read of a pointer can access any region in memory, go out of bounds or overlap with existing pointers. Control flow is also unstructured. Program execution can jump to any point in the code, and jumps can be dynamic. Resolving these indirections is a challenge. Formal semantics are often unavailable for low-level architectures, requiring any analysis to deal with uncertainty. The aforementioned challenges will be addressed in this paper. Another challenge is obtaining assembly or low-level code from binaries [32]. We consider this out of scope, since this problem is more or less orthogonal.

Logics that reason over reachability triples have been studied extensively under various names (must+ [2,3], Backwards Under-Approximative Triples [24], Lisbon Triples [26], Outcome Logic [34]). They revolve around triples of the following definition:

$$\langle P \rangle \; p \; \langle Q \rangle \equiv \forall \sigma \in \Sigma \cdot P(\sigma) \implies \exists \sigma' \in \Sigma \cdot \sigma \xrightarrow{p} \sigma' \wedge Q(\sigma')$$

Here, p is a program under investigation and Q is a postcondition. Intuitively, the triple formulates that any state σ satisfying the precondition P will reach the postcondition with at least one of its execution paths. It is herein different from commonly known program logics such as Hoare Logic [19] which reasons over program correctness, and Reverse Hoare Logic [33] and Incorrectness Logic [26] which both reason over total reachability. A more thorough discussion on the relation between these logics, can be found elsewhere [25,34]. From now on, we will refer to this kind of triples as reachability triples.

In this paper, we consider postcondition Q to be *fixed* and thus study the problem: can we define a function τ that given program p and postcondition Q computes a precondition such that $\langle \tau(p, Q) \rangle \; p \; \langle Q \rangle$ holds? Moreover, we consider program p to be low-level code.

The relevance of such a function τ, is that it allows the generation of inputs that lead to *unwanted* states. In low-level code, an unwanted state can be a candidate for an exploit. For example, a state in which the top of the stack frame is overwritten is unwanted, as it may lead to an exploit. Taking as postcondition such an unwanted state and applying function τ can either show that the unwanted state is unreachable, or provide information on how to reach it.

The first step is to formalize an academic programming language similar to the well-known WHILE [19] language. Whereas WHILE is intended to be an abstract model of high-level programming languages, this paper proposes JUMP as an abstract model of low-level representations of executable behavior such as assembly or LLVM IR [21]. The language JUMP is characterized by being low-level, having unstructured control flow (jumps instead of loops) and an unstructured flat memory model. Moreover, it is *non-deterministic*, allowing us to model the uncertainty of the semantics of various constructs found in executables. Even state-of-the-art research into semantics of instruction sets are not able to provide deterministic semantics for all instructions [12,17]. Any static analysis over low-level code thus must be able to deal with the non-determinism caused by undefined behavior of instructions.

We then define a function τ in two forms: 1.) in Isabelle/HOL [25, 19, 11], and 2.) a mirrored implementation in Haskell. The Isabelle/HOL version allows a formal proof of soundness and completeness; we know that the search space describes only actual reachability evidence, and that it describes all possible ways to reach the intended state.

Algorithmically, the approach presented in this paper boils down to backwards symbolic execution (BSE) [9,10,13,15]. What this paper aims to do, is to relate backwards symbolic execution to a program logic, analogous to how forwards symbolic execution is related to Hoare logic. By formulating BSE as a precondition-transformation function over reachability triples, we can formally reason over soundness and completeness.

Limitations of this approach include that the search space becomes infinite. This is a necessary consequence of soundness and completeness. However, finding one path from assertion to initial state suffices and thus there is no need for full search space traversal to find bugs and vulnerabilities. Various research exists that combine BSE with dealing with loops, but the focus of this paper is to show how precondition-generation for reachability logic allows finding unwanted states in low-level code. Additionally, the characterisation of unwanted states, i.e., which postcondition to start with, is now chosen manually. Automating this characterisation is out of scope.

The Haskell implementation allows experimentation on several litmus tests, as well as on two larger case studies. It shows how a search space is generated, traversed and preconditions are found. Application of this approach to large real-world programs is explicitly left as future work. All results, source code and the formalized proof of correctness in Isabelle/HOL are publicly available[1].

In summary, this paper presents the following contributions:

- A formal foundation for reasoning over reachability in low-level languages.
- A sound and complete precondition-generation algorithm for (single-path) reachability triples.

---

[1] https://github.com/niconaus/low-level-reachability.

This paper is the first to provide a formal foundation for reasoning over reachability in low-level languages, in particular, formulate BSE as precondition-transformation function over reachability triples.

Section 2 introduces the JUMP language. Section 3 presents the reachability triples precondition generation mechanism. Litmus tests are described in Sect. 4 and Sect. 5 presents two case studies. Related work is discussed in Sect. 6 before we conclude in Sect. 7.

2   The JUMP Language

The JUMP language is intended as an abstract representation of low-level languages such as LLVM IR [21] or assembly. It has no explicit control flow; instead it has jumps to addresses. It consists of basic *blocks* of elementary statements that end with either a jump or an exit. Blocks are labeled with addresses. Memory is modeled as a mapping from addresses to values. Variables from a set $\mathcal{V}$ represent registers and flags. The *values* stored in variables and memory are words (bit-vectors) of type $\mathcal{W}$.

The following design decisions have been made regarding JUMP.

Non-determinism. We explicitly include *non-determinism* through an `Obtain` statement that allows to retrieve some value out of a set. Non-determinism allows modeling of external functions whose behavior is unknown, allows dealing with uncertain semantics of assembly instructions and allows modeling user-input and IO. The `Obtain` statement is the only source of non-determinism in JUMP.

Unstructured Memory. Memory essentially consists of a flat mapping of addresses to values. There is no explicit notion of heap, stack frame, data section, or global variables. This is purposefully chosen as it allows to reason over pointer aliasing. For example, it allows Reachability Triples to formulate statements as "the initial value of this pointer should be equal to the initial value of register `rsp`" which is interpreted as a pointer pointing to the return address at the top of the stack frame. Note that registers are treated as variables in JUMP.

No Structured Control Flow. All control flow happens either through jumps, conditional jumps or indirect jumps. Indirect control flow is typically introduced by a compiler in case of switch statements, callbacks, and to implement dynamic dispatch. Note that a normal instruction such as the x86 instruction `ret` implicitly is an indirect jump as well.

Definition 1. *A* JUMP *program* p *is defined as the pair* (a_0, blocks) *where* a_0 *is the entry address, and* blocks *a mapping from addresses to blocks. A block is defined by the grammar in Fig. 1.*

A block consists of a sequence of zero or more statements, followed by either a jump, conditional jump, indirect jump or `Exit`, where `Exit` merely indicates that a program has ended. The conditional jump jumps to the address a_1 only

Block
$\underline{b}$ ::= $\underline{s}$; $\underline{b}$ | Exit   Sequence, exit
    | Jump a | CJump $\underline{e}$ a_1 a_2 | IJump $\underline{e}$ Jump, conditional jump, indirect jump

Statement
$\underline{s}$ ::= Assign v $\underline{e}$ Variable assignment
    | Obtain v Where $\underline{e}$ Nondeterministic assign
    | Store $\underline{e}_1$ $\underline{e}_2$ Store v in address e

Expression
$\underline{e}$ ::= w | v | *$\underline{e}$ | $\underline{e}_1$ $\oplus$ $\underline{e}_2$ | $\neg\underline{e}$ Value, variable, deref, bin op, not

$\oplus \in \{+, -, \times, \%, <, \leq, =, \neq, >, \geq, \wedge, \vee, \ldots\}$ Binary operators

Fig. 1. The JUMP language syntax.

if the given expression evaluates to non-zero, otherwise to address a_2. The indirect jump calculates the value of $\underline{e}$ and jumps to the block at that address. *Statements* can be assignments or stores. A deterministic assignment writes the value of expression $\underline{e}$ to variable v. A nondeterministic assignment, denoted as Obtain v Where $\underline{e}$, obtains some value w that satisfies $\underline{e}[v := w]$, and writes it to variable v. Note that since expressions can read from memory, using the C-style *e notation, an assignment can model a load instruction. A store writes the value that results from evaluating $\underline{e}_2$ into the memory location that is obtained by evaluating $\underline{e}_1$. *Expressions* consist of values, variables, dereferencing, binary operations and negation.

The state consists of values assigned to variables and memory. Memory is defined as an array-like structure. Two memory operations are provided, namely reading and writing. Function write is of type $\mathcal{A} \times \mathcal{W} \times \mathcal{M} \to \mathcal{M}$ and function read is of type $\mathcal{A} \times \mathcal{M} \to \mathcal{W}$.

We assume values can bijectively be cast to addresses and we do so freely.

Definition 2. *A state σ is a tuple* (mem, vars) *where* mem *is of type $\mathcal{M}$ and* vars *are of type $\mathcal{V} \to \mathcal{W}$.*

Semantics are expressed through transition relations $\longrightarrow_J$, $\longrightarrow_B$ and $\longrightarrow_S$ that respectively define state transitions induced by programs, blocks, and statements (see Fig. 2). For example, notation $p : \sigma \longrightarrow_J \sigma'$ denotes a transition induced by program p from state σ to state σ'. Notation $\sigma \vdash \underline{e} = w$ denotes the evaluation of expression $\underline{e}$ in state σ to value w.

The semantics are largely straightforward. A program defined by an entry address a_0 and a mapping blocks from addresses to basic blocks, is evaluated by evaluating the block pointed to by the entry address. A conditional jump is evaluated by evaluating the condition, and then the target block. Indirect jumps are evaluated in a similar manner, by evaluating the expression to obtain the block to jump to. The nondeterministic assignment NDASSIGN is non-standard, and evaluates expression $\underline{e}$ after substituting the variable v for some value w. For any value w where expression $\underline{e}$ evaluates to non-zero, a transition may occur. A STORE evaluates expression $\underline{e_1}$ producing some address a, and evaluates $\underline{e_2}$ and writes its value to the corresponding region in memory. A LOAD uses function read to read from memory. All other expression evaluations are omitted because they are standard.

$$
\text{PROG} \quad \frac{\text{blocks}(a_0) \,:\, \sigma \longrightarrow_B \sigma'}{(a_0, \text{blocks}) \,:\, \sigma \longrightarrow_J \sigma'}
$$

$$
\text{SEQ} \quad \frac{\underline{s} \,:\, \sigma \longrightarrow_S \sigma' \quad \underline{b} \,:\, \sigma' \longrightarrow_B \sigma''}{\underline{s};\underline{b} \,:\, \sigma \longrightarrow_B \sigma''}
$$

$$
\text{EXIT} \quad \overline{\text{Exit} \,:\, \sigma \longrightarrow_B \sigma}
$$

$$
\text{JUMP} \quad \frac{\text{blocks}(a) \,:\, \sigma \longrightarrow_B \sigma'}{\text{Jump } a \,:\, \sigma \longrightarrow_B \sigma'}
$$

$$
\text{IJUMP} \quad \frac{\sigma \vdash \underline{e} = a \quad \text{blocks}(a) \,:\, \sigma \longrightarrow_B \sigma'}{\text{IJump } \underline{e} \,:\, \sigma \longrightarrow_B \sigma'}
$$

$$
\text{CJUMPLEFT} \quad \frac{\sigma \vdash \underline{e} \neq 0 \quad \text{blocks}(a_1) \,:\, \sigma \longrightarrow_B \sigma'}{\text{CJump } \underline{e} \; a_1 \; a_2 \,:\, \sigma \longrightarrow_B \sigma'}
$$

$$
\text{CJUMPRIGHT} \quad \frac{\sigma \vdash \underline{e} = 0 \quad \text{blocks}(a_2) \,:\, \sigma \longrightarrow_B \sigma'}{\text{CJump } \underline{e} \; a_1 \; a_2 \,:\, \sigma \longrightarrow_B \sigma'}
$$

$$
\text{ASSIGN} \quad \frac{(\text{mem}, \text{vars}) \vdash \underline{e} = w}{\textbf{Assign } v \; \underline{e} \,:\, (\text{mem}, \text{vars}) \longrightarrow_S (\text{mem}, \text{vars}[v/w])}
$$

$$
\text{STORE} \quad \frac{(\text{mem}, \text{vars}) \vdash \underline{e_1} = a \quad (\text{mem}, \text{vars}) \vdash \underline{e_2} = w}{\textbf{Store } \underline{e_1} \; \underline{e_2} \,:\, (\text{mem}, \text{vars}) \longrightarrow_S (\text{write}(a, w, \text{mem}), \text{vars})}
$$

$$
\text{NDASSIGN} \quad \frac{(\text{mem}, \text{vars}) \vdash \underline{e}[v/w] \neq 0}{\textbf{Obtain } v \textbf{ Where } \underline{e} \,:\, (\text{mem}, \text{vars}) \longrightarrow_S (\text{mem}, \text{vars}[v/w])}
$$

$$
\text{LOAD} \quad \frac{(\text{mem}, \text{vars}) \vdash \underline{e} = a \quad \text{read}(a, \text{mem}) = w}{(\text{mem}, \text{vars}) \vdash *\underline{e} = w}
$$

Fig. 2. Semantics of JUMP. Rules for evaluation of expressions are omitted, except for the dereference operator.

3   Precondition Generation

Precondition generation has its basis in reachability triples, as defined in Sect. 1. Motivation for choosing reachability triples as our underlying logic, is that it is the only program logic triple that is suitable for generating inputs automatically. Hoare Logic [19] requires reasoning over all paths, and thus needs manually written loop invariants. Reverse Hoare Logic [33] and Incorrectness Logic [26] allow for an over-approximation of the set of input states, leading to false positives. For a more in-depth discussion on the differences between these logics, and the advantage of using reachability triples, we refer to work by Zilberstein et al. [34].

Using the reachability triple definition from Sect. 1, we can now define our precondition generation function. The central idea is to formulate a transformation function τ that takes as input 1.) a program p, and 2.) a post-condition Q, and produces as output a disjunctive *set* of preconditions. This transformation function follows the recursive structure of JUMP, i.e., we formulate functions τ_J, τ_B and τ_S that perform transformations relative to a program, a block and a statement respectively.

Predicate
$$P ::= \exists\, i \in \mathbb{N} \cdot \underline{e} \wedge P \mid \underline{e} \quad \text{Existential quantification, expression}$$

Predicates P are expressions (true if and only if they evaluate to non-zero), but can also contain outermost existential quantifiers. The predicate $\exists i \in \underline{e} \cdot P$ means there exists a value w for i such that both $\underline{e}[i/w]$ and $P[i/w]$ hold.

When applied statement-by-statement, the τ-functions populate the precondition search space. This search space is an acyclic graph, with symbolic predicates as vertices and the initial postcondition as the root. It contains a labeled edge (Q, s, P) if and only if application of function τ_S for statement s and postcondition Q produces a set containing precondition P.

Given a program p and a postcondition Q defined in the predicate language above, a transformation is *sound* if it generates preconditions P that form a reachability triple. Soundness means that a generated precondition actually represents an initial state that non-deterministically leads to the Q-state. To define soundness, we first define the notion of a reachability triple relative to blocks, instead of a whole program as in Sect. 1:

Definition 3. *A reachability triple for block b is defined as:*

$$\langle P \rangle\, b\, \langle Q \rangle \equiv \forall \sigma \in \Sigma \cdot P(\sigma) \implies \exists \sigma' \cdot b\, :\ \sigma \longrightarrow_{\mathrm{B}} \sigma' \wedge Q(\sigma')$$

We restate this definition to stress that a reachability triple over block b intuitively means that precondition P leads to the desired state when running the block *and subsequent blocks jumped to, until an exit*, i.e., not just running the instructions within block b itself. This is due to the nature of the transition relation $\longrightarrow_{\mathrm{B}}$ (see Fig. 2). A similar definition can also be made for statements: a reachability triple $\langle P \rangle\, s\, \langle Q \rangle$ for statement s is defined for transition relation $\longrightarrow_{\mathrm{S}}$ and thus concerns the execution of the individual statement s only.

Definition 4. *Function τ_J is* sound, *if and only if, for any program p and postcondition Q:*

$$\forall P \in \tau_J(p, Q) \cdot \langle P \rangle\, p\, \langle Q \rangle$$

Similarly, soundness is defined for blocks and statements, with the only difference that the precondition for blocks and statements is constructed by combining the predicate and path condition in conjunction.

Figure 3 shows the transformation functions. Function τ_P starts at the entry block of the program. The program is then traversed in the style of a *right fold* [30]: starting at the entry block, the program is traversed up to an exit point, from which postcondition transformation happens. Function τ_B is identical to standard weakest precondition generation in the cases of sequence and exit. In the case of a conditional jump, two paths are explored. Either path could lead to a precondition, as long as the branching conditions remain satisfiable. In case of an indirect jump, all possible addresses that can be jumped to, are explored.

Function τ_S is standard in case of deterministic assignment. In case of nondeterministic assignment, according to the execution semantics, some value i needs to be found that fulfills the condition $\underline{e}$. That existentially quantified value is substituted for variable v in the post-condition.

Program:

$$\tau_J(p, Q) \qquad\qquad = \tau_B(\text{blocks}(a_0), Q)$$

Block:

$$\tau_B(\underline{s};\underline{b}, Q) \qquad\qquad = \bigcup\{\tau_S(\underline{s}, P) \mid P \in \tau_B(\underline{b}, Q)\}$$
$$\tau_B(\texttt{Jump}\,\underline{e}\,\,a_1\,\,a_2, Q) = \{P_1 \wedge \underline{e} \mid P_1 \in \tau_b(\text{blocks}(a_1), Q)\}$$
$$\qquad\qquad \cup\{P_2 \wedge \neg\underline{e} \mid P_2 \in \tau_b(\text{blocks}(a_2), Q)\}$$
$$\tau_B(\texttt{IJump}\,\underline{e}, Q) \qquad = \{P \wedge \underline{e} \equiv a \mid P \in \tau_b(\text{blocks}(a), Q), a \in \text{dom}(\text{blocks})\}$$
$$\tau_B(\texttt{Exit}, Q) \qquad\qquad = \{Q\}$$

Statement:

$$\tau_S(\texttt{Assign}\,\,v\,\,\underline{e}, Q) \qquad = \{Q[v/\underline{e}]\}$$
$$\tau_S(\texttt{Obtain}\,\,v\,\,\texttt{Where}\,\underline{e}, Q) = \{\exists i \in \underline{e} \cdot Q[v/i]\}$$
$$\tau_S(\texttt{Store}\,\,\underline{e}\,\,v, Q) \qquad = \{Q' \wedge \phi \mid (Q', \phi) \in \tau_{\texttt{store}}(\underline{e}, v, Q)\}$$

Fig. 3. Precondition generation functions

$$\tau_{\texttt{store}}(\underline{e}_1, \underline{e}_2, w) \qquad\qquad = \{(c, \textit{True})\}$$
$$\tau_{\texttt{store}}(\underline{e}_1, \underline{e}_2, v) \qquad\qquad = \{(x, \textit{True})\}$$
$$\tau_{\texttt{store}}(\underline{e}_1, \underline{e}_2, *\underline{e}_p) \qquad = \{(*\underline{e}_p, \underline{e}_1 \neq \underline{e}_p), (\underline{e}_2, \underline{e}_1 = \underline{e}_p)\}$$
$$\tau_{\texttt{store}}(\underline{e}_1, \underline{e}_2, \neg\underline{e}_p) \qquad = \{(\neg\underline{e}'_p, \phi) \mid (\underline{e}'_p, \phi) \in \tau_{\texttt{store}}(\underline{e}_1, \underline{e}_2, \underline{e}_p)\}$$
$$\tau_{\texttt{store}}(\underline{e}_1, \underline{e}_2, \underline{e}_{p1} \oplus \underline{e}_{p2}) \quad = \{(\underline{e}'_{p1} \oplus \underline{e}'_{p2}, \phi_1 \wedge \phi_2) \mid (\underline{e}'_{p1}, \phi_1) \in \tau_{\texttt{store}}(\underline{e}_1, \underline{e}_2, \underline{e}_{p1})$$
$$\qquad\qquad , (\underline{e}'_{p2}, \phi_2) \in \tau_{\texttt{store}}(\underline{e}_1, \underline{e}_2, \underline{e}_{p2})\}$$
$$\tau_{\texttt{store}}(\underline{e}_1, \underline{e}_2, \exists i \in \underline{e}_p \cdot P) = \{(\exists i \in \underline{e}'_p \cdot P', \phi_1 \wedge \phi_2) \mid (\underline{e}'_p, \phi_1) \in \tau_{\texttt{store}}(\underline{e}_1, \underline{e}_2, \underline{e}_p)$$
$$\qquad\qquad , (P', \phi_2) \in \tau_{\texttt{store}}(\underline{e}_1, \underline{e}_2, P)\}$$

Fig. 4. Case definitions for precondition of store

In the case of memory assignment, predicate transformation is a bit more complex. Consider the following example:

$$\texttt{Store}\,\,x\,\,42;\,\,\texttt{Store}\,\,y\,\,43\,\,\langle *x = 42\rangle$$

If memory regions x and y alias, then $*x$ will be 43 after execution. The postcondition $*x \equiv 42$ can only hold if x and y are separate.

We explicitly encode assumptions about memory separation into the generated preconditions. The $\tau_{\texttt{store}}$ function listed in Fig. 4 takes care of this. It takes as input expression $\underline{e}_1$ that describes a memory pointer, expression $\underline{e}_2$ which is the value to be written, and the postcondition P. It returns a set of tuples (Q, ϕ) where Q is the precondition and ϕ provides the pointer-relations under which that substitution holds. For example, we have $\tau_{\texttt{store}}(a_1, v, *a_2 = 42) = \{(*a_2 = 42, a_1 \neq a_2), (v = 42, a_1 = a_2)\}$. This indicates two possible substitutions when transforming postcondition into precondition:

$$\langle *a_2 = 42\rangle\,\,\texttt{Store}\,\,a_1\,\,v\,\,\langle *a_2 = 42\rangle\,\,\text{if}\,\,a_1 \neq a_2$$
$$\langle v = 42\rangle\,\,\,\,\texttt{Store}\,\,a_1\,\,v\,\,\langle *a_2 = 42\rangle\,\,\text{if}\,\,a_1 = a_2$$

All other cases of $\tau_{\texttt{store}}$ merely propagate the case generation.

There are no special rules for dealing with loops. Instead, loops are unrolled by the precondition generation. In the case of infinite iterations, the reachability search space will be infinitely large. To deal with this search space, we order and prune the space. Theorem 1 states a basic property of reachability triples that is used for the purpose of pruning. Section 4 describes how the space is ordered to manage large search spaces.

Theorem 1 (Preservation of unsatisfiability). *For any program p and conditions P and Q such that $\langle P \rangle\ p\ \langle Q \rangle$,*

$$(\forall \sigma' \cdot Q(\sigma') \implies \textit{False}) \implies (\forall \sigma \cdot P(\sigma) \implies \textit{False})$$

The above can directly be concluded from the definition of a reachability triple, as given at the beginning of this section. Once an unsatisfiable condition is generated, the precondition generation can be halted, and the condition discarded.

We validate our precondition generation function by proving it is both sound and complete. Theorems 2 and 3 define these respective properties.

Theorem 2 (Soundness of precondition generation). *Functions τ_P, τ_B and τ_S are sound.*

Theorem 3 (Completeness of precondition generation).

$$\frac{\textit{termination}(p,P) \qquad \textit{no\_indirections}(p)}{\langle P \rangle\ p\ \langle Q \rangle \implies \exists P' \in \tau_J(p,Q) \wedge (P \implies P')}$$

Having both soundness and completeness means that the reachability space defines all and only valid preconditions for a certain program and postcondition.

Both theorems, including 1.) the syntax and semantics of JUMP, 2.) the syntax and semantics of the predicates, and 3.) the functions τ have been formally proven correct in the Isabelle/HOL theorem prover. The proof, including a small example of precondition generation within Isabelle/HOL, constitutes roughly 1000 lines of code. Proof scripts are publicly available[2]. To prove completeness, Theorem 3 imposes two restrictions. One, we require execution of a program p under a state described by P to terminate. If a program does not terminate, it is impossible to construct a P' for this program, and therefore completeness does not hold. Two, we show the theorem holds for programs without indirect jumps. The predicate no_indirections(p) ensures that the JUMP program does not contain an IJump instruction. In practice however, this premise has little to no impact. Every JUMP program containing indirect jumps, can be converted to one with only direct jumps, by encoding a jump-table like structure using blocks and conditional jumps. Given that P is a precondition for program p and postcondition Q, the precondition generation will generate a P' that is non-strictly weaker than P. An equivalent of Theorem 3 also holds for τ_S and τ_B.

---

[2] https://github.com/niconaus/low-level-reachability.

4   Litmus Tests

This section presents two litmus tests that demonstrate the application of reachability triples and its precondition generation algorithm to low-level code. We have a prototype implementation available in Haskell, in which we have tested these examples[3].

The prototype implements the τ functions similar to how they are presented above. The τ functions are defined as non-deterministic functions, building up a tree as a search space. Branches at the same level originate from a conditional, and deeper branches indicate a jump. On top of that, basic simplification is applied to the generated predicates, to make them more readable.

The precondition search space can be infinitely large. The implementation builds up the search space as a tree structure. This orders the search space, making it feasible to search the infinite space in a structured way. Although some rudimentary ordering is done, efficiently searching and reducing the reachability space is explicitly left as future work. The implementation includes an SMT solver, for deciding the satisfiability of the computed preconditions.

4.1   Infinite Reachability Space: Long Division

Our first litmus test demonstrates conditional jumps, loops, infinite reachability space and post-condition pruning. Figure 5 lists the program blocks on the left. The blocks are labeled #0 though #3, with block #0 the entry point. Variables x and y signify the input. The program divides x by y, by means of long division. If x is larger than y, the result of the division is returned in variable i. The variable x is updated, and after execution holds the remainder from division.

In this case, we want to derive that a state is reachable which clearly should not be, to show that there is a bug in the program. The program behaves incorrectly when after execution, the remainder stored in x is equal to or larger than the divisor y. We use this, $x \geq y$, as our postcondition.

The right side of Fig. 5 represents precondition generation. Conditions shown in this Figure are left unsimplified for the purpose of illustration. We start back to front. Exit does not alter the postcondition, so we just copy it. Then, we either execute block 0, 1 or 2, depending on what condition holds. If we came directly from block 0, then $x < y$ must hold, so our precondition is $x \geq y \land x < y$, which is false, indicated by the lightning bolt. If we came from block 1, then $\neg(x \geq y)$ must have held. Block 1 updates x with $x - y$, leading to the precondition $(x - y) \geq y \land \neg((x - y) \geq y)$. Note that this precondition is unsatisfiable. From Theorem 1, we know that we can halt exploration of this particular path.

The last block to look at, is block 2. To arrive here, we must have had that $\neg(x > y)$. The body of block 2 updates x, and we end up with $(x - y) \geq y \land \neg((x - y) > y)$. Here, we see the loop unfolding at work. We have executed the loop body once, and the τ function generates two alternatives. We exit the

---

[3] https://github.com/niconaus/low-level-reachability.

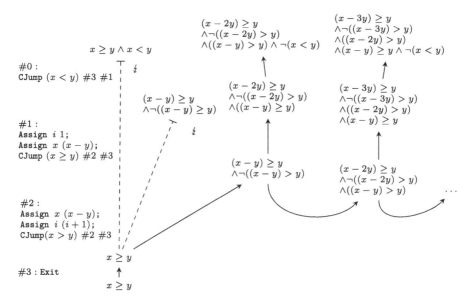

Fig. 5. Precondition generation for long division example. A dashed arrow leads to an unsatisfiable precondition.

loop, indicated by the arrow pointing up, or we run another iteration, indicated by the arrow pointing right.

Ending the loop at this point again leads to a precondition that is satisfiable. Completing the calculation, leads us to the first viable precondition for the postcondition $x \geq y$.

The precondition function τ does not stop at this point. A second unrolling step is shown in the Figure. It will continue to unroll the loop an infinite amount of times, making the reachability space infinitely large. By ordering the space as shown in this example, we can perform a breadth first search, starting with the smallest number of unrolling. While this does make the space more manageable, the search space is still potentially infinite. In such a case, if no satisfiable precondition exists, breadth first search will never terminate.

4.2   Indirect Jumps

Our next litmus test demonstrates how reachability triples and its precondition generation deals with indirect jumps. Switch-statements consisting of many cases are often compiled into jump tables. These are typically combined with a guard for values not handled by the jump table. Figure 6 shows a model of this.

Execution starts at block 0. Here, y is set to 0, and the conditional jump checks if x is smaller than 1 or larger than 4. If so, we jump to exit. If not, we jump to block 1, which is the start of our guard. The indirect jump jumps to the block label stored in x. Blocks 2, 3, and 4 signify the guard options.

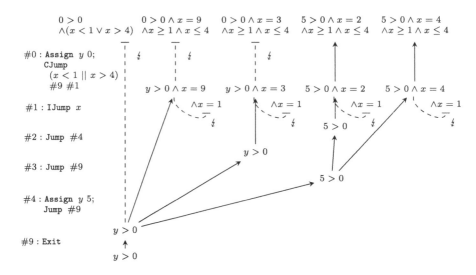

Fig. 6. Precondition generation for indirect jump example.

As a postcondition, we select $y > 0$. This postcondition does not necessarily encode a program error, but does allow us to demonstrate how our approach deals with indirection.

Starting at block 9, we again work our way up the execution back to front. We refrain from a step-by-step explanation of the precondition generation, and instead focus on the behavior of precondition generation involving indirection. Block 1 contains the indirect jump. As can be seen from the precondition generation graph, we have to explore every possible jump target when we get to block 1, including a jump to itself. This generates a large number of paths, but many of these explorations generate unsatisfiable preconditions. Potentially, an indirect jump can jump to any address, but in practice, the number of paths explored is limited by the conditions that must hold.

5   Case Studies

In this section, we present our results of applying precondition generation to two bigger examples. Out goal with these examples is to demonstrate the feasibility of our approach, but we leave application to real-world binaries as future work.

5.1   Faulty Partitioning for Quicksort

The core of any quicksort algorithm is the partitioning algorithm. One well-known partitioning algorithm is the one invented by Tony Hoare [18] which selects a *pivot* element and then transforms an input data set into two smaller sets, depending on relative ordering of elements in the data set to the pivot. This scheme seems superficially very simple, but it is very easy to get wrong.

For instance, the following algorithm has a superficially plausible variant of this partitioning scheme, which is "nearly correct".

```
void quicksort(int a[], size_t N) {
  if(N <= 1) return;
  int pivot = a[rand()%N];
  int i = 0, j = N-1;
  while(i <= j) {
    while(i < j  && a[i] <= pivot) i++;
    while(i <= j && a[j] >= pivot) j--;
    swap(&a[i++], &a[j--]);
  }
  quicksort(a, j+1);
  quicksort(a+i, N-i);}
```

The partitioning scheme can be translated into a JUMP program relatively easily; selection of the pivot can be modeled using a non-deterministic assign.

We are interested in detecting out-of-bounds memory access. We add bounds checks to the program, and thus our postcondition is $(i < 0) \vee (i \geq N)$. Running the resultant program through our implementation for an array of size 3 will then generate an exploit-precondition: the program can go out of bounds if the following condition holds:

$$\exists i.0 \leq i \leq 2 \wedge a[i] \leq a[0] \wedge a[i] \leq a[1] \wedge a[i] \leq a[2] \wedge a[0] > a[i]$$

Informally, this conditions says that a[0] is not the minimal element of the array. The reason for this is that if the minimal element is chosen as a pivot, and a[0] is not equal to it, the first inner loop will simply fall through, and after the second loop, i will become -1, pointing outside the array before the swap occurs. A fix for this would be make the swap conditional, replacing it with:

```
if(i <= j) swap(&a[i++], &a[j--]);
```

This will in fact prevent any out-of-bound memory access. However, another way any version of quicksort can fail dramatically is when the recursive calls are performed with incorrect parameters. For example if $i = 0$ or $j = N$ at the end of the partitioning scheme, we will end up in a infinite recursive loop. If we specify this as a post-condition of the partitioning scheme, we find that the same preconditions are generated as before.

The functional correctness of the partitioning scheme can also be examined— that is, is it actually the case that all the elements moved towards the the left-hand side of the array are less-or-equal to the pivot, and that the elements to the right are greater-or-equal than the pivot? To examine this, we can specify as an exploit condition that the input to the first recursive invocation of quicksort contains an element greater than the pivot; this finds no satisfiable conditions (as it is not true). However, specifying this for input sent to the second invocation of quicksort instead, our prototype will essentially start generating counter-examples. For example, if the first element is the pivot, and strictly less than the middle element but strictly higher than the third element, partitioning fails.

5.2 Karatsuba

Several assembly routines for multiplying multi-precision integers on an 8-bit AVR controller were verified by Schoolderman [29]. It was discovered that some of these routines could compute incorrect results if their arguments aliased with the memory location intended to store the result. A full verification like this appears to require significant effort; however, if we are only interested in finding aliasing bugs, reachability triples seem ideally suited to find these.

We focused on the smallest routine exhibiting the problem: the $48 \times 48 \rightarrow$ 96-bit multiplication routine as originally developed by Hutter and Schwabe [20]. This routine computes a product of two 48-bit integers using Karatsuba's method, splitting its inputs into two 24-bit halves, and performing a three $24 \rightarrow$ 48-bit multiplications with these, combining the results.[4] In the process, the lowest 24-bits of the result are known early on and written to memory before the upper half of the inputs is read, causing an aliasing bug.

To model this in JUMP, registers and the carry flags are modeled as JUMP variables, whereas the memory space is modeled using JUMP addresses. Every AVR instruction is modeled by a sequence of JUMP statements. For example, the instruction ADD $a0$, $a1$ can be expressed by the sequence:

$$\textsf{Assign } tmp \ (a0 + a1);$$
$$\textsf{Assign } a0 \ (tmp \bmod 256);$$
$$\textsf{Assign } carry \ (tmp \ / \ 256)$$

Adding the appropriate binary operators to the syntax of Fig. 1, every instruction required for the program (which are only a handful) can be modeled, allowing the entire multiplication routine (consisting of 136 instructions) to be expressed as a JUMP program. The memory accesses, which operate on three bytes at a time, were modeled as a single memory operations on a three-byte memory region.

As seen in Sect. 4, generated preconditions can be fairly verbose, and we expected that in this case as well. To remedy this somewhat, we extended the Haskell implementation with constant folding and other simplifications to more efficiently manage the search space of possible preconditions, and pruning areas of the search space which can easily be determined to be impossible. In a more production-oriented setting, SMT solving and/or a robust expression simplifier can be used to do this more efficiently than our naive Haskell implementation.

For the precondition, we look at the case $X \cdot Y$ where $X = Y = 2^{24}$. Clearly the expected result should be $X \cdot Y = 2^{48}$, i.e. the 96-bit result should consist of 12 bytes, all of which contain 0, except for the seventh byte which should hold 1. As a postcondition, we therefore specify that this byte does *not* hold 1.

Running the JUMP version of the 48-bit Karatsuba code through our analysis resulted in a handful of preconditions. Some of these simplify to *False*, as they

---

[4] To be more precise, this method uses the fact that $(2^w X_h + X_l)(2^w Y_h + Y_l) = (1 + 2^w)(2^w X_h Y_h + X_l Y_l) - 2^w(X_l - X_h)(Y_l - Y_h)$.

express impossible aliasing conditions—an SMT solver would be able to discard these easily. However, 7 preconditions remained which are completely plausible and satisfiable, which fall into three categories:

- X, Y alias, and their high 24-bits overlap with the low 24-bits of the result
- X, Y are disjoint, and of them partially overlaps with the result as before
- X, Z are partially aliased, and one of them partially overlaps with the result

Which are exactly the case we would expect: the issue is being caused by either (or both) inputs sharing their high 24-bits with the low 24-bits of the output location. Had we not chosen the fixed input values for X and Y, this case would have generated more complex preconditions, however, this case shows that there is an easy instance where these would be satisfied.

6   Related Work

As mentioned in Sect. 1, the relation described by reachability triples has been studied before under different names. Möller, O'Hearn and Hoare [24] describe what they call Backwards Under-Approximative Triples. They do not develop a precondition generation algorithm for these triples, but merely reflect on the triples with regards to over-approximate triples.

The must+ relation used in works by Ball (et al.) [2,3] also describes an under-approximative transition relation in the context of abstract interpretation. A must+ transition is defined such that if an abstract transition exists, given a concrete state that relates to the abstract state before execution, a concrete post-state also exists. Instead of doing precondition generation, their aim is to use this relation in a model transition system, to ultimately generate test cases that cover the entire reachable state space.

Zilberstein et al. [34] refer to this exact same relation as Outcome Logic (OL). They argue why OL is better suited for reasoning over reachability, compared to existing program logics. Deduction rules are presented, and the paper includes several example proofs over Outcome Logic triples.

To the best of our knowledge, these logics and triples have never been applied to automatically reason over reachability in low-level code.

Many other approaches to do reachability analysis exist. Dynamic logic [16] allows reasoning over the execution of a program. Use of modal operators □ and ◇ allows for reasoning that something is necessarily the case or possibly the case, respectively. For example, stating $\langle p \rangle a$ means that after performing program p, it is possible for a to hold. Reachability triples go beyond this by including the state before execution in the relation, crucial for the intended purpose, as well as defining precondition generation.

Rosu et al. [28] and the continuation of that work by Ştefănescu et al. [31] introduce Reachability Logic for non-deterministic languages. Their logic serves as a proof system that allows for user-assisted reachability proofs over programs. Reachability Logic is language agnostic, and has its basis in Hoare Logic. As mentioned in Sect. 2, Hoare Logic is unsuitable for automatically generating reachability evidence, and these arguments also extend to Reachability Logic.

Recent work by Asadi et al. [1] describes an under-approximative reachability analysis for linear and polynomial systems. They define the reachability problem as a finite system of linear inequalities and use Farkas' lemma [14] to solve it. Their approach is able to handle theoretical benchmarks that were previously beyond reach. For the purpose of automatic reachability analysis for low-level programs however, their system is too restrictive.

Symbolic execution is another popular method for reasoning over reachability. Symbolic execution runs a program with symbols instead of actual input. Running the program with these symbolic inputs results in a complete overview of the programs behavior. Symbolic execution is extensively used for software testing [4,6,7]. Cadar and Sen [8] provide a great overview of the applications of symbolic execution for this purpose. The biggest downside of symbolic execution is that it describes the complete program behavior, and therefore quickly becomes infeasible, due to the many paths to be described.

Symbolic backward execution (SBE) attempts to mitigate the downside of reasoning over all possible paths by targeting a specific program point. Charreteur and Gotlieb present a method for generating test input based on SBE for Java bytecode [11]. Dinges and Agha augment this approach with concrete execution as well [13]. As mentioned earlier, SBE relates to reachability triples, as Hoare logic relates to forward symbolic execution. SBE provides a concrete algorithm, and potential optimizations such as loop invariant generation, to compute preconditions. Our work provides a formal foundation for reasoning over reachability in low level languages, as opposed to a purely algorithmical solution.

7   Conclusion

In this paper, we have studied automated reachability analysis over low-level code based on formal logic. We define low-level code as code with unstructured control flow, unstructured memory model and non-determinism. The use of formal logic based on reachability triples allows us to prove that generated preconditions will lead to a certain post-condition. The formal logic is based on reachability triples, which under various names have been studied earlier in related work [2,3,24,26,34]).

The precondition generation that has currently been implemented is relatively naive, and may get stuck in an infinite search. In order to apply this kind of reasoning to real-world programs, we believe that further research on efficient ways of traversing the program and compositional reasoning are needed.

Acknowledgements. This work is supported by the Defense Advanced Research Projects Agency (DARPA) and Naval Information Warfare Center Pacific (NIWC Pacific) under Contract No. N66001-21-C-4028, by DARPA under Agreement No. HR00112090028, and by the US Office of Naval Research (ONR) under grants N00014-17-1-2297 and N00014-18-1-2665.

References

1. Asadi, A., Chatterjee, K., Fu, H., Goharshady, A.K., Mahdavi, M.: Polynomial reachability witnesses via stellensätze. In: Freund, S.N., Yahav, E. (eds.) PLDI '21: 42nd ACM SIGPLAN International Conference on Programming Language Design and Implementation, Virtual Event, Canada, June 20–25, 2021, pp. 772–787. ACM (2021)

2. Ball, T.: A theory of predicate-complete test coverage and generation. In: de Boer, F.S., Bonsangue, M.M., Graf, S., de Roever, W.-P. (eds.) FMCO 2004. LNCS, vol. 3657, pp. 1–22. Springer, Heidelberg (2005). https://doi.org/10.1007/11561163_1

3. Ball, T., Kupferman, O., Yorsh, G.: Abstraction for falsification. In: Etessami, K., Rajamani, S.K. (eds.) CAV 2005. LNCS, vol. 3576, pp. 67–81. Springer, Heidelberg (2005). https://doi.org/10.1007/11513988_8

4. Boyer, R.S., Elspas, B., Levitt, K.N.: Select-a formal system for testing and debugging programs by symbolic execution. ACM SigPlan Notices **10**(6), 234–245 (1975)

5. Buchanan, E., Roemer, R., Shacham, H., Savage, S.: When good instructions go bad: generalizing return-oriented programming to RISC. In: Ning, P., Syverson, P.F., Jha, S. (eds.) Proceedings of the 2008 ACM Conference on Computer and Communications Security, CCS 2008, Alexandria, Virginia, USA, October 27–31, 2008, pp. 27–38. ACM (2008)

6. Burch, J.R., Clarke, E.M., McMillan, K.L., Dill, D.L., Hwang, L.J.: Symbolic model checking: 1020 states and beyond. Inf. Comput. **98**(2), 142–170 (1992)

7. Cadar, C., Dunbar, D., Engler, D.R., et al.: Klee: unassisted and automatic generation of high-coverage tests for complex systems programs. In: OSDI. vol. 8, pp. 209–224 (2008)

8. Cadar, C., Sen, K.: Symbolic execution for software testing: three decades later. Commun. ACM **56**(2), 82–90 (2013)

9. Chalupa, M., Strejcek, J.: Backward symbolic execution with loop folding. In: Dragoi, C., Mukherjee, S., Namjoshi, K.S. (eds.) Static Analysis - 28th International Symposium, SAS 2021, Chicago, IL, USA, October 17–19, 2021, Proceedings. Lecture Notes in Computer Science, vol. 12913, pp. 49–76. Springer (2021). https://doi.org/10.1007/978-3-030-88806-0_3

10. Chandra, S., Fink, S.J., Sridharan, M.: Snugglebug: a powerful approach to weakest preconditions. In: Proceedings of the 2009 ACM SIGPLAN Conference on Programming Language Design and Implementation, PLDI 2009, Dublin, Ireland, June 15–21, 2009, pp. 363–374 (2009)

11. Charreteur, F., Gotlieb, A.: Constraint-based test input generation for java bytecode. In: IEEE 21st International Symposium on Software Reliability Engineering, ISSRE 2010, San Jose, CA, USA, 1–4 November 2010, pp. 131–140. IEEE Computer Society (2010)

12. Dasgupta, S., Park, D., Kasampalis, T., Adve, V.S., Roşu, G.: A complete formal semantics of x86–64 user-level instruction set architecture. In: Proceedings of the 40th ACM SIGPLAN Conference on Programming Language Design and Implementation, pp. 1133–1148 (2019)

13. Dinges, P., Agha, G.A.: Targeted test input generation using symbolic-concrete backward execution. In: Crnkovic, I., Chechik, M., Grünbacher, P. (eds.) ACM/IEEE International Conference on Automated Software Engineering, ASE '14, Vasteras, Sweden - September 15–19, 2014, pp. 31–36. ACM (2014)

14. Farkas, J.: Theorie der einfachen ungleichungen. J. für die reine und angewandte Mathematik (Crelles Journal) **1902**(124), 1–27 (1902)

15. Gulwani, S., Juvekar, S.: Bound analysis using backward symbolic execution. Technical Report MSR-TR-2004-95, Microsoft Research (2009)

16. Harel, D.: Dynamic logic. In: Handbook of philosophical logic, pp. 497–604. Springer (1984). https://doi.org/10.1007/978-94-017-0456-4_2

17. Heule, S., Schkufza, E., Sharma, R., Aiken, A.: Stratified synthesis: automatically learning the x86–64 instruction set. In: Proceedings of the 37th ACM SIGPLAN Conference on Programming Language Design and Implementation, pp. 237–250 (2016)

18. Hoare, C.A.R.: Algorithm 64: quicksort. Commun. ACM **4**(7), 321 (1961)

19. Hoare, C.A.R.: An axiomatic basis for computer programming. Commun. ACM **12**(10), 576–580 (1969)

20. Hutter, M., Schwabe, P.: Multiprecision multiplication on AVR revisited. J. Cryptogr. Eng. **5**(3), 201–214 (2015)

21. Lattner, C., Adve, V.S.: LLVM: A compilation framework for lifelong program analysis & transformation. In: 2nd IEEE / ACM International Symposium on Code Generation and Optimization (CGO 2004), 20–24 March 2004, San Jose, CA, USA, pp. 75–88 (2004)

22. Le, Q.L., Raad, A., Villard, J., Berdine, J., Dreyer, D., O'Hearn, P.W.: Finding real bugs in big programs with incorrectness logic. Proc ACM Programm. Lang. **6**(OOPSLA1), 1–27 (2022)

23. Miller, M.: Trends, challenge, and shifts in software vulnerability mitigation, 2019. www.github.com/microsoft/MSRC-Security-Research/raw/master/presentations/2019_02_BlueHatIL/2019_01 (2019)

24. Möller, B., O'Hearn, P., Hoare, T.: On algebra of program correctness and incorrectness. In: Fahrenberg, U., Gehrke, M., Santocanale, L., Winter, M. (eds.) RAMiCS 2021. LNCS, vol. 13027, pp. 325–343. Springer, Cham (2021). https://doi.org/10.1007/978-3-030-88701-8_20

25. Naus, N., Verbeek, F., Schoolderman, M., Ravindran, B.: Reachability logic for low-level programs. CoRR abs/2204.00076 (2022)

26. O'Hearn, P.W.: Incorrectness logic. Proc. ACM Program. Lang. 4(POPL), 10:1–10:32 (2020)

27. Raad, A., Berdine, J., Dang, H., Dreyer, D., O'Hearn, P.W., Villard, J.: Local reasoning about the presence of bugs: Incorrectness separation logic. In: Computer Aided Verification - 32nd International Conference, CAV 2020, Los Angeles, CA, USA, July 21–24, 2020, Proceedings, Part II, pp. 225–252 (2020)

28. Rosu, G., Stefanescu, A., Ciobâcă, Ş., Moore, B.M.: One-path reachability logic. In: 28th Annual ACM/IEEE Symposium on Logic in Computer Science, LICS 2013, New Orleans, LA, USA, June 25–28, 2013, pp. 358–367. IEEE Computer Society (2013)

29. Schoolderman, M.: Verifying branch-free assembly code in why3. In: Paskevich, A., Wies, T. (eds.) VSTTE 2017. LNCS, vol. 10712, pp. 66–83. Springer, Cham (2017). https://doi.org/10.1007/978-3-319-72308-2_5

30. Sheard, T., Fegaras, L.: A fold for all seasons. In: Proceedings of the Conference On Functional Programming Languages And Computer Architecture, pp. 233–242 (1993)

31. Ştefănescu, A., Ciobâcă, Ş, Mereuta, R., Moore, B.M., Şerbănută, T.F., Roşu, G.: All-path reachability logic. In: Dowek, G. (ed.) RTA 2014. LNCS, vol. 8560, pp. 425–440. Springer, Cham (2014). https://doi.org/10.1007/978-3-319-08918-8_29

32. Verbeek, F., Bockenek, J.A., Fu, Z., Ravindran, B.: Formally verified lifting of c-compiled x86–64 binaries. In: Jhala, R., Dillig, I. (eds.) PLDI '22: 43rd ACM

SIGPLAN International Conference on Programming Language Design and Implementation, San Diego, CA, USA, June 13–17, 2022. pp. 934–949. ACM (2022)

33. de Vries, E., Koutavas, V.: Reverse hoare logic. In: Software Engineering and Formal Methods - 9th International Conference, SEFM 2011, Montevideo, Uruguay, November 14–18, 2011. Proceeding, pp. 155–171 (2011)

34. Zilberstein, N., Dreyer, D., Silva, A.: Outcome logic: A unifying foundation for correctness and incorrectness reasoning. CoRR abs/2303.03111 (2023)

Testing a Formally Verified Compiler

David Monniaux, Léo Gourdin$^{(\boxtimes)}$, Sylvain Boulmé, and Olivier Lebeltel

Univ. Grenoble Alpes, CNRS, Grenoble INP, Verimag, Grenoble, France
`leo.gourdin@univ-grenoble-alpes.fr`

Abstract. We report on how we combine tests and formal proofs while developing extensions to the CompCert formally verified compiler.

Keywords: Software Engineering · Formal Proofs · Experimental Validation

1 Introduction

CompCert is a formally verified compiler, which compiles a large fragment of the C programming language to assembly code. "Formally verified" means that there is a machine-checked proof (here with the Coq proof assistant) that if *compilation succeeds*, the possible executions of this assembly code match those of the C source [9]. Hence, CompCert's formal proof aims at forbidding *miscompilation*, i.e., compiled programs with unexpected behaviors.

Miscompilations being potentially very unsafe for final users, eradicating them is highly desirable. However, according to [25], in mainline compilers—without formal proof—such as GCC and LLVM, more than half of the bugs in optimization passes are miscompilations. This indicates that eradicating them is nonetheless very difficult with standard software engineering methods.

While developing new features for CompCert, we realized that formal proofs were not enough, and that testing was required. We thus greatly extended the testing system present in the GitHub repository of CompCert. This paper describes the challenges that we experienced and the solutions we found.[1]

Here are some incorrect behaviors not prevented by CompCert's formal proof and that we experienced. (1) **Unexpected compilation failure** (compiler internal error): the formal proof assumes that compilation succeeds; always failing would trivially satisfy this criterion. Failing when incorrect behavior occurs protects against miscompilation, as detailed in §2. (2) **Compilation timeout**: compilation may loop forever or take prohibitively long. (3) **Error during assembling or linking**: reasons for this range from details in the syntax comment of certain assemblers to the use of short branch instructions.[2]

The above behaviors are not miscompilations, but compile-time errors. In contrast, the following may lead to miscompilation, revealing issues in the

---

Work partially supported by the LabEx PERSYVAL-Lab (ANR-11-LABX-0025-01).

[1] Get our code on `https://gricad-gitlab.univ-grenoble-alpes.fr/certicompil/Chamois-CompCert`.

[2] A short branch and its target must be close, which may be false on large functions.

V. Prevosto and C. Seceleanu (Eds.): TAP 2023, LNCS 14066, pp. 40–48, 2023.
https://doi.org/10.1007/978-3-031-38828-6_3

Trusted Computing Base (TCB) which the formal proof relies on. (4) **Source semantics mismatch**: the C language is surprisingly complicated, and its semantics as formally defined in CompCert may diverge from the informal one defined in the standard, or in CompCert's manual. (5) **Assembly semantics mismatch**: the semantics of assembly language, plus platform-dependent peculiarities (e.g., how to access global symbols), may contain unexpected pitfalls (such as out-of-range operands resulting in a wrap-around behavior). Furthermore, some instructions present in CompCert's "assembly" languages are actually macros expanded by trusted (unverified) OCaml code. Some of these macros were inexactly specified, for instance by forgetting a clobbered register—this went unnoticed as long as the compiler did not take advantage of the value in that register being preserved [11]. (6) **Assembly language mis-expansion or misprinting**: we also found rare miscompilations in the expansion or printing of macros-instructions. For instance, a rarely selected instruction was misprinted; our macro-instruction for stack frame allocation did something incorrect but that almost always worked.

Some of these issues had not been detected for months, which indicated that testing was insufficient. We thus gradually developed a testing and continuous integration framework, which we ported to the other targets supported by CompCert, leading to new discoveries [11].

Here is an outline of the paper. Section 2 explains how we deliberately rely on compiler failures—issue (1) above—in order to simplify our formal proofs. Indeed, compiler failures seem a lesser evil than other issues, and testing is anyway necessary for these other issues. The remainder of the paper examines methods for identifying all these issues. Section 3 introduces an extended suite of tests. When a new bug is triggered, we describe in Sect. 4 how to produce a minimal example. CompCert's TCB is intended to be as small as possible, but it is almost inevitable to rely on trusted parts for both ends of the pipeline: the C and assembly semantics, as well as the expansion of assembly macro-instructions. Details about these sensitive parts and possible solutions are provided in Sect. 5. Another important aspect of testing is the benchmarking: measuring the performance of the generated code faithfully is not trivial, and require a rigorous strategy. Section 6 covers this topic, and presents our evaluation toolkit to compile, execute, and analyze representative benchmarks with multiple compilers, including CompCert. Finally, Sect. 7 concludes.

2   Formally Verified Defensive Tests

CompCert's formal proof assumes compilation success, and states nothing in case of failure. This allows for *Formally Verified Defensive Programming* (FVDP) [1]: complex computations are delegated to efficient functions, called *oracles*, whose implementations are both *untrusted* and hidden from formal proofs; only a *defensive test* of their result is formally verified.

For example, we introduced a hash-consing factory, formally verified using only defensive pointer equality tests [1, §3.3.2][21, §4.4]. We use *translation validation* [14,17,23], in particular by *symbolic execution*, an approach for compiler testing [6,19]: the same formally verified translation validator is used to check many untrusted transforms [22]. We validate fixpoints, computed using imperative data structures that cannot be easily modeled in Coq, by a verified checker [12].

Such a design induces simpler formal proofs, high modularity, while allowing for arbitrarily complex oracles.

In short, FDVP is a systematic approach for turning miscompilations into compiler failures (behavior (1) of §1). It helps us formally prove the absence of miscompilation (w.r.t. the TCB). Furthermore, such a compiler failure helps in debugging; the uncaught exception raised by the compiler directly points to the issue: either an incorrect oracle or a too coarse defensive test. For this, we still need testing for compiler failures extensively.

3   Test Suite for Compiler Correctness

AbsInt markets a version of CompCert suitable for qualification for safety-critical applications, e.g. nuclear power plants and avionics [7]. To our knowledge, this involves a large test suite, including the standard compliance suite SuperTest.[3] This test suite not being publically available, we extended the regression tests of CompCert's GitHub repository[4] with tests produced by off-the-shelf random generators, a form of *compiler fuzzing* [10], as well as the gcc "torture test" suite. The purpose of adding new tests here is to avoid both compile-time errors (especially failures and timeouts in our translation validators) and any form of miscompilation. Testing can help identify the six bad behaviors mentioned in §1. For each program generator i (items (a) and (b) below), N_i programs are generated by varying the random seed of the generator from 0 to $N_i - 1$, ensuring reproducibility. (a) **Csmith 2.3.0 & YarpGen 1.1**:[5] The produced code—which is supposed to be compilable and devoid of undefined behaviors—is compiled with both CompCert and gcc and run on the target processor or an instruction set simulator (e.g. qemu). The results are then compared (*differential testing*). Yet this code may fail to terminate, thus a timeout is used; the test is considered valid if both programs yield the same value, or fail to terminate within the timeout. The timeout value is large enough to avoid cases where only one program, better optimized, terminates while the other does not, but would with more time. (b) **CCG**:[6] Its programs are not expected to run correctly, so we thus just test that they compile correctly. (c) **gcc 12.2.0 tests**: Finally,

---

[3] See https://www.absint.com/ and https://solidsands.com/products/supertest.

[4] See directory "**test**" of https://github.com/AbsInt/CompCert/.

[5] https://github.com/csmith-project/csmith [24] with packed structures (gcc extension) disabled. https://github.com/intel/yarpgen (One random seed value is excluded because on ARM it leads to register allocation causing out of memory. Large auto-generated programs causing resource exhaustion in the compiler is not considered a bug [8]).

[6] https://github.com/Mrktn/ccg. We disabled the generation of ternary conditional operators with omitted middle operand, a gcc extension not supported by CompCert.

we added gcc's C torture tests, both for compilation only and for compilation + execution, except those that relied on gcc-specific extensions (such as SIMD vectors), gcc-specific behaviors on undefined or unspecified cases, and those that tested the limits of the compiler (i.e. very large number of declarations).

Each newly added generator or suite triggered new bugs (in our own extensions, or in upstream recent extensions not yet covered by AbsInt's tests). The full test suite, including the three items above, is triggered from continuous integration for a variety of targets.[7] Generally, test cases that triggered bugs had to be reduced (§4) before the bug could be investigated. In addition to making us more confident about the reliability of our validators by detecting compilation failures (§2), the tests helped to discover miscompilations (§5) and intolerable compilation running-times. We have also another framework for evaluating the performances of the generated code, briefly described in §6 (the test suite of this section is not designed to measure performance).

4   Reducing Test Cases

Random and application test cases are often too large for the compiler developer to identify bugs. Finding a reduced test case that exhibits the same bug is the first step for understanding what went wrong [4]. Reducing cases by hand is tedious and error-prone; we thus automated this task using C-Reduce.[8]

C-Reduce takes as input a C program (possibly several source or header files) and a predicate (typically a shell script), which must be satisfied by this original program, and gradually reduces the program by removing or simplifying declarations and statements, as long as the predicate is satisfied, until a minimal test case is produced. A timeout may be specified for evaluating the predicate, as well as other parameters (e.g. the number of cores for parallel execution).

On a compiler failure, the predicate is easy to write: simply execute the compiler and check that it crashes with the same error. For a timeout error, run the compiler with a timeout and check that it really reaches the timeout. For assembling (resp. linking) errors, check that the compiler runs successfully, but that assembling (resp. linking) fails with the same error.

When the error is miscompilation, the predicate is much harder to write. The main test is then to compile the program with CompCert and another compiler (gcc or clang), run both versions (on either the target processor or an instruction set simulator), and compare execution results: miscompilation is detected if their results diverge (either they print different values, or the version produced by CompCert crashes while the other does not). However, this criterion works only if the program does not have undefined behavior. Indeed, if a program has undefined behavior, such as reading from an uninitialized variable, it is normal that it gives one result with one compiler, another with another compiler. Unfortunately, if given the opportunity by a lax predicate, C-Reduce will

---

[7] x86, x86-64, AArch64, ARMv7 with software and hardware floating-point, 32-bit PowerPC, 64-bit RISC-V, KVX. This even led us to find bugs in qemu for PowerPC.

[8] https://embed.cs.utah.edu/creduce/ [18].

write programs that have undefined behavior: this is what usually happens if one removes statements haphazardly from a program, such as statements that initialize variables. The predicate should thus refuse programs that have undefined behavior.

An obvious method is to compile the program using gcc and/or clang and run the resulting program under Valgrind,[9] which checks for undefined behaviors at the object code level, such as accessing data outside currently allocated blocks, or branching (or conditionally moving data) according to a test on uninitialized values. In addition, if both gcc and clang are used, the program should give exactly the same output. Another approach is to compile the program using gcc and/or clang using the "sanitizers", which insert code that detects at runtime that certain undefined behaviors have happened. The categories of bugs that Valgrind and the "sanitizers" can detect overlap, but are not identical.

However, running the program under an instruction set simulator or under Valgrind is costly. It is thus very beneficial to exclude programs that evidently are likely to exhibit undefined behavior prior to running them. We ask gcc and clang to print error (as opposed to warning) messages when they discover certain undefined behaviors such as the use of an uninitialized variable.

Finally, some sanity checks on programs results are performed: for reducing a miscompilation bug that results in the gcc and CompCert versions printing out different checksums (e.g. for programs generated by Csmith), we check that the output indeed includes a line printing out a checksum. See details in the long version of this paper on https://hal.science/hal-04096390.

5   Checking the Trusted Computing Base

Formal C semantics [issue (4) of §1] Two mismatches between the C formal semantics of CompCert and that of the standard were identified: (a) memory allocation is supposed to always return a valid pointer (e.g. not NULL), unlike the standard's malloc function; (b) storing a bitfield in an otherwise uninitialized structure, then reading from it, yields an undefined (uninitialized) value whereas it should yield the value stored (truncated to the appropriate size); this is because initialized-ness is defined at word level, not bit level.

The second one was identified when using CompCert's reference C interpreter on reduced test cases. Neither can currently cause miscompilation, because CompCert's optimizations do not exploit these shortcuts of the formal semantics.

Unit testing of the assembly (macro-)instructions [issues (5) and (6) of §1] The formally verified part of CompCert ends with an abstraction of assembly code: (a) machine instructions are seen as operating over values, with the value datatype defined as a disjoint union of 32- and 64-bit integers, 32- and 64-bit floating-point values, and pointers, whereas in reality they are all bitstrings; pointers are pairs of a block identifier and an offset within this block, whereas in reality they are (in a flat memory model) just integers; (b) memory copy, used

---

[9] https://valgrind.org/ [15, 16, 20].

either as an intrinsic or for implementing C structure assignment, is a macro whose expansion depends on the block size; (c) memory is seen as independent blocks, and it is impossible to move from one to another by pointer arithmetic; each stack frame is an independent block; macros implement the creation and destruction of stack frames by expanding into a sequence that saves the previous frame's address and adjusts the stack pointer; (d) certain basic operations may be macro-instructions: taking the address of a global symbol may entail splitting it between high- and low-order bits or more complicated schemes;[10] on a 32-bit platform, adding two 64-bit numbers split in 32-bit registers involves propagating carry bits, which may not be reflected in the assembly semantics; etc.

The expansion of macro-instructions—miscompilation (6) of §1—has been identified as the main source of miscompilation bugs in CompCert (which, however, remain rare) [11], especially if they involve case analyses over arguments (register aliasing, constants): rarely exercised cases could be incorrect. Also, in some cases, wrong but syntactically correct instructions were printed.

Possibly, the definition of the formal semantics of the regular assembly instructions—mismatch (5) of §1—could also feature incorrect corner cases. However, our testing approach currently lacks a complete unit testing system that would match the semantics of abstract (pseudo-)instructions in their formal specification to that on the target processor. Such testing would not only need to check that the result values of the instruction fit the specification, whether these values are in processor registers or in memory, but also that values that the specification lists as unmodified were unaffected. Based on our coverage measurements, our tests do not validate the entire OCaml code of the TCB.

6   Testing the Performance of Generated Code

Developing a new pass require ensuring that its results are not only *beneficial* on every target, but also that it does not *interfere* with existing optimizations [2]. Since most instruction set simulators are not capable of counting cycles, we measure and compare the code performance of various CompCert configurations directly on the target core. Firstly, such measures are often subject to many *subtle biases* [13], among which are the runtime environment, the size of the benchmarks, as well as decisions by the operating system kernel: frequency scaling, migration between cores, etc. We address this by running multiple execution of each test, and by forcing the process to remain on the same core (e.g. with `taskset`), under the same shell environment. Then, we average out the different executions to filter them when the *relative standard deviation* exceeds a certain threshold (*noise elimination*), so that too small or unreliable tests are removed.

Secondly, for the comparison to GCC or Clang to be *fair*, we have to compare compilers on a common basis of applicable transformations. Notably, we disable options that would not be correct in the CompCert semantics—e.g. "fast-math",

---

[10] E.g., we implemented using symbols in thread-local storage (TLS) because some platforms put some C library globals in TLS even if the program is not multithreaded.

or replacing $ab + c$ by a fused multiply-add,[11] and instruction set extensions that CompCert cannot use—e.g., vector (SIMD) instructions.

For the measure to be *representative* and to avoid concluding on an overfitted subset of benchmarks, we combine several test suites: (a) an extended version of LLVMtest[12] (various concrete applications); (b) the computational oriented PolyBench;[13] the embedded oriented suites (c) MiBench [5] and (d) TACLeBench [3]; (e) and our own test suite with multiple types of tests (from small sorting algorithms to OCaml or GCC whole applications). See details in the long version of this paper on https://hal.science/hal-04096390.

We developed a performance measuring toolkit,[14] based on a JSON configuration that details, for each compiler to measure, sets of options to compare. Shell scripts then automatically (a) build; (b) copy to the target machine (e.g. via `rsync`); (c) run N times on a fixed core; and (d) gather tests results as CSV files. Finally, a Python/Pandas script filters and analyses CSVs to yield (in text or as a plot) the observed gains w.r.t. a reference compiler with options set pair.

7   Conclusion on Testing Formally Verified Software

Extensive testing on formally verified software is necessary for at least two reasons. First, the formal specification may not guarantee all the properties expected by users, but only *critical* ones (e.g. no miscompilation for CompCert). Second, critical bugs may still remain, because the formal specification might not exactly fit reality. However, in this case, critical bugs are in the—much smaller and simpler—TCB. For example, in our experience, bugs in CompCert's TCB are fixed a few days after their discovery. This seems to contrast with critical bugs in usual optimizing compilers which remain, on average, more than one year before being fixed [25].

Moreover, *formally verified defensive testing*—as introduced in §2—may drastically reduce the overall proof effort. It is also much more powerful for finding bugs of untrusted optimizations than usual testing: it detects all their miscompilation bugs for a given input file, without even running the code they generate. In contrast, in a usual compiler devoid of independent verification of the optimization passes, some of the bugs that we detected because compilation aborted would have resulted in miscompilation, which may have been unnoticed by usual testing.

Acknowledgement. We thank Xavier Leroy for his useful feedbacks on a preliminary version of this paper.

---

[11] An "fma" rounds differently from a × followed by a +. Replacing the latter by the former thus is a semantic change, which runs afoul of CompCert's soundness criteria.

[12] https://github.com/lac-dcc/Benchmarks.

[13] http://web.cs.ucla.edu/~pouchet/software/polybench/.

[14] Our benchmarks and toolkit: https://gricad-gitlab.univ-grenoble-alpes.fr/certicompil/chamois-benchs.

References

1. Boulmé, S.: Formally Verified Defensive Programming (efficient Coq-verified computations from untrusted ML oracles). Habilitation à diriger des recherches, Université Grenoble-Alpes (Sep 2021). www.hal.archives-ouvertes.fr/tel-03356701, see also www.verimag.imag.fr/boulme/hdr.html
2. Curtsinger, C., Berger, E.D.: STABILIZER: Statistically Sound Performance Evaluation. In: ASPLOS'2013, pp. 219–228. ACM (2013). https://doi.org/10.1145/2451116.2451141
3. Falk, H., et al.: TACLeBench: A benchmark collection to support worst-case execution time research. In: Schoeberl, M. (ed.) 16th International Workshop on Worst-Case Execution Time Analysis (WCET 2016). OpenAccess Series in Informatics (OASIcs), vol. 55, pp. 2:1–2:10. Schloss Dagstuhl-Leibniz-Zentrum für Informatik, Dagstuhl, Germany (2016)
4. GCC bugs. www.gcc.gnu.org/bugs/
5. Guthaus, M., Ringenberg, J., Ernst, D., Austin, T., Mudge, T., Brown, R.: MiBench: A free, commercially representative embedded benchmark suite. In: Proceedings of the Fourth Annual IEEE International Workshop on Workload Characterization. WWC-4 (Cat. No.01EX538), pp. 3–14. IEEE, Austin, TX, USA (2001). https://doi.org/10.1109/WWC.2001.990739, www.ieeexplore.ieee.org/document/990739/
6. King, J.C.: Symbolic execution and program testing. Commun. ACM **19**(7), 385–394 (1976). https://doi.org/10.1145/360248.360252
7. Kästner, D., et al.: CompCert: Practical experience on integrating and qualifying a formally verified optimizing compiler. In: ERTS 2018: Embedded Real Time Software and Systems. SEE (Jan 2018). https://xavierleroy.org/publi/erts2018_compcert.pdf
8. Leroy, X.: Answer to CompCert bug #137. www.github.com/AbsInt/CompCert/issues/137#issuecomment-243353529
9. Leroy, X.: Formal verification of a realistic compiler. Commun. ACM **52**(7) (2009). https://doi.org/10.1145/1538788.1538814
10. Marcozzi, M., Tang, Q., Donaldson, A.F., Cadar, C.: Compiler fuzzing: how much does it matter? Proc. ACM Program. Lang. **3**(OOPSLA), 155:1–155:29 (2019). https://doi.org/10.1145/3360581
11. Monniaux, D., Boulmé, S.: The trusted computing base of the compcert verified compiler. In: European Symposium on Programming Languages and Systems (ESOP '22). Lecture Notes in Computer Science, vol. 13240, pp. 204–233. Springer (2022). https://doi.org/10.1007/978-3-030-99336-8_8
12. Monniaux, D., Six, C.: Formally verified loop-invariant code motion and assorted optimizations. ACM Trans. Embed. Comput. Syst. **22**(1), 3:1–3:27 (2023). https://doi.org/10.1145/3529507
13. Mytkowicz, T., Diwan, A., Hauswirth, M., Sweeney, P.F.: Producing Wrong Data Without Doing Anything Obviously Wrong! In: ASPLOS'2009, pp. 265–276. ACM (2009). https://doi.org/10.1145/1508244.1508275
14. Necula, G.C.: Translation validation for an optimizing compiler. In: Programming Language Design and Implementation (PLDI), pp. 83–94. Association for Computing Machinery (2000). https://doi.org/10.1145/349299.349314
15. Nethercote, N., Seward, J.: How to shadow every byte of memory used by a program. In: Krintz, C., Hand, S., Tarditi, D. (eds.) Proceedings of the 3rd International Conference on Virtual Execution Environments, VEE 2007, San Diego, California, USA, June 13–15, 2007, pp. 65–74. ACM (2007). https://doi.org/10.1145/1254810.1254820

16. Nethercote, N., Seward, J.: Valgrind: a framework for heavyweight dynamic binary instrumentation. In: Ferrante, J., McKinley, K.S. (eds.) Proceedings of the ACM SIGPLAN 2007 Conference on Programming Language Design and Implementation, San Diego, California, USA, June 10–13, 2007, pp. 89–100. ACM (2007). https://doi.org/10.1145/1250734.1250746

17. Pnueli, A., Siegel, M., Singerman, E.: Translation validation. In: Tools and Algorihtms for the Construction and Analysis of Systems (TACAS). Lecture Notes in Computer Science, vol. 1384, pp. 151–166. Springer (1998). https://doi.org/10.1007/BFb0054170

18. Regehr, J., Chen, Y., Cuoq, P., Eide, E., Ellison, C., Yang, X.: Test-case reduction for C compiler bugs. In: Vitek, J., Lin, H., Tip, F. (eds.) ACM SIGPLAN Conference on Programming Language Design and Implementation, PLDI '12, Beijing, China - June 11–16, 2012, pp. 335–346. ACM (2012). https://doi.org/10.1145/2254064.2254104

19. Samet, H.: Compiler testing via symbolic interpretation. In: Gosden, J.A., Johnson, O.G. (eds.) Proceedings of the 1976 Annual Conference, Houston, Texas, USA, October 20–22, 1976, pp. 492–497. ACM (1976). https://doi.org/10.1145/800191.805648

20. Seward, J., Nethercote, N.: Using Valgrind to detect undefined value errors with bit-precision. In: Proceedings of the 2005 USENIX Annual Technical Conference, April 10–15, 2005, Anaheim, CA, USA, pp. 17–30. USENIX (2005). www.usenix.org/events/usenix05/tech/general/seward.html

21. Six, C., Boulmé, S., Monniaux, D.: Certified and efficient instruction scheduling: application to interlocked VLIW processors. Proc. ACM Program. Lang. 4(OOP-SLA), 129:1–129:29 (2020). https://doi.org/10.1145/3428197, https://hal.science/hal-02185883

22. Six, C., Gourdin, L., Boulmé, S., Monniaux, D., Fasse, J., Nardino, N.: Formally Verified Superblock Scheduling. In: Certified Programs and Proofs (CPP '22). Philadelphia, United States (Jan 2022). https://doi.org/10.1145/3497775.3503679, https://hal.science/hal-03200774

23. Tristan, J.B., Leroy, X.: Formal verification of translation validators: A case study on instruction scheduling optimizations. In: Proceedings of the 35th ACM Symposium on Principles of Programming Languages (POPL'08), pp. 17–27. ACM Press (Jan 2008) https://xavierleroy.org/publi/validation-scheduling.pdf

24. Yang, X., Chen, Y., Eide, E., Regehr, J.: Finding and understanding bugs in C compilers. In: Programming Language Design and Implementation (PLDI), pp. 283–294. Association for Computing Machinery (2011). https://doi.org/10.1145/1993498.1993532

25. Zhou, Z., Ren, Z., Gao, G., Jiang, H.: An empirical study of optimization bugs in gcc and llvm. J. Syst. Softw.**174**, 110884 (2021). https://doi.org/10.1016/j.jss.2020.110884, https://www.sciencedirect.com/science/article/pii/S0164121220302740

Formal Models

Certified Logic-Based Explainable AI –
The Case of Monotonic Classifiers

Aurélie Hurault[1]([✉]) [iD] and Joao Marques-Silva[2] [iD]

[1] IRIT, Université de Toulouse, Toulouse, France
`aurelie.hurault@enseeiht.fr`
[2] IRIT, CNRS, Toulouse, France
`joao.marques-silva@irit.fr`

Abstract. The continued advances in artificial intelligence (AI), including those in machine learning (ML), raise concerns regarding their deployment in high-risk and safety-critical domains. Motivated by these concerns, there have been calls for the verification of systems of AI, including their explanation. Nevertheless, tools for the verification of systems of AI are complex, and so error-prone. This paper describes one initial effort towards the certification of logic-based explainability algorithms, focusing on monotonic classifiers. Concretely, the paper starts by using the proof assistant Coq to prove the correctness of recently proposed algorithms for explaining monotonic classifiers. Then, the paper proves that the algorithms devised for monotonic classifiers can be applied to the larger family of *stable* classifiers. Finally, confidence code, extracted from the proofs of correctness, is used for computing explanations that are guaranteed to be correct. The experimental results included in the paper show the scalability of the proposed approach for certifying explanations.

Keywords: Formal Explainability · Certification

1 Introduction

The ongoing advances in Artificial Intelligence (AI), including in Machine Learning (ML), raise concerns about whether human decision makers can trust the decisions made by systems of AI/ML, and even whether they are able to fathom them. Aiming to address these concerns, the field of eXplainable AI (XAI) [7–9] has witnessed massive interest [6]. Explainability has also been proposed as a core component of efforts for the verification of ML models [25].

Unfortunately, most work on XAI offers no guarantees of rigor. Model-agnostic XAI approaches [16,23,24] represent one such example. As a result of the lack of guarantees of rigor, there is by now comprehensive evidence [10,11,14] that confirms the lack of rigor of non-formal XAI approaches. These results are troublesome, especially in application domains where rigor is paramount. To address the limitations of non-formal XAI, there has been work on formal XAI (FXAI) [17,19]. Formal explanations are logically defined and model-based, and

V. Prevosto and C. Seceleanu (Eds.): TAP 2023, LNCS 14066, pp. 51–67, 2023.
https://doi.org/10.1007/978-3-031-38828-6_4

so guarantee the correctness of computed explanations, as long as (i) the representation of the ML model is adequate; and (ii) the implemented algorithms are correct. Unfortunately, algorithms can exhibit bugs, as can their implementations. Hence, besides the need to explain and/or verify AI/ML models, and in settings that are deemed of high-risk or that are safety-critical, the certification of computed explanations is bound to become a required step.

This paper represents a first step in the direction of certifying the computation of explanations. Concretely, we use the Coq proof assistant to prove the correctness of recently proposed explanation algorithms for monotonic classifiers. The insights from the proof of correctness also serve to generalize the algorithms proposed for monotonic classifiers to a more general class of stable classifiers. Finally, the proofs of correctness are used to generate confidence code, which can be used for computing explanations that are guaranteed to be correct.

The paper is organized as follows. Section 2 introduces the notation and definitions used throughout the paper. Section 3 briefly overviews the computation of explanations in the case of monotonic classifiers [18]. Section 4 details the approach for the proofs of correctness and demonstrates that the results can be applied to a broader category of classifiers we named *stable*. Section 5 provides evidence to the scalability of certified explainers for *stable* classifiers. Finally, Sect. 6 concludes the paper.

2   Preliminaries

We follow the notation and definitions used in earlier work [18].

Classification Problems. A classification problem is defined on a set of features $\mathcal{F} = \{1, \ldots, N\}$ and a set of classes $\mathcal{K} = \{c_1, c_2, \ldots, c_M\}$. Each feature $i \in \mathcal{F}$ takes values from a domain $\mathcal{D}_i$. Domains are ordinal and bounded, and each domain can be defined on boolean, integer or real values. If $x_i \in \mathcal{D}_i$, then $\lambda(i)$ and $\mu(i)$ denote respectively the smallest and largest values that x_i can take, i.e. $\lambda(i) \leq x_i \leq \mu(i)$. Feature space is defined by $\mathbb{F} = \mathcal{D}_1 \times \mathcal{D}_2 \times \ldots \times \mathcal{D}_N$. The notation $\mathbf{x} = (x_1, \ldots, x_N)$ denotes an arbitrary point in feature space, where each x_i is a variable taking values from $\mathcal{D}_i$. Moreover, the notation $\mathbf{v} = (v_1, \ldots, v_N)$ represents a specific point in feature space, where each v_i is a constant representing one concrete value from $\mathcal{D}_i$. An *instance* denotes a pair $(\mathbf{v}, c)$, where $\mathbf{v} \in \mathbb{F}$ and $c \in \mathcal{K}$. An ML classifier $\mathcal{M}$ is characterized by a non-constant *classification function* κ that maps feature space $\mathbb{F}$ into the set of classes $\mathcal{K}$, i.e. $\kappa : \mathbb{F} \to \mathcal{K}$. Since we assume that κ is non-constant, then the ML classifier $\mathbb{M}$ is declared *nontrivial*, i.e. $\exists \mathbf{a}, \mathbf{b} \in \mathbb{F}, \kappa(\mathbf{a}) \neq \kappa(\mathbf{b})$.

Monotonic Classifiers. Given two points in feature space $\mathbf{a}$ and $\mathbf{b}$, $\mathbf{a} \leq \mathbf{b}$ if $a_i \leq b_i$, for all $i \in \{1, \ldots, N\}$. A set of classes $\mathcal{K} = \{c_1, \ldots, c_M\}$ is *ordered* if it respects a total order $\preccurlyeq$, with $c_1 \preccurlyeq c_2 \preccurlyeq \ldots \preccurlyeq c_M$. An ML classifier $\mathbb{M}$ is fully monotonic if the associated classification function is monotonic, i.e. $\mathbf{a} \leq \mathbf{b} \Rightarrow \kappa(\mathbf{a}) \preccurlyeq \kappa(\mathbf{b})$[1]. Throughout the paper, when referring to a monotonic

---

[1] The paper adopts the classification of monotonic classifiers proposed in earlier work [5].

classifier, this signifies a fully monotonic classifier. In addition, the interaction with a classifier is restricted to computing the value of $\kappa(\mathbf{v})$, for some point $\mathbf{v} \in \mathbb{F}$, i.e. the classifier will be viewed as a black-box.

As a monotonic classifier, we used a heart failure prediction in the Sect. 5, which depends on age and certain medical measures such as diabetes and platelet count. It is natural to expect the classifier to exhibit monotonicity, i.e., as age or diabetes levels increase, the risk of heart failure should also increase.

Stable Classifiers. An ML classifier is *stable* if the associated classification function respects $\forall \mathbf{a}, \mathbf{b}, \mathbf{c} \in \mathbb{F}, \mathbf{a} \le \mathbf{b} \le \mathbf{c} \wedge \kappa(\mathbf{a}) = \kappa(\mathbf{c}) \Rightarrow \kappa(\mathbf{a}) = \kappa(\mathbf{b}) = \kappa(\mathbf{c})$. As for monotonic classifiers, an order relation is needed on each domain $\mathcal{D}_i$. However, classes do not need to be ordered. All monotonic classifiers are *stable*. Not all stable classifiers are monotonic.

Intuitively, a *stable* classifier can be thought of as relaxing the requirement of monotonicity by not imposing a specific order on the classes. In other words, if two points in the feature space receive the same prediction from the classifier, then all points between them should also receive the same prediction.

Logic-Based Explainability. We now define formal explanations. For brevity, we only provide a brief introduction to logic-based explainability.

Prime implicant (PI) explanations [26] denote a minimal set of literals (relating a feature value x_i and a constant v_i from its domain $\mathcal{D}_i$) that are sufficient for the prediction.[2]. Formally, given $\mathbf{v} = (v_1, \ldots, v_N) \in \mathbb{F}$ with $\kappa(\mathbf{v}) = c$, an AXp is any minimal subset $\mathcal{X} \subseteq \mathcal{F}$ such that,

$$\forall (\mathbf{x} \in \mathbb{F}).\left[\bigwedge_{i \in \mathcal{X}}(x_i = v_i)\right] \rightarrow (\kappa(\mathbf{x}) = c) \tag{1}$$

We associate a predicate WAXp with (1), such that any set $\mathcal{X} \subseteq \mathcal{F}$ for which WAXp($\mathcal{X}$) holds is referred to as a *weak* AXp. Thus, every AXp is a weak AXp that is also subset-minimal. AXp's can be viewed as answering a 'Why?' question, i.e. why is some prediction made given some point in feature space. A different view of explanations is a contrastive explanation [21], which answers a 'Why Not?' question, i.e. which features can be changed to change the prediction. A formal definition of contrastive explanation is proposed in recent work [12]. Given $\mathbf{v} = (v_1, \ldots, v_N) \in \mathbb{F}$ with $\kappa(\mathbf{v}) = c$, a CXp is any minimal subset $\mathcal{Y} \subseteq \mathcal{F}$ such that,

$$\exists (\mathbf{x} \in \mathbb{F}).\bigwedge_{j \in \mathcal{F} \setminus \mathcal{Y}}(x_j = v_j) \wedge (\kappa(\mathbf{x}) \ne c) \tag{2}$$

Moreover, we associate a predicate WCXp with (2), such that any set $\mathcal{Y} \subseteq \mathcal{F}$ for which WCXp($\mathcal{Y}$) holds is referred to as a *weak* CXp. Thus, every CXp is a weak CXp that is also subset-minimal. Building on the results of R. Reiter in model-based diagnosis [12,22] proves a minimal hitting set (MHS) duality relation between AXp's and CXp's, i.e. AXp's are MHSes of CXp's and vice-versa. Furthermore, it can be shown that both predicates WAXp and WCXp are

---

[2] PI-explanations can be formulated as a problem of logic-based abduction, and so are also referred to as abductive explanations (AXp) [13]. More recently, AXp's have been studied from a knowledge compilation perspective [1].

monotone. An important consequence of this observation is that one can then use efficient oracle-based algorithms for finding AXp's and/or CXp's [20]. Thus, as long as one can devise logic encodings for an ML classifier (and this is possible for most ML classifiers), then (1) and (2), and access to a suitable reasoner, offer a solution for computing one AXp/CXp.

Recent years witnessed a rapid development of logic-based explainability, with practically efficient solutions devised for a growing number of ML models. Overviews of these results are available [17,19].

3   Explanations for Monotonic Classifiers

In [18], the authors proposed algorithms for computing explanations of a black-box monotonic classifier. Algorithms 1 and 2 compute the abductive and contrastive explanations of the prediction of a feature $\mathbf{v}$, for a classifier κ with a set of features $\mathcal{F}$. For all features $i \in \mathcal{F}$, $\mathbf{v}_i$ must be bounded between $\lambda(i)$ and $\mu(i)$.

Algorithm 1. findAXp $\mathcal{F}$ $\mathbf{v}$

1   $\mathbf{v}_l \leftarrow (\mathbf{v}_1, ..., \mathbf{v}_N)$
2   $\mathbf{v}_u \leftarrow (\mathbf{v}_1, ..., \mathbf{v}_N)$
3   $(C, D, P) \leftarrow (\mathcal{F}, \emptyset, \emptyset)$
4   **for all** $i \in \mathcal{F}$ **do**
5       $(\mathbf{v}_l, \mathbf{v}_u, C, D) \leftarrow \mathsf{FreeAttr}(i, \mathbf{v}, \mathbf{v}_l, \mathbf{v}_u, C, D)$
6   **if** $\kappa(\mathbf{v}_l) \neq \kappa(\mathbf{v}_u)$ **then**
7           $(\mathbf{v}_l, \mathbf{v}_u, D, P) \leftarrow \mathsf{FixAttr}(i, \mathbf{v}, \mathbf{v}_l, \mathbf{v}_u, C, P)$
8   **endif**
9   **endfor**
10 **return** P

Algorithm 2. findCXp $\mathcal{F}$ $\mathbf{v}$

1   $\mathbf{v}_l \leftarrow (\lambda(1), ..., \lambda(N))$
2   $\mathbf{v}_u \leftarrow (\mu(1), ..., \mu(N))$
3   $(C, D, P) \leftarrow (\mathcal{F}, \emptyset, \emptyset)$
4   **for all** $i \in \mathcal{F}$ **do**
5       $(\mathbf{v}_l, \mathbf{v}_u, C, D) \leftarrow \mathsf{FixAttr}(i, v, \mathbf{v}_l, \mathbf{v}_u, C, D)$
6   **if** $\kappa(\mathbf{v}_l) = k(\mathbf{v}_u)$ **then**
7           $(\mathbf{v}_l, \mathbf{v}_u, D, P) \leftarrow \mathsf{FreeAttr}(i, \mathbf{v}, \mathbf{v}_l, \mathbf{v}_u, C, P)$
8   **endif**
9   **endfor**
10 **return** P

Algorithm 3. FreeAttr i v $\mathbf{v}_l$ $\mathbf{v}_u$ A B	**Algorithm 4.** FixAttr i v $\mathbf{v}_l$ $\mathbf{v}_u$ A B
1 $\mathbf{v}_l \leftarrow (\mathbf{v}_{l1}, ... \lambda(i), ..., \mathbf{v}_{lN})$	1 $\mathbf{v}_l \leftarrow (\mathbf{v}_{l1}, ... \mathbf{v}_i, ..., \mathbf{v}_{lN})$
2 $\mathbf{v}_u \leftarrow (\mathbf{v}_{u1}, ... \mu(i), ..., \mathbf{v}_{uN})$	2 $\mathbf{v}_u \leftarrow (\mathbf{v}_{u1}, ... \mathbf{v}_i, ..., \mathbf{v}_{uN})$
3 $(A, B) \leftarrow (A \setminus \{i\}, B \cup \{i\})$	3 $(A, B) \leftarrow (A \setminus \{i\}, B \cup \{i\})$
4 **return** (v_l, v_u, A, B)	4 **return** $(\mathbf{v}_l, \mathbf{v}_u, A, B)$

The idea behind the algorithms is to analyze the features one by one and determine whether they have an impact on the decision. In abductive explanations, two points in the feature space are tested with the minimum and maximum values for the feature being tested. If the classifications are different, then that feature has an impact on the answer and is included in the explanation to answer the question "Why?". In contrastive explanations, two points in the feature space are tested with the minimum and maximum values for all features except the one being tested. If the classification is the same, and since the classifier is not trivial, the feature must be changed to alter the classification value, answering the question "Why not?" and is included in the explanation. For pedagogical reasons, this explanation is simplified: in the algorithm, the features are tested while considering the responses obtained for the features previously tested.

4 Proofs

The aim of this work is threefold: to prove the correctness of the algorithms, to extract the confidence code from the proof of correctness, and to investigate whether the monotonicity constraint of the classifiers can be relaxed.

To achieve these objectives, we used a proof assistant that allows code extraction: Coq[3].

The Coq proof, the Python codes used to generate and check the models, and the OCaml code used to run the experiments (Sect. 5) are available at this link: https://github.com/hurault/tap23.

4.1 Coq

Coq is a proof assistant that is built on a programming language called Gallina, which allows expressing mathematical theorems and software specifications. This language combines higher-order logic and functional programming. Coq provides a command language for defining functions and predicates, stating theorems and specifications, and developing formal proofs interactively. The proofs can then be checked by a small certification "kernel". Additionally, Coq allows the extraction of certified programs into languages such as OCaml, Haskell, or Scheme.

---

[3] https://coq.inria.fr.

4.2   The Coq Formalization

To ensure compatibility with Coq, it was necessary to modify the method used to encode the original algorithms (1, 2, 3, and 4), while ensuring that the changes facilitated the proof of termination and correctness, as well as code generation.

In Coq, the data structures are homogeneous, so all features should have the same type T. That is, for all i in $\mathcal{F}$, $\mathcal{D}_i = T$. This type T requires a total order relation. This may seem restrictive, but all digital types, for example, meet these constraints. A point in feature space is represented by a list of elements of type T. The output of the classifier has type Tk. The only requirement on Tk is the existence of a decidable equality (Tk_eq_dec). C and D are not used and are dropped, while P is coded by a list of naturals (indexes of the features).

The original iterative way of coding the algorithms has been replaced by a recursive version that is more in line with the Coq environment. For the abductive (resp. contrastive) explanation, two auxiliary functions are required: findAXp_aux which adds parameters that correspond to the variables of the original algorithm and findAXp_aux_j that corresponds to the loop. To ease the proof of termination for Coq, the parameter j that indicates the feature to analyze is chosen to be strictly decreasing.

The Coq version of algorithm 1 is presented in algorithm 5. A similar transformation has been carried out for findCXp.

An auxiliary function is also needed for FreeAttr. The Coq version of the original algorithm 3 is given in algorithm 6. Equivalent transformations are also done for FixAttr.

The Coq formalization of the AXp property (Eq. 1) is given in algorithm 7. Equivalent formalization is done for the CXp property (Eq. 2).

The formalization of the algorithms and their Coq proof can be found in the file Coq/AXp_CXp_Stable_nfeatures.v.

4.3   Results

In [18], the authors proposed algorithms and argued for their correctness for monotonic classifiers. In our paper, we provide a proof of their correctness and relax the monotonicity constraint on the classifier to a more general class of classifiers known as *stable* classifiers.

The AXp finder algorithm is proven correct for stable classifiers.

Theorem 1.

$$\forall k : (list\ T \to Tk), \mathsf{stable}\ k \to ($$
$$\forall v : list\ T, length\ v = N$$
$$\wedge\ \forall j \in [0, N[, \lambda(j) \leq v_j \leq \mu(j)$$
$$\to \mathsf{is\_AXp}\ k\ v\ (\mathsf{findAXp}\ k\ v)$$
$$)$$

Proof. Done with Coq.   □

Algorithm 5. findAXp κ **v**

```
1   (* Find the abductive explanation of v *)
2   (* j : (N-j) the feature to check *)
3   (* p : the feature before (N-j) that are part of the explanation *)
4   (* j is decreasing for Coq to proof the termination *)
5   Fixpoint findAXp_aux_j (k: list T → Tk) (j:nat) (v vl vu: list T) (p:list nat)
6   {struct j}: list nat :=
7   match j with
8   | 0 ⇒ p
9   | S jminus1 ⇒
10    let '(nvl,nvu) := freeAttr (N−j) vl vu in
11    match T_eq_dec (k nvl) (k nvu) with
12    | false ⇒ let '(nvl,nvu,np) := fixAttr (N−j) v nvl nvu p in
13                  findAXp_aux_j k jminus1 v nvl nvu np
14    | true ⇒ findAXp_aux_j k jminus1 v nvl nvu p
15      end
16  end.
17
18  (* Find the abductive explanation of v *)
19  (* i : the feature to check *)
20  (* p : the feature before i that are part of the explanation *)
21  Definition findAXp_aux (k: list T → Tk) (i:nat) (v vl vu: list T) (p:list nat):
22  list nat :=
23    findAXp_aux_j k (N−i) v vl vu p.
24
25  (* Find the abductive explanation of v *)
26  Program Definition findAXp (k: list T → Tk) (v: list T) : list nat :=
27    findAXp_aux k 0 v v v nil.
```

Algorithm 6. FreeAttr i $\mathbf{v}_l$ $\mathbf{v}_u$

```
1   (* Replace the i-th elements of the list vl and vu *)
2   by a value determined by n *)
3   Fixpoint freeAttr_aux (i:nat) (n:nat) (vl:list T) (vu:list T) :=
4     match i,vl,vu with
5     | 0,_:: ql,_:: qu ⇒ ((lambda n)::ql,(mu n):: qu)
6     | _,tl:: ql,tu:: qu ⇒ let (rl,ru) := freeAttr_aux (i−1) n ql qu
7                          in (tl:: rl,tu:: ru)
8     |_,_,_ ⇒ (vl,vu)
9     end.
10
11  (* Replace the i-th elements of the lists vl and vu *)
12  by lambda i and mu i *)
13  Definition freeAttr (i:nat) (vl:list T) (vu:list T) := freeAttr_aux i i vl vu.
```

Algorithm 7. is_AXp

```
1   Definition is_weak_AXp (k : list T → Tk) (v: list T) (p:list nat) : Prop :=
2       forall (x: list T),
3       List.length v = N
4       (* x in feature space *)
5     ∧ List.length x = N
6       (* the values of the features of x are in the bounds *)
7       (* led is the relation order in feature space *)
8     ∧ (forall (j:nat), j>=0 ∧ j< N
9         → (led (lambda j) (get j x) ∧ led (get j x) (mu j)))
10      (* the values of the feature constraints in the explanation
11        are the same in x and v *)
12    ∧ (forall (j:nat), j>=0 ∧ j< N
13        → ((mem j p ∧ get j x = get j v) ∨ (not (mem j p))))
14      → k(x)=k(v).
15
16  Definition is_AXp (k : list T → Tk) (v: list T) (p:list nat) : Prop :=
17      (* satisfy the equation of AXp *)
18      is_weak_AXp k v p
19    ∧ (* no subset satisfies the equation of AXp *)
20      forall (q:list nat), (is_strict_subset q p) → not (is_weak_AXp k v q).
```

The CXp finder algorithm is proved correct for stable and nontrivial classifiers.

Theorem 2.

$$\forall k : (list\ T \to Tk), \text{not\_trivial } k \wedge \text{stable } k \to ($$

$$\forall v : list\ T, length\ v = N$$
$$\wedge\ \forall j \in [0, N[, \lambda(j) \le v_j \le \mu(j)$$
$$\to \text{is\_CXp } k\ v\ (\text{findCXp } k\ v)$$
$$)$$

Proof. Done with Coq.

4.4 Proof Sketch

Here is the proof sketch for the algorithm computing abductive explanations. The same structure is used for contrastive explanations.

1. A property R, depending on $\kappa, i, \mathbf{v}, \mathbf{v}_l, \mathbf{v}_u$ and p is identified and proven to be true for the initial values of findAXp_aux i.e. $R(\kappa, 0, \mathbf{v}, \mathbf{v}, \mathbf{v}, nil)$ (lemma R_init_Axp).
2. The property R is proven to be preserved by the two recursive cases of the algorithm:

(a) $R(\kappa, i, \mathbf{v}, \mathbf{v}_l, \mathbf{v}_u, p)$
   $\wedge(\mathbf{nv}_l, \mathbf{nv}_u) = \mathsf{freeAttr}(i, \mathbf{v}, \mathbf{v}_l, \mathbf{v}_u, p)$
   $\wedge(\mathbf{nnv}_l, \mathbf{nnv}_u, np) = \mathsf{fixAttr}(i, \mathbf{v}, \mathbf{nv}_l, \mathbf{nv}_u, p)$
   $\rightarrow R(\kappa, i+1, \mathbf{v}, \mathbf{nnv}_l, \mathbf{nnv}_u, np)$

(b) $R(\kappa, i, \mathbf{v}, \mathbf{v}_l, \mathbf{v}_u, p)$
   $\wedge(\mathbf{nv}_l, \mathbf{nv}_u) = \mathsf{freeAttr}(i, \mathbf{v}, \mathbf{v}_l, \mathbf{v}_u, p)$
   $\rightarrow R(\kappa, i+1, \mathbf{v}, \mathbf{nv}_l, \mathbf{nv}_u, p)$

R is in fact a conjunction of several sub-properties, each of these R_i properties is handled by the lemmas preserveRiCas2_AXp and preserveRiCas3_AXp for case (a) and case (b).

3. A second property E, depending on $\kappa, i, \mathbf{v}, \mathbf{v}_l, \mathbf{v}_u$ and p is identified and proven to be implied by R i.e. $R(\kappa, i, \mathbf{v}, \mathbf{v}_l, \mathbf{v}_u, p) \rightarrow E(\kappa, i, \mathbf{v}, \mathbf{v}_l, \mathbf{v}_u, p)$ (lemma R_implies_E_findAXp).
4. The last step proves that E in the terminal case, i.e. $E(\kappa, N, \mathbf{v}, \mathbf{v}_l, \mathbf{v}_u, p)$, implies that p is an abductive explanation of $\mathbf{v}$ for κ (theorem axp_all).

R : The property R is a conjunction of ten or eleven properties that are listed in Fig. 1. These properties are about the size of the lists used for representing an instance of the feature space (R_0) and the bounded properties of the elements of these lists (R_1). R_4, R_6, R_7, and R_9 explicitly state the values of $\mathbf{v}_l$ and $\mathbf{v}_u$ depending on i (the current feature), λ, μ, $\mathbf{v}$, and p. R_5 and R_8 give some information about p: it is sorted and can only contain features that have been reviewed. $R10$ explains the consequences for a feature x of being part of the explanation p. R_2 links the value of $\kappa(\mathbf{v})$, $\kappa(\mathbf{v}_l)$, and $\kappa(\mathbf{v}_u)$.

E : The property E is a conjunction of three properties that are listed in Fig. 2. E_1 states that the explanation is a weak explanation. E_2 states that the explanation is sorted and E_3 explains the consequences for a feature x of being part of an explanation. E_2 and E_3 are necessary to prove that the explanation is subset-minimal.

Additional Lemmas. The proof of preservation of R requires lemmas on FreeAttr and FixAttr, such as the preservation of list size, bounded properties of features, and modification of only the i-th element. In total, 137 lemmas are necessary to prove the two correctness theorems for the algorithms.

4.5   Computing Explanations that Are Guaranteed to Be Correct

Let us recall that the objective of this work is to compute explanations that are guaranteed to be correct. We have proof that if a classifier is stable, the algorithms generate correct explanations. To have confidence in a tool's generated explanations, one must have confidence in the algorithm's implementation and in the stability of the classifiers.

	findAXp_aux κ i $\mathbf{v}$ $\mathbf{v}_l$ $\mathbf{v}_u$ p	findCXp_aux κ i $\mathbf{v}$ $\mathbf{v}_l$ $\mathbf{v}_u$ p
R_0	List.length $\mathbf{v} = N$ List.length $\mathbf{v}_l = N$ List.length $\mathbf{v}_u = N$	idem
R_1	$\forall j \in [0, N[, \lambda(j) \leq \mathbf{v}_j \leq \mu(j)$ $\forall j \in [0, N[, \lambda(j) \leq \mathbf{v}_{lj} \leq \mu(j)$ $\forall j \in [0, N[, \lambda(j) \leq \mathbf{v}_{uj} \leq \mu(j)$	idem
R_2	$\kappa(\mathbf{v}_l) = \kappa(\mathbf{v}_u) = \kappa(\mathbf{v})$	$\kappa(\mathbf{v}_l) \neq \kappa(\mathbf{v}_u)$
R_3	$i \geq 0$	idem
R_4	$\forall j \in [0, N[,$ $\lambda(j) = \mathbf{v}_{lj} \wedge \mu(j) = \mathbf{v}_{uj}$ $\vee\ \mathbf{v}_j = \mathbf{v}_{lj} \wedge \mathbf{v}_j = \mathbf{v}_{uj}$	not needed
R_5	$\forall j \in [0, N[, j \geq i \rightarrow j \notin p$	idem
R_6	$\forall j \in [0, N[, j \in p \rightarrow$ $\mathbf{v}_j = \mathbf{v}_{lj} \wedge \mathbf{v}_j = \mathbf{v}_{uj}$	$\forall j \in [0, N[, j \in p \rightarrow$ $\lambda(j) = \mathbf{v}_{lj} \wedge \mu(j) = \mathbf{v}_{uj}$
R_7	$\forall j \in [0, N[, j < i \wedge j \notin p \rightarrow$ $\lambda(j) = \mathbf{v}_{lj} \wedge \mu(j) = \mathbf{v}_{uj}$	$\forall j \in [0, N[, j \geq i \rightarrow$ $\lambda(j) = \mathbf{v}_{lj} \wedge \mu(j) = \mathbf{v}_{uj}$
R_8	is_sorted p	idem
R_9	$\forall j \in [0, N[, j \geq i \rightarrow$ $\mathbf{v}_j = \mathbf{v}_{lj} \wedge \mathbf{v}_j = \mathbf{v}_{uj}$	$\forall j \in [0, N[, j < i \wedge j \notin p \rightarrow$ $\mathbf{v}_j = \mathbf{v}_{lj} \wedge \mathbf{v}_j = \mathbf{v}_{uj}$
R_{10}	$\forall x, x_0, x_1, p = x_0 @(x :: x_1) \rightarrow$ $\exists nv_l, nv_u, (\forall j \in [0, N[,$ $((p \in x_1 \vee j > x) \wedge$ $\mathbf{v}_j = nv_{lj} \wedge \mathbf{v}_j = nv_{uj})$ $\vee$ $(\neg(p \in x_1 \vee j > x) \wedge$ $\lambda(j) = nv_{lj} \wedge \mu(j) = nv_{uj}))$ $\wedge$ $\kappa(nv_l) \neq \kappa(nv_u)$	$\forall x, x_0, x_1, p = x_0 @(x :: x_1) \rightarrow$ $\exists nv_l, nv_u, (\forall j \in [0, N[,$ $((p \in x_1 \vee j > x) \wedge$ $\lambda(j) = nv_{lj} \wedge \mu(j) = nv_{uj})$ $\vee$ $(\neg(p \in x_1 \vee j > x) \wedge$ $\mathbf{v}_j = nv_{lj} \wedge \mathbf{v}_j = nv_{uj}))$ $\wedge$ $\kappa(nv_l) = \kappa(nv_u)$

Fig. 1. Invariants

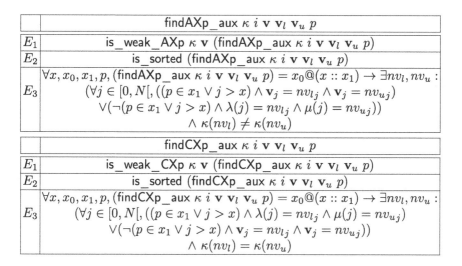

findAXp_aux κ i **v** $\mathbf{v}_l$ $\mathbf{v}_u$ p
E_1 is_weak_AXp κ **v** (findAXp_aux κ i **v** $\mathbf{v}_l$ $\mathbf{v}_u$ p)

	findAXp_aux κ i **v** $\mathbf{v}_l$ $\mathbf{v}_u$ p
E_1	is_weak_AXp κ **v** (findAXp_aux κ i **v** $\mathbf{v}_l$ $\mathbf{v}_u$ p)
E_2	is_sorted (findAXp_aux κ i **v** $\mathbf{v}_l$ $\mathbf{v}_u$ p)
E_3	$\forall x, x_0, x_1, p, (\text{findAXp\_aux } \kappa\, i\, \mathbf{v}\, \mathbf{v}_l\, \mathbf{v}_u\, p) = x_0 @ (x :: x_1) \rightarrow \exists nv_l, nv_u :$ $(\forall j \in [0, N[, ((p \in x_1 \lor j > x) \land \mathbf{v}_j = nv_{l_j} \land \mathbf{v}_j = nv_{u_j})$ $\lor (\neg(p \in x_1 \lor j > x) \land \lambda(j) = nv_{l_j} \land \mu(j) = nv_{u_j}))$ $\land \kappa(nv_l) \neq \kappa(nv_u)$

	findCXp_aux κ i **v** $\mathbf{v}_l$ $\mathbf{v}_u$ p
E_1	is_weak_CXp κ **v** (findCXp_aux κ i **v** $\mathbf{v}_l$ $\mathbf{v}_u$ p)
E_2	is_sorted (findCXp_aux κ i **v** $\mathbf{v}_l$ $\mathbf{v}_u$ p)
E_3	$\forall x, x_0, x_1, p, (\text{findCXp\_aux } \kappa\, i\, \mathbf{v}\, \mathbf{v}_l\, \mathbf{v}_u\, p) = x_0 @ (x :: x_1) \rightarrow \exists nv_l, nv_u :$ $(\forall j \in [0, N[, ((p \in x_1 \lor j > x) \land \lambda(j) = nv_{l_j} \land \mu(j) = nv_{u_j})$ $\lor (\neg(p \in x_1 \lor j > x) \land \mathbf{v}_j = nv_{l_j} \land \mathbf{v}_j = nv_{u_j}))$ $\land \kappa(nv_l) = \kappa(nv_u)$

Fig. 2. Post conditions

Confidence on the Implementation. Coq is used to extract OCaml code that is certified as correct, i.e. it validates proven properties. We can provide a certified tool that computes correct explanations.

The generated OCaml code is not modified, but it is reorganized. The *.mli* file generated by Coq is converted into a signature module (with some additional functions), while the *.ml* file generated by Coq is converted into a functor that conforms with the signature module and is parameterized by a dataset (file OCaml/explain.ml). For each dataset, the axioms (N, T, Tk, Tk_eq_dec, λ, and μ) need to be realized (file OCaml/dataset.ml). k is implemented using the pyml library[4], which allows for an efficient binding between the OCaml generated by Coq and the Python used to generate and run classifiers (file Ocaml/runAXpCXp.ml).

Confidence on the Stablity of the Classifiers. The literature commonly employs the monotonicity constraint more frequently than the stability constraint. As far as we are aware, no tool exists that guarantees model stability while several tools offer ways to force monotony: XGBoost[5] [3], COMET[6] [27], Deep Lattice Network (DLN)[7] [28] or Certified Monotonic Neural Networks[8] [15].

None of those tools is certified as correct, so we have developed a Python program, using XGBoost, that check the stability (file XGBoost/verif_stable.py)

---

[4] https://github.com/thierry-martinez/pyml.
[5] https://xgboost.readthedocs.io/en/stable/tutorials/monotonic.html.
[6] https://github.com/AishwaryaSivaraman/COMET.
[7] https://www.tensorflow.org/lattice/overview.
[8] https://github.com/gnobitab/CertifiedMonotonicNetwork.

and monotonicity (file XGBoost/verif_mono.py) of a classifier through **exhaustive testing** on the predictions of the training and testing datatsets. In the next section, it will be shown that three out of the four models used are monotonic, but one is not. However, since the predictions are stable, the model can still be used.

5   Experiments

In this section, we present a series of experiments aimed at demonstrating the feasibility and scalability of our approach. Through these experiments, we illustrate how our method can address the challenges we have identified and provide tangible evidence of its potential benefits.

5.1   Datasets

Four datasets are used from https://www.kaggle.com and can be found in the XGBoost/dataset repository:

- Car Evaluation Data Set[9]
- Heart Failure Prediction[10]
- Placement data full class[11]
- The Complete Pokemon Dataset[12]

Some modifications, such as feature digitization, removal of non-digital features, removal of incomplete instances, and modification of some output features for certain instances, are done to make the datasets monotonic.

Name	nb instances	nb features	nb classes
Heart	299	11	2
Car	1728	6	4
Placement	148	7	4
Pokemon	800	31	2

Fig. 3. Properties of the datasets

A summary of the properties of the datasets is presented in Fig. 3.

5.2   Models

XGBoost[13] [3] is used to create models that exhibit monotonicity. The Python code can be found in the file XGBoost/build_mono.py. As explain previously, after generating the model, a Python program is used to perform a test to ensure that its predictions on the dataset adhere to both the monotonicity and stability constraints.

---

[9] https://www.kaggle.com/datasets/elikplim/car-evaluation-data-set.
[10] https://www.kaggle.com/datasets/andrewmvd/heart-failure-clinical-data.
[11] https://www.kaggle.com/datasets/barkhaverma/placement-data-full-class.
[12] https://www.kaggle.com/datasets/rounakbanik/pokemon.
[13] https://xgboost.readthedocs.io/en/stable/.

Name	Accuracy	Monotonic ?	Stable ?	Size of the json file
Heart	71.72%	No	Yes	59.9Kio
Car	99.12%	Yes	Yes	650.9Kio
Placement	63.27%	Yes	Yes	19.0 Kio
Pokemon	98.86%	Yes	Yes	48.1 Kio

Fig. 4. Properties of the models generated by XGBoost

A summary of the properties of the models is presented in Fig. 4.

5.3 Computing Explanations

To use the certified code (see Sect. 4.5), the axioms N, T, Tk, $\mathsf{Tk\_eq\_dec}$, λ, and μ need to be implemented for each dataset. The N axiom is provided in Fig. 3. For the four datasets $T = float$, $T_k = int$, and $\mathsf{Tk\_eq\_dec}$ is the equality on int. λ and μ are extracted from the datasets.

The experiment are run in a Dell Inc. Latitude 7400 with 32Gio RAM and 8 Intel® Core™ i7-8665U CPU @ 1.90GHz. The operating system is Ubuntu 22.04.2 LTS (64 bits). The execution time is compute using the Linux time command.

Name	Average size AXp	Average size CXp	Time for the entire dataset	Time for 100 instances (proportion)
Heart	2.45	1.61	user 0m24.991s sys 0m0.909s	0m8.358s 0m0.304s
Car	2.39	1.27	user 6m1.489s sys 0m1.704s	0m20.919s 0m0.098s
Placement	2.14	1.51	user 0m8.493s sys 0m0.864s	0m8.739s 0m0.584s
Pokemon	1.71	2.76	user 2m47.066s sys 0m1.600s	0m20.883s 0m0.200s

Fig. 5. Properties of the explanations

A summary of the explanation properties is given in Fig. 5. As can be observed, the explanation sizes are generally small, which confirms the interest in computing AXp and CXp explanations and helps to explain the model.

The algorithm makes $2 * N$ calls to κ, which is linear in the number of features. This enables the code to scale effectively with larger feature sets. The number of features explains the difference in computation times for the different models and in particular why the execution time, reduced to 100 instances, is more important for the *pokemon* dataset which has three times more features than the others. Even if the *car* model has only six features, the execution time is higher than expected. We assume that this is due to the size of the generated model. Despite this, the computation time for calculating explanations of several hundred instances is reasonable considering that the code is written for certification rather than optimization.

As an example, Fig. 6 shows the distribution of features in the explanations for the heart dataset and model.

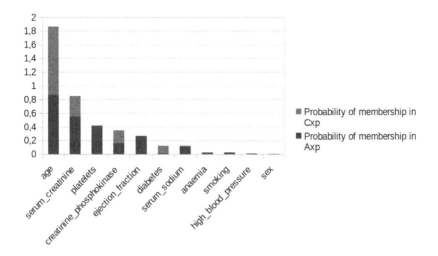

Fig. 6. Probability for a feature to be in the explanations

Our analysis reveals that, certain features are found to only contribute to the abductive explanations (*platelets*), while others are only relevant to the contrastive explanations (*diabetes*). This highlights the importance of distinguishing between these types of explanations when interpreting the classifier's behavior.

5.4   Comparison with Direct Mono-Language Implementation

To evaluate the effectiveness of the certified code, the algorithms were coded in Python (file XGBoost/find_xp.py) and run on the same models and dataset as the certified code. The comparison of the execution time is presented in the table in Fig. 7.

Except for the model *car*, we can notice that the code generated by Coq takes around 25% more user time and 5% more system time. The difference in execution time is due to the fact that the code was written to facilitate proof, not efficiency, and calls to classifiers are cross-language. However, despite this, the execution times are still reasonable and demonstrate the dual benefits of the work: proving that the algorithm is correct and providing a proof of concept for the use of certified correct code.

Name		OCaml generated code	Python code	Additional time
Heart	user	0m24.991s	0m19.672s	27%
	sys	0m0.909s	0m0.880s	3%
Car	user	6m1.489s	1m2.110s	482%
	sys	0m1.704s	0m1.115s	52%
Placement	user	0m8.493s	0m6.712s	26.5%
	sys	0m0.864s	0m0.792s	9%
Pokemon	user	2m47.066s	2m15.932s	22.9%
	sys	0m1.600s	0m1.516s	5.5%

Fig. 7. Execution time comparison between the OCaml generated code and a Python code

6   Conclusions

Explainability is posed to prove instrumental in delivering trustworthy AI, including in high-risk and safety-critical application domains. Unfortunately, informal XAI approaches offer no guarantees of rigor, and so their use in high-risk and safety-critical domains could be disastrous. There has been recent work on formal explainability, which offers guarantees of rigor in computed explanations. However, implemented algorithms (and some times their description) may not be correct.

This paper takes a first step towards delivering certified explanations. The paper considers monotonic classifiers, proves the correctness of proposed algorithms, and extracts confidence code from the proofs of correctness. The experimental results validate the scalability of the work.

Future work will extend the certification of formal explainability algorithms to classifiers more complex than the monotonic case. For tractable explainability problems, we envision adopting an approach similar to the one described in this paper. For more complex explainability problems, e.g. when the decision problems are (co-)NP-complete or even Σ_2^P/Π_2^P-hard, we envision adopting solutions similar to those used in the case of automated reasoners, especially SAT solvers [2,4].

References

1. Audemard, G., Koriche, F., Marquis, P.: On tractable XAI queries based on compiled representations. In: KR, pp. 838–849 (2020)
2. Biere, A., Heule, M., van Maaren, H., Walsh, T. (eds.): Handbook of Satisfiability - Second Edition, Frontiers in Artificial Intelligence and Applications, vol. 336. IOS Press (2021). https://doi.org/10.3233/FAIA336
3. Chen, T., Guestrin, C.: XGBoost: a scalable tree boosting system. In: Proceedings of the 22nd ACM SIGKDD International Conference on Knowledge Discovery and Data Mining (KDD '16), pp. 785–794. ACM, New York (2016). https://doi.org/10.1145/2939672.2939785

4. Cruz-Filipe, L., Marques-Silva, J., Schneider-Kamp, P.: Formally verifying the solution to the Boolean pythagorean triples problem. J. Automat. Reason. **63**(3), 695–722 (2018). https://doi.org/10.1007/s10817-018-9490-4

5. Daniels, H., Velikova, M.: Monotone and partially monotone neural networks. IEEE Trans. Neural Netw. **21**(6), 906–917 (2010)

6. Guidotti, R., Monreale, A., Ruggieri, S., Turini, F., Giannotti, F., Pedreschi, D.: A survey of methods for explaining black box models. ACM Comput. Surv. **51**(5), 93:1–93:42 (2019)

7. Gunning, D.: Explainable artificial intelligence (xai). dARPA-BAA-16-53 (2016). https://www.darpa.mil/attachments/DARPA-BAA-16-53.pdf

8. Gunning, D., Aha, D.W.: Darpa's explainable artificial intelligence (XAI) program. AI Mag. **40**(2), 44–58 (2019). https://doi.org/10.1609/aimag.v40i2.2850

9. Gunning, D., Stefik, M., Choi, J., Miller, T., Stumpf, S., Yang, G.: XAI - explainable artificial intelligence. Sci. Robot. **4**(37) (2019). https://doi.org/10.1126/scirobotics.aay7120

10. Huang, X., Marques-Silva, J.: The inadequacy of shapley values for explainability. arXiv preprint CoRR abs/2302.08160 (2023). arXiv:2302.08160

11. Ignatiev, A.: Towards trustable explainable AI. In: IJCAI, pp. 5154–5158 (2020)

12. Ignatiev, A., Narodytska, N., Asher, N., Marques-Silva, J.: From contrastive to abductive explanations and back again. In: AIxIA, pp. 335–355 (2020)

13. Ignatiev, A., Narodytska, N., Marques-Silva, J.: Abduction-based explanations for machine learning models. In: AAAI, pp. 1511–1519 (2019)

14. Ignatiev, A., Narodytska, N., Marques-Silva, J.: On validating, repairing and refining heuristic ML explanations. CoRR abs/1907.02509 arXiv preprint (2019) arXiv:1907.02509

15. Liu, X., Han, X., Zhang, N., Liu, Q.: Certified monotonic neural networks. Adv. Neural Inf. Process. Syst. **33** (2020)

16. Lundberg, S.M., Lee, S.: A unified approach to interpreting model predictions. In: NeurIPS, pp. 4765–4774 (2017)

17. Marques-Silva, J.: Logic-based explainability in machine learning. CoRR abs/2211.00541 arXiv preprint (2022). arXiv:2211.00541

18. Marques-Silva, J., Gerspacher, T., Cooper, M.C., Ignatiev, A., Narodytska, N.: Explanations for monotonic classifiers. In: ICML, pp. 7469–7479 (2021)

19. Marques-Silva, J., Ignatiev, A.: Delivering trustworthy AI through formal XAI. In: AAAI, pp. 12342–12350 (2022)

20. Marques-Silva, J., Janota, M., Mencía, C.: Minimal sets on propositional formulae, problems and reductions. Artif. Intell. **252**, 22–50 (2017). https://doi.org/10.1016/j.artint.2017.07.005

21. Miller, T.: Explanation in artificial intelligence: insights from the social sciences. Artif. Intell. **267**, 1–38 (2019)

22. Reiter, R.: A theory of diagnosis from first principles. Artif. Intell. **32**(1), 57–95 (1987)

23. Ribeiro, M.T., Singh, S., Guestrin, C.: "Why should I trust you?": Explaining the predictions of any classifier. In: KDD, pp. 1135–1144 (2016)

24. Ribeiro, M.T., Singh, S., Guestrin, C.: Anchors: high-precision model-agnostic explanations. In: AAAI, pp. 1527–1535 (2018)

25. Seshia, S.A., Sadigh, D., Sastry, S.S.: Toward verified artificial intelligence. Commun. ACM **65**(7), 46–55 (2022). https://doi.org/10.1145/3503914

26. Shih, A., Choi, A., Darwiche, A.: A symbolic approach to explaining Bayesian network classifiers. In: IJCAI, pp. 5103–5111 (2018)

27. Sivaraman, A., Farnadi, G., Millstein, T.D., den Broeck, G.V.: Counterexample-guided learning of monotonic neural networks. In: Larochelle, H., Ranzato, M., Hadsell, R., Balcan, M., Lin, H. (eds.) Advances in Neural Information Processing Systems 33: Annual Conference on Neural Information Processing Systems 2020, NeurIPS 2020 (December), pp. 6–12. Virtual (2020). https://proceedings.neurips.cc/paper/2020/hash/8ab70731b1553f17c11a3bbc87e0b605-Abstract.html
28. You, S., Ding, D., Canini, K.R., Pfeifer, J., Gupta, M.R.: Deep lattice networks and partial monotonic functions. In: Guyon, I., et al. (eds.) Advances in Neural Information Processing Systems 30: Annual Conference on Neural Information Processing Systems 2017 (December), pp. 4–9, 2017. Long Beach, CA, USA, pp. 2981–2989 (2017), https://proceedings.neurips.cc/paper/2017/hash/464d828b85b0bed98e80ade0a5c43b0f-Abstract.html

Context Specification Language for Formally Verifying Consent Properties on Models and Code

Myriam Clouet[1]([✉]), Thibaud Antignac[2], Mathilde Arnaud[1], and Julien Signoles[1]

[1] Université Paris-Saclay, CEA List, 91120 Palaiseau, France
{myriam.clouet,mathilde.arnaud,julien.signoles}@cea.fr
[2] CNIL (Commission nationale de l'informatique et des libertés), 3 place de Fontenoy, TSA 80715, 75334 Paris CEDEX 07, France
tantignac@cnil.fr

Abstract. Recent privacy laws and regulations raise the stakes in verifying that software systems respect user consent. The current state of the art shows that privacy by design and formal methods can help. Still, ensuring the validity of privacy properties, in particular consent properties, at different stages of software development, is hard. This paper proposes a step towards solving this issue by introducing a new tool, named CASTT, that allows software engineers to verify consent properties at two different development stages: system modeling and code verification. To describe the system, this paper introduces a new formal context specification language, named CSpeL, to specify the key elements involved in consent and their relationships. The tool is evaluated on two use cases targeting different application domains: healthcare and website. We also evaluate the correctness and the efficiency of our tool.

Keywords: Privacy · Specification Language · Formal Verification

1 Introduction

Personal data processing occurs in many application domains : web services, voice assistants, or healthcare systems, to name but a few. Laws and regulations have been established around the world to govern such processing, e.g. GDPR in Europe, the Privacy Act in Australia or the Act on The Protection of Personal Information in Japan. Failure to comply with these laws can be punished by

---

Thibaud Antignac—The views, opinions, and positions expressed in this article are those of this author and not of the institution to which he belongs. This work was mostly done while the author was at CEA LIST.

substantial fines, which have been recently applied to Google[1] and WhatsApp[2]. Hence, verifying that a system respects expected privacy properties is crucial.

Formal methods provides a set of techniques based on logic, mathematics, and theoretical computer science used for specifying, developing and verifying software and hardware systems [22]. In particular, it can be used for privacy property verification [33]. Another way to provide privacy guarantees is to follow the *privacy by design* principle, which requires controllers to "both at the time of the determination of the means for processing and at the time of the processing itself, implement appropriate technical and organizational measures" [15]. In this regard, the controllers have to integrate these measures at early development stages [2]. More generally, ensuring compliance of a software system with respect to privacy requires to verify that the expected privacy properties hold during all the system lifecycle. It usually involves different abstraction levels (corresponding to the lifecycle development steps), which complicates the verification process.

Consent-related properties are particular as they relate to an agreement between interested parties concerning personal data processing [12]. These properties, even if disjointedly taken into account by legal departments, can be ignored at design time and are usually not checked at all at implementation and verification stages, which may lead to serious issues regarding this legal basis.

This paper proposes an approach to verify consent properties at two different development stages, modeling and code verification, as illustrated in Fig. 1. First, a model specification language, named CSpeL, allows engineers to formally specify key system elements with regards to two specific consent properties. Second, this paper introduces a new tool, CASTT, to verify the aforementioned properties on traces from a model (at Model Level), on traces from a program (at Program Level), or directly on a program.

This tool has been applied on use cases from two application domains at both model and program levels. Correctness and efficiency evaluations have been carried out to demonstrate the usefulness of our approach.

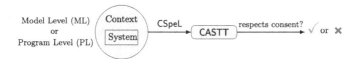

Fig. 1. High-level view of the contributions: CSpeL and CASTT.

More precisely, our contributions are the following:

- CSpeL, a **new formal context specification language** of the key elements involved in two specific consent properties: *purpose compliance*, stating that

---

[1] https://www.bbc.com/news/technology-46944696.
[2] https://www.bbc.com/news/technology-58422465.

personal data are only processed for granted purposes, and *necessity compliance*, stating that personal data are only processed when needed.
- CASTT, a **new verification tool** that includes:
  - a **method to verify** purpose and necessity compliance on traces from a model or from a program; and
  - a **translation mechanism** from CSpeL to the ACSL specification language [5] that allows the user to verify the purpose and necessity compliance on C source code;
- an **empirical evaluation** of CASTT on **use cases** from two different application domains, namely healthcare and website, that illustrates the usefulness of the overall approach.

The paper is organized as follows: Sect. 2 presents the related work while Sect. 3 introduces a running example used to illustrate our approach. Then, Sect. 4 details CSpeL, and shows how to use it to specify a system, while Sect. 5 presents CASTT and the associated verification process. Finally, Sect. 6 provides the results of the experimental evaluation of CASTT, and Sect. 7 concludes and discusses future works.

2   Related Work

Several existing approaches to verify formal properties at both model and program levels. Among them, the B method [1] allows engineers to specify behaviors of a system in B, and to refine this model iteratively down to a concrete executable model. Conversely, Greenaway et al. [18] propose a tool for abstracting the C semantics into higher-level specifications. However, these approaches target safety properties, expressing how the program is expected to behave. Regarding security properties, existing approaches consider either model or program level. For instance, Bernhard et al. [7] specify a new model of voting protocol satisfying specific formal properties, such as secrecy [29], while Dufay et al. [14] specify a JML-based language and use static analysis to verify a non interference property.

Table 1. Comparison of Consent-related Approaches.

Solution	Formal properties	ML	PL	Language	Tool	Verification method
[3]		✓	×	unnamed	×	Smart contracts
[6]		✓	×	CAPVerDE	CAPVerDE	SMT solvers
[31]		✓	×	unnamed	DataProVe	Ad-hoc algorithm
[24]		✓	×	Prolog	Prolog-based	Runtime verification
[25]	×	×	✓	unnamed	Poly	Policy enforcement framework
[32]	×	×	✓	unnamed	CASTOR	Semantic mapping
[19]	×	×	✓	OpenAPI	OpenAPI	Policy enforcement framework
[21]	×	×	✓	JIF	JIF	Information flow control
[this paper]		✓	✓	CSpeL	CASTT & Frama-C	Ad-hoc algorithm & Frama-C plug-in

Table 1 compares works verifying formal consent-related properties at model level (ML) or program level (PL). Consent properties target why personal data is processed and not who has access to the data and are thus complementary. Some approaches verify consent properties at model level: they rely on smart contracts for blockchains [3], a specific architecture design and verification using SMT solvers [6], a policy language and an architecture description language [31], or logs to verify actions scheduling [24]. Three approaches rely on tools: Bavendiek et al. [6], and Ta and Eiza [31] use their own tool, while de Montety et al. use Prolog [24]. However, none of these approaches check any implementation.

Other approaches propose solutions to ensure consent at Program Level, but they do not target verification at Model Level. Also, they do not formalize the verified consent property, but rather follow some privacy principles, typically GDPR's *data protection by design and by default* [15]. These solutions rely on extending some permission model in a policy enforcement framework [25], on a dedicated specification language and static analysis based on semantic mapping [32], on extending an OpenAPI as a policy enforcement framework [19], or on information-flow control [21]. All of them rely on tools: Hayati and Abadi [21] use an existing tool, not initially designed for privacy. Similary, Nauman et al. [25], and Grünewald et al. [19] extend existing tools to tackle privacy concerns. Tokas et al. [32] prefer to implement a dedicated tool from scratch.

To sum up, our solution is the only one that targets both model and program levels for verifying consent-related properties. It is also the only one able to verify a formally-specified consent property at program level. Our verification method uses an ad-hoc algorithm for offline runtime verification and Frama-C plug-ins for runtime or static verification using abstract interpretation or SMT solvers.

3   Running Example

This section presents our running example, which is adapted from an example of Petkovic et al. [26]. This example introduces a hospital information system that processes patients' data, named EPR (for **E**lectronic **P**atient **R**ecord). Each EPR contains some personal data (e.g., date of birth), and some non-personal data (e.g., drug dosages). The medical staff may use the hospital information system to process EPRs for two different purposes: providing treatment to patients (**Treatment**) or performing a clinical trial (**Research**). In both cases, doctors should ask for an access to patients' personal data at some point during the treatment or the clinical trial when they need them.

In the following, Sect. 3.1 introduces a model of this system, Sect. 3.2 the key implementation elements, and Sect. 3.3 the goals that we aim to achieve.

3.1   Model of the Hospital Information System

At model level, we use BPMN [10] to model the hospital information system: Fig. 2 defines a process **P1** corresponding to purpose **Treatment**, while Fig. 3 defines another process **P2** corresponding to purpose **Research**. Each BPMN process P_i contains a start element S_i, a final element E_i, and different tasks T_{ij}, executed sequentially one after the other. Some tasks use EPR when executed.

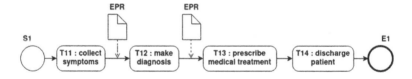

Fig. 2. Healthcare system at ML - Process P1: Treatment.

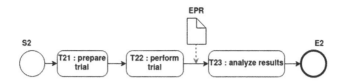

Fig. 3. Healthcare system at ML - Process P2: Research.

Process **P1** contains four tasks. Task **T11** collects the patient's symptoms, which are part of her **EPR**. Then, using this data, Task **T12** makes a diagnosis, which also uses the patient's **EPR**. Next, Task **T13** prescribes a medical treatment. Finally, Task **T14** corresponds to the patient's discharge.

Process **P2** only contains three tasks. Task **T21** prepares the trial, which is then performed by Task **T22**. This latter uses the patient's **EPR** for producing statistics. Finally, Task **T23** analyzes the results.

3.2   Implementation of the Information System

Figure 4 introduces some key elements of a C implementation of the hospital information system, while Table 2 shows the relationships between the BPMN models and the code, as explained below.

As seen in the previous section, BPMN processes **P1** and **P2** perform different tasks, possibly handling EPR. Some of these tasks and the associated EPR processing are manually executed (typically, by a doctor) and are thus not present in the code. For instance, preparing the clinical study (Task **T21**), or discharging the patient (Task **T14**) are manual unimplemented actions. The other tasks and associated EPR processing are implemented by C functions: task **T13** is implemented by the function `makePrescr` while task **T23** is implemented by the function `computeStats` and uses the necessary pieces of EPRs provided by the function `getData` (from **T22**). Therefore, we can consider that the whole process **P1** is represented at code level by the single function `makePrescr`, while the whole process **P2** is represented by the pair of functions `getData` and `computeStats`. Some tasks handle EPRs. At code level, an EPR is implemented

```
/*-- EPR Datatype --*/
typedef struct {char date[SIZE]; char medicine[SIZE];} Dos;
typedef struct { int id; char name[SIZE]; char birthdate[SIZE];
    Dos dosList[NB_D];...} Patient;
typedef struct { char birthdateList[NB][SIZE];
    char sexList[NB][SIZE]; Dos dosList[NB_D];
} TrialData ;

/*-- Processes' Tasks --*/
Patient makePrescr(Dos newd, Patient p) { ... }
TrialData getData(Patient patientList[NB]) { ... }
int computeStats(TrialData data) { ... }

/*-- Testing the system --*/
int main() {
    ...
    patient = makePrescr(newd, patient);
    TrialData d = getData(list1);
    int res = computeStats(d);
    return 0;
}
```

Fig. 4. Code snippet of the healthcare system.

Table 2. Mapping between the BPMN model and the code.

ML	PL
P1	Patient makePrescr(Dos newd, Patient p)
P2	TrialData getData(Patient patientList[NB_PATIENT])
	int computeStats(TrialData data)
EPR	Patient, TrialData, Dos

by three C data structures, namely Dos, Patient, and TrialData. Dos represents the drug dosage. By itself, it does not contain any personal data. Patient represents a patient. It contains personal data such as the name or the date of birth, and the list of prescribed treatments. TrialData represents data used for statistical computations during the clinical trial. It also contains personal data such as collections of dates of birth and genders, and medical prescriptions.

3.3 Goal

Thereafter we assume that the BPMN model can be simulated to generate execution traces. Whether the code is executable only impacts the usable code-level verification methods, as explained in Sect. 5.2 and it is not mandatory. In this paper, our goal consists in checking whether the hospital information system processes EPRs according to each patient's consent at model and program levels. Checking consent properties at both levels is necessary. Indeed, some invalid actions may relate to manual tasks that are only represented in the model. Conversely, invalid actions can also be introduced during implementation. Whether we verify that *some* execution traces or *all* traces respect the data subject's consent depends on the chosen verification technique(s) as explained in Sect. 5.2.

Section 4 explains how to describe the hospital information system at model and implementation stages with the same language, named CSpeL. Then, Sect. 5 introduces a tool, named CASTT, that allows verifying a consent property on execution traces (Sect. 5.1) and on a C implementation (Sect. 5.2).

4 Specifying a System with CSpeL

CSpeL is a language designed to formally specify both a system in a privacy context and an execution trace, in order to verify consent properties. Section 4.1 presents how to formally model a system and Sect. 4.2 how to represent en execution. Next, Sect. 4.3 formalizes the consent properties that we verify. Finally, Sect. 4.4 introduces the CSpeL grammar used in practice.

4.1 Model of a System

First, we need to define formally a notion of context. In the following, we use $\top$ (resp. $\bot$) to denote the Boolean value "true" (resp. "false").

Definition 1 (Context). *A context $\mathcal{C}$ is a 6-tuple $(S, D, P, \gamma, \pi, \nu)$ where S is a set of processes, D a set of personal data, and P a set of purposes. The total function $\gamma \triangleq D \times P \to bool$ represents the data subject consent for the use of each piece of personal data, for each purpose. The total functions $\pi \triangleq S \to \mathcal{P}(P)$ and $\nu \triangleq S \to \mathcal{P}(D)$ return, for each process of the system, the purposes of the process, and the personal data needed respectively.*

Example 1. The following context represents the BPMN model of Sect. 3.1:

$$
\begin{aligned}
S &\triangleq \{P1; P2\}; & \pi &\triangleq P1 \mapsto \{Treatment\} \\
D &\triangleq \{EPR\}; & P2 &\mapsto \{Research\}; \\
P &\triangleq \{Treatment; Research\}; & \nu &\triangleq P1 \mapsto \{EPR\} \\
\gamma &\triangleq (EPR, Treatment) \mapsto \top & P2 &\mapsto \{EPR\}; \\
& (EPR, Research) \mapsto \bot;
\end{aligned}
$$

In this instance, the user consented to the use of his personal data for Treatment purposes only. Similarly, we can define a context representing the system at code level introduced in Sect. 3.2:

$$
\begin{aligned}
S &\triangleq \{\texttt{makePrescr}; \texttt{getData}; \texttt{computeStats}\}; & \pi &\triangleq \texttt{makePrescr} \mapsto \{Treatment\} \\
D &\triangleq \{Patient, TrialData\}; & \texttt{getData} &\mapsto \{Research\} \\
P &\triangleq \{Treatment; Research\}; & \texttt{computeStats} &\mapsto \{Research\}; \\
\gamma &\triangleq (Patient, Treatment) \mapsto \top & \nu &\triangleq \texttt{makePrescr} \mapsto \{Patient\} \\
& (Patient, Research) \mapsto \bot; & \texttt{getData} &\mapsto \{Patient, TrialData\} \\
& (TrialData, Treatment) \mapsto \bot; & \texttt{computeStats} &\mapsto \{TrialData\}. \\
& (TrialData, Research) \mapsto \bot;
\end{aligned}
$$

The elements necessary for verifying the desired consent properties can be modeled thanks to this formalism. In particular, modeling purposes apart from processes is important to accurately verify consent. Indeed, user consent is defined via purposes, while processes, as entities handling personal data, are the targets for verification. There is no one-to-one correspondence between processes and purposes, thus the need for function π.

4.2   Execution Traces

We check system behavior w.r.t consent properties through trace analysis. This section introduces the notion of traces, while the consent properties will be defined in Sect. 4.3. Our traces are abstract enough to represent traces generated either from a model (usually, by simulation) or from a program run, yet expressive enough to allow us to formally specify consent properties.

Definition 2 (Execution Trace). *Let* $\mathcal{C} = (S, D, P, \gamma, \pi, \nu)$ *be a context,* $\{\sigma_i\}_{i \in \mathbb{N}} \subseteq S$, *and* $\{d_i\}_{i \in \mathbb{N}}$ *be a set of (personal or non personal) data. The execution traces of* $\mathcal{C}$ *are defined by the following grammar:*

$$T :: = \epsilon | Handle(\sigma_i, d_i); T.$$

ϵ *is the empty trace; event* $Handle(\sigma_i, d_i); T$ *means that* σ_i *processes data* d_i

It is worth noting that data in execution traces can be personal or non-personal. Also, only one piece of data at a time is processed in each event. Also, traces might directly be represented by (unordered) sets of events and not by sequences. We have chosen sequences because this is quite a standard formalism for traces and should help future extensions, without adding too much complexity in the current version.

Example 2. Consider the BPMN model introduced in Sect. 3.1. The trace $Handle(P1, EPR); \epsilon$ (resp. $Handle(P2, EPR); \epsilon$) denotes the handling of EPR by process $P1$ (resp. $P2$), while the trace $Handle(P1, EPR); Handle(P2, EPR); \epsilon$ denotes the handling of EPR by process $P1$ followed by the handling of EPR by process $P2$. At code level, the trace

$$Handle(\texttt{makePrescr}, Patient); Handle(\texttt{makePrescr}, Dos); \epsilon$$

denotes the execution of function `makePrescr` on a patient for delivering some prescription. As function `makePrescr` processes two pieces of data, namely *Patient* and *Dos*, the trace is composed with two events. Similarly,

$$Handle(\texttt{getData}, Patient); Handle(\texttt{getData}, TrialData);$$
$$Handle(\texttt{computeStats}, TrialData); \quad \epsilon$$

denotes the execution of function `getData`, with two distinct events as two pieces of data are processed, before computing statistics with `computeStats`.

4.3   Consent Properties

Our goal consists in verifying that an execution trace T respects a consent property *Prop* in a context $\mathcal{C}$, noted $\mathcal{C}, Prop \vdash T$. Consent refers to many different yet related notions [30]. In this paper, we focus on the notions of *purpose* and *data necessity*. More precisely, when some personal data is processed, we would like to check that the data subject agreed to at least one of the process's purposes and that the personal data is necessary to the process. We formally express these properties through the notions of *purpose compliance* and *necessity compliance*.

Definition 3 (Purpose Compliance). *An event of data processing Handle* (σ, d) *is purpose-compliant with respect to a context* $C \triangleq (S, D, P, \gamma, \pi, \nu)$ *if and only if consent was granted to at least one of the process' purposes, i.e.:*

$$C, Purpose_{Comp} \vdash Handle(\sigma, d) \iff \begin{cases} d \notin D & ; \; or \\ \exists p \in \pi(\sigma), \gamma(d, p) = \top. \end{cases}$$

Definition 4 (Necessity Compliance). *An event of data processing Handle* (σ, d) *is necessity-compliant with respect to a context* $C \triangleq (S, D, P, \gamma, \pi, \nu)$ *if and only if the personal data is necessary for the processing, i.e.:*

$$C, Necessity_{Comp} \vdash Handle(\sigma, d) \iff \begin{cases} d \notin D & ; \; or \\ d \in \nu(\sigma). \end{cases}$$

These notions of *purpose compliance* and *necessity compliance* are extended to execution traces thanks to the inference rules given in Fig. 5. The empty trace is *purpose-compliant* (resp. *necessity-compliant*) with respect to any context, while a non-empty trace is *purpose-compliant* (resp. *necessity-compliant*) if and only if all its events are *purpose-compliant* (resp. *necessity-compliant*).

$$\frac{}{C, Prop \vdash \epsilon} \qquad \frac{C, Prop \vdash Handle(\sigma, d) \quad C, Prop \vdash T}{C, Prop \vdash Handle(\sigma, d); T}$$

with $Prop \in \{Purpose_{Comp}; Necessity_{Comp}\}$

Fig. 5. Trace Consent Compliance.

Example 3. In our running example, at model level, consent was granted to process *EPR* for purpose *Treatment* but not *Research*. The purpose of *P1* is *Treatment* and the purpose of *P2* is *Research*. Thus $Handle(P1, EPR); \epsilon$ is *purpose-compliant* and $Handle(P2, EPR); \epsilon$ is not *purpose-compliant*[3]. As *EPR* is needed for *P1* and for *P2*, both of these traces are *necessity-compliant*.

At program level, the trace

$$Handle(\texttt{makePrescr}, Patient); Handle(\texttt{makePrescr}, Dos); \epsilon$$

is *purpose-compliant*, because consent was granted for the processing of *Patient* for purpose *Treatment* associated with `makePrescr` and *Dos* is not a personal data. However the trace

---

[3] Proof of this claim and the following ones are in Appendix B.

$Handle(\texttt{getData}, Patient); Handle(\texttt{getData}, TrialData);$

$Handle(\texttt{computeStats}, TrialData); \quad \epsilon$

is not *purpose-compliant*, because the purpose of `getData` is *Research* and consent for the use of *Patient* (or *TrialData*) is not granted for this purpose.

As `makePrescr` needs *Patient*, the first trace is *necessity-compliant*. Similarly, `getData` needs *Patient*, *TrialData*, and `computeStats` needs *TrialData*, thus the second trace is also *necessity-compliant*.

4.4   Concrete Language

The formalism introduced so far lets us define the generic notions of *purpose compliance* and *necessity compliance* for any executable system. However, since these notions over the system are specified by a quite abstract notion of context, they are not convenient for working engineers. To circumvent this issue, this section introduces the practical language CSpeL linking these notions to executable systems. It can be used either at model level, or at program level.

Figure 6 gives the formal syntax of CSpeL. Literals d, σ, and p are strings that respectively denote a data element, a process and a purpose. A CSpeL model M is a context C, possibly followed by a trace T.

$$
\begin{array}{ll}
M ::= & C \mid CT \\
C ::= & \texttt{\textbackslash context}\{S,D,P,\gamma,\pi,\nu,IS\} \\
& \mid \texttt{\textbackslash context}\{S,D,P,\gamma,\pi,\nu\} \\
S ::= & \texttt{\textbackslash process}\{\Sigma Set\} \\
D ::= & \texttt{\textbackslash personalData}\{DSet\} \\
P ::= & \texttt{\textbackslash purposes}\{PSet\} \\
\gamma ::= & \texttt{\textbackslash isGranted}\{TSet\} \\
\pi ::= & \texttt{\textbackslash hasPurposes}\{APSet\} \\
\nu ::= & \texttt{\textbackslash needData}\{ADSet\} \\
IS ::= & \texttt{\textbackslash init}\{\Sigma Set\} \\
T ::= & \texttt{\textbackslash trace}\{\ PCSet\ \}
\end{array}
$$

$$
\begin{array}{ll}
\Sigma Set ::= & \sigma \mid \sigma, \Sigma Set \\
DSet ::= & d \mid d,\ DSet \\
PSet ::= & p \mid p,\ PSet \\
TSet ::= & (\texttt{d:p}) \mid (\texttt{d:p}),\ TSet \\
APSet ::= & (\sigma{:}\{PSet\}) \mid (\sigma{:}\{PSet\}),\ APSet \\
ADSet ::= & (\sigma{:}\{DSet\}) \mid (\sigma{:}\{DSet\}),\ ADSet \\
PCSet ::= & \texttt{\textbackslash handle}(\sigma,\ \texttt{d});\ PCSet \mid \texttt{VOID}
\end{array}
$$

Fig. 6. CSpeL grammar.

A context (keyword \context), contains elements matching those in Definition 1. It may also contain a process set to specify where the elements are initialized, IS. The set S (resp. D, and P) of processes is introduced by the keyword \process (resp. \personalData, and \purposes). Similarly, the total function γ (resp. π, and ν) is introduced by the keyword \isGranted (resp. \hasPurposes, and \needData). Each keyword maps elements from the function's domain to elements from the function's co-domain. Currently, there is no check that the functions defined in this way are total.

A trace is introduced by the keyword \trace. It is a sequence *PCSet* of data processing. The empty sequence is VOID. An event of data processing in a trace is introduced by the keyword \handle and associates a process to a data.

Example 4. The model defined in Example 1 could be specified in CSpeL as:

```
\model{\context{\process{P1;P2},\personalData{EPR},
                \purposes{Treatment;Research},\isGranted{(EPR:Treatment)},
                \hasPurposes{ (P1: { Treatment }),(P2: { Research })},
                \needData{ (P1: { EPR }),(P2: { EPR }) }},
        \trace{\handle(P1,EPR); VOID }}
```

As we have seen, CSpeL allows formally specifying both a system in a privacy context and an execution trace, independently of its level of abstraction (Model or Program). Thanks to this, we can easily verify consent properties.

5   Verifying Consent with CASTT

We develop the CASTT tool as a Frama-C plug-in in order to verify consent properties from a specification written in CSpeL. Frama-C [4] is an open source extensible analysis platform for C code. It provides many plug-ins for analyzing C source code extended with formal annotations written in the ACSL specification language [5]. Its three main verification plug-ins are E-ACSL [28], Eva [9] and WP [8]. E-ACSL is a runtime assertion checker [11] that verifies ACSL properties during concrete program runs, Eva is a static tool based on abstract interpretation [27] that raises alarms on any potential undefined behavior and invalid ACSL property, and WP relies on deductive methods [20] for proving ACSL properties thanks to associated provers, such as Alt-Ergo [13]. As explained later, we use all of them on our case studies, together with CASTT. CASTT can be used in two ways: to check either a trace written in CSpeL, or a C code w.r.t. a CSpeL file. The first usage targets offline runtime verification [16] of traces representing system executions at model or code level. The second one specifically targets verification of C code, either statically or dynamically.

First, Sect. 5.1 details CASTT's offline runtime verification. Then, Sect. 5.2 explains CASTT's translation to ACSL.

5.1   CSpeL Offline Runtime Verification

Offline runtime verification checks properties on complete system executions. As shown in Fig. 7, CASTT can verify that some specific trace of a system, described in CSpeL, satisfies the consent properties expressed in Definition 3 and in Sect. 4.3. Currently, the traces are manually written, but they could be automatically generated from a simulated model or from program runs.

Algorithm 1 illustrates trace analysis in order to reach this goal. It is implemented in CASTT. For each event in the trace, it verifies whether the data being processed is in the personal data set. If so, the algorithm checks whether the data subject previously agreed to one of the purposes associated to the process: the trace is invalid if there is no such agreement. It also checks whether the data

Fig. 7. Use of CASTT.

is necessary to the processing: the trace is invalid if the data is not necessary. The evaluation continues until all events have been checked. The trace is valid only if all events are valid. For completeness, we do not stop the algorithm at the first invalid event. The complexity of this algorithm is linear.

Algorithm 1: Trace Evaluation

Input: A context and a trace
Output: Evaluation result

1 is_valid = True ; // void trace is valid
2 **while** *trace is not void* **do**
3 | (process, data) ← trace.current event;
4 | trace ← trace.next();
5 | **if** *data ∈ context.personal data* **then**
6 | | is_consented = False ; // purpose compliance
7 | | **foreach** *purpose ∈ context.hasPurposes(process)* **do**
8 | | | **if** *context.isGranted(data, purpose)* **then**
9 | | | | is_consented = True ;
10 | | is_necessary = False ; // necessity compliance
11 | | **if** *data ∈ context.needData(process)* **then**
12 | | | is_necessary = True ;
13 | | is_valid = is_valid && is_consented && is_necessary
14 **return** *is_valid;*

5.2 Consent Verification on C Source Code

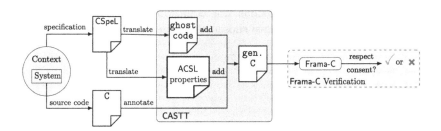

Fig. 8. Functional View of CASTT for Verifying Consent on C Code.

Figure 8 shows the functional view of CASTT, together with Frama-C, for verifying our properties defined in Sect. 4.3 on a C source code. CASTT takes as inputs a consent specification written in CSpeL and a C source code in order to generate a new C source code extended with ACSL annotations that encode the CSpeL specification. Then, any Frama-C analyzer can be used to verify the ACSL annotations embedded in this generated code. Verifying all of them implies that the original properties are satisfied. In practice, the user can rely on E-ACSL, Eva, WP, or a combination of them, for verifying the generated code.

We do not detail how the code and the ACSL annotations are generated from a given CSpeL file and a C source code: we just give a few insights, in Table 3. The sets of personal data and purposes, respectively specified by \personalData and \purposes, are translated to enumeration types in the generated code. Based on these sets, CASTT generates a matrix Consent that specifies, for each personal data, for which purposes the data subject has granted consent. This matrix is declared as ghost code, which is a set of stateful ACSL annotations that do not interfere with the user's C code: ghost code cannot modify the state of the original program [17]. The command \isGranted is used to generate ghost statements that initialize this ghost matrix in the processes specified with \init. Similarly the matrix Need is initialized thanks to the command \needData. This matrix specifies which data are necessary for each process.

For each statement in the program functions (i.e., process), if it corresponds to processing of a personal data, ACSL assert clauses, that correspond to our properties, are generated. For *purpose compliance*, the clause checks that consent was granted to process this data for at least one of the function purposes. For *necessity compliance*, the clause checks that the data is necessary to this function. These are defined by the user in the CSpeL file through \personalData and \hasPurposes. Thereafter, for any ACSL annotation /*@ assert Consent[d][p] == 1;*/ (resp. /*@ assert Need[σ][d] == 1;*/) with d a personal data, p a purpose and σ a function name, the used Frama-C verification plug-in(s) will try to check that these properties are satisfied. Note that whether non-reachable properties are verified depends on the chosen plug-in(s). This way, it ensures that the user agreed to the processing of data d for purpose p (resp. that the data d is necessary for the function σ). One may observe that the content of the matrix Need remains unchanged after having been initialized. Therefore, instead of these assertions, one could directly write /*@ assert 1; */ or /*@ assert 0; */. We have chosen the current version for readability.

Table 3. Code Generation Snippets.

CSpeL Definition	Generated Code Snippet
\personalData	`enum _PersonalData {TRIALDATA = 0, PATIENT = 1}` `typedef enum _PersonalData PersonalData;`
\purposes	`enum _Purposes {RESEARCH = 0, TREATMENT = 1}` `typedef enum _Purposes Purposes;`
\personalData & \purposes	`/*@ ghost bool Consent[2][2];*/`
\process & \personalData	`/*@ ghost bool Need[3][2];*/`
\personalData & \purposes & \isGranted & \init	`/*@ ghost Consent[PATIENT][RESEARCH] = 0; */` `/*@ ghost Consent[PATIENT][TREATMENT] = 1; */` `/*@ ghost Consent[TRIALDATA][RESEARCH] = 0; */` `/*@ ghost Consent[TRIALDATA][TREATMENT] = 0; */`
\process & \personalData & \needData & \init	`/*@ ghost Need[MAKEPRESCR][PATIENT] = 1; */` `/*@ ghost Need[MAKEPRESCR][TRIALDATA] = 0; */` `/*@ ghost Need[GETDATA][PATIENT] = 1; */` `/*@ ghost Need[GETDATA][TRIALDATA] = 1; */`
\personalData & \hasPurposes	`/*@ assert Consent[PATIENT][TREATMENT] == 1; */`
\personalData	`/*@ assert Need[MAKEPRESCR][PATIENT] == 1; */`

6   Experimentation and Evaluation

This section presents our experimentation for evaluating our tool CASTT. First, Sect. 6.1 presents our use cases. Then, Sect. 6.2 (resp. 6.3) evaluates CASTT's trace analysis (resp. verification process at code level) on these use cases. The first use case is the healthcare running example already introduced in Sect. 3. The second use case is a website system, focusing on two purposes: keeping track of purchases and targeted advertising. For each use case and each abstraction level (model or code), a file specifying the CSpeL context is provided as input to CASTT. At code level, the use case's source code is also given as input. Even if our evaluation is still preliminary, it allows us to come to a few positive conclusions. Future work includes extending our evaluation to larger examples.

The evaluations were performed on a PC with a 2 GHz Intel Xeon CPU and 32 GB of RAM. We used CASTT with the public version of Frama-C[4] as of 9/29/2022 (git commit 3c453a2b). Our evaluation relies on a home-made shell script executing the necessary commands for running CASTT and Frama-C as well as a Python script for graphics generation. We have also implemented trace

---

[4] https://git.frama-c.com/pub/frama-c.

and function call generators to evaluate our tool on examples containing traces with up to $1,000,000$ events, and programs with up to $3,000$ function calls[5] .

6.1 Examples Used

We successfully executed our analysis using CASTT, both at model and program level, on the running example presented in Sect. 3. All the valid and invalid executions were detected.

Our running example Healthcare is a simplified version of the example of Petkovic et al. [26]. For our offline runtime verification evaluation we use the complete version, called **Purpose Control** in the following, that is more complex (with pools containing various tasks, events, conditional branches and message transfers), using the trace verification functionality of CASTT.

Since they do not provide a C implementation, we have implemented another use case concerning a different application domain (website) for evaluating CASTT's code verification functionality. In this use case, some functions have various purposes (and not just one as the previous example).

6.2 Offline Runtime Verification Evaluation

We evaluate CASTT's offline runtime verification with the following Research Questions in mind:

RQ1 *Can CASTT successfully verify a consent property on a trace from a model/program and detect the invalid traces?*

RQ2 *Is CASTT usable on large traces?*

For answering Question **RQ1**, we run a correctness script using CASTT. This script executes the following command on various CSpeL files, corresponding to various applicative domains and different levels (ML and PL), : where `file.cspel` is the name of the test file:

```
frama-c -castt-verify-trace \
    -castt-consent-file <testFile.cspel>
```

Table 4. Experimental Results for CASTT's Trace Analysis.

Example	LVL	NbTests	Size of traces	Valid traces detected	Invalid traces detected
Healthcare	ML	6	1 to 3 events	✓	✓
	PL	6	2 to 6 events	✓	✓
Website	ML	9	1 to 5 events	✓	✓
	PL	9	5 to 24 events	✓	✓
*Purpose Control	ML	10	1 to 20 events	✓	✓

---

[5] All the resources to run our experimentation are available in CASTT repository.

Each experiment instantaneously (i.e., in less than a second) provides its results, which are summarized in Table 4. This table presents, for each use case and each abstraction level, the number of analyzed CSpeL files, the minimum and maximum number of events in the trace, and whether the validity statuses were correctly detected. Our experiments include as many valid traces as invalid traces. These results demonstrate that CASTT always provides the expected verdict on our examples, both at model and program level. Therefore, we can positively answer Research Questions **RQ1**.

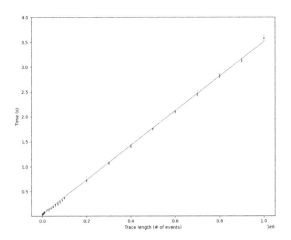

Fig. 9. Time for trace verification depending on the analyzed trace size

To answer Question **RQ2**, we run a script measuring time efficiency. This script executes the previous command on CSpeL files corresponding to one use case, but with various sizes of traces (containing from 10 to 1, 000, 000 events). The script executes the verification 10 times for each size and calculates the mean of the verification time. Results are shown on Fig. 9 (the x-scale is 1e6). This demonstrates that the trace verification algorithm is time linear. It also shows that large traces, i.e. with 1, 000, 000 events, are verified by CASTT in less than 4 s. Therefore, we can positively answer **RQ2**.

6.3   Translation Mechanism Evaluation

We evaluate the translation mechanism of CASTT with the following Research Questions in mind:

RQ3 *Can CASTT successfully verify systems at PL by translating a CSpeL file for a PL tool, so that the PL tool always detects invalid traces?*
RQ4 *Does CASTT reduce the number of hand-written specifications?*
RQ5 *Is CASTT usable on large code (i.e. with many lines and function calls)?*

For answering Question **RQ3**, we run a correctness script, which executes the following commands:

```
frama-c <source_file.c>                      \
  -castt-annotate                            \
  -castt-consent-file <context.cspel> \
  -then-last                                 \
  -print -ocode <annotated_file.c>
```

and then `frama-c -<analyzer> <annotated_file.c>` on various use cases. Here, option `-analyzer` is either `-eva` for running Eva or `-wp` for running WP. We also monitor the code generated by CASTT with E-ACSL for dynamic verification. In this case, we run: `e-acsl-gcc.sh -c <annotated_file.c> -O <monitored_binary>` and then `./<monitored_binary>.e-acsl`

Table 5. Frama-C Code Verification Experimental Results.

Plug-in	Expected Result	Meaning	Evaluation
WP	all goals are proved	Valid	✓
Eva	all assertions are valid		✓
E-ACSL	no error is raised at runtime		✓
WP	some goals are not proved	Invalid	✓
Eva	some assertions are invalid		✓
E-ACSL	an error is raised at runtime		✓

All experiments instantaneously provide their results, which are summarized in Tables 5 and 6. The first table shows, for each Frama-C plug-in, the meaning of the expected result for our approach, and whether the actual result matches our expectations. For this evaluation with Eva and WP, we manually check the results in the Frama-C GUI. For E-ACSL, the error raised at runtime specifies which ACSL annotation is not satisfied at runtime. Our experimentation shows that CASTT, combined with any of the three main Frama-C's verification plug-ins, can successfully verify consent compliance of the provided code. Therefore, we can positively answer Research Questions **RQ3**. Table 6 presents, for each test case, the number of lines of code in the original source file, the number of lines generated by CASTT, the number of lines needed for WP, and the length of the CSpeL model. An example of CASTT generated file is given in Appendix A. As shown in the Table, in our examples, CSpeL files are used to generate files 3 to 5 times their size in lines. These generated lines amount to 60% to 75% of the source file. Thus, we can positively answer **RQ4**.

To answer Question **RQ5**, we run a script measuring efficiency. This script executes the previous commands on a same C source file (except for the number of function calls) and a same CSpeL file. We use a function call generator to increase the number of function calls in the main function of the source file. Because the WP plug-in is not designed to manage this kind of test, we do not include it in our results (WP is modular and does not depend on the main).

Table 6. CASTT's Code Generation Experimental Results.

Example	Healthcare			Website			
	T1	T2	T3	T1	T2	T3	
# **original lines of code**	53	54	50	121	122	121	60-75%
# **generated lines by CASTT**	33	35	33	92	94	90	× 3-5
# **lines in CSpeL file**	10			18			

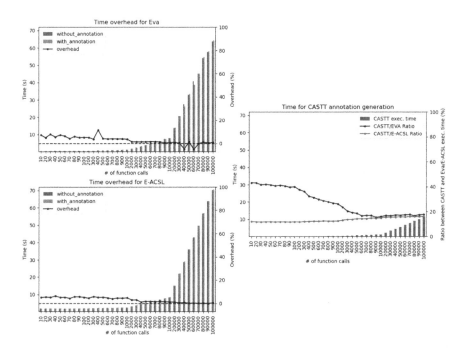

Fig. 10. Execution time by number of function calls

Figure 10 shows our results obtained from files containing between 10 to 100,000 function calls. For each size, we execute the test 10 times and calculate the time mean. We compute the time for the verification with and without the annotations generated by CASTT, to calculate the overhead generated by our approach. This evaluation shows that the time for CASTT annotation generation is negligible compared to the time of the verification plug-ins. It also shows that our generated annotations do not slow down too much the verification process (usually less than 10% for Eva and usually less than 5% for E-ACSL), and the bigger the size of the original program the smaller the overhead. In particular, our evaluation includes a code with 1,000,000 function calls. In this case, the overhead for Eva is about 1.6%, while it is 0.50% for E-ACSL. CASTT runs much faster than Eva or E-ACSL. In particular, it is always at least 5 times faster as soon as you exceed 5,000 events. Therefore, we can positively answer **RQ5**.

7   Conclusion and Perspectives

This paper presents two consent properties, *purpose compliance* and *necessity compliance*, and the CSpeL context specification language that formally describes systems targeting these properties. CSpeL is used by its companion tool, CASTT, in order to verify these properties at both model and program levels.

CASTT can be used to check these properties for some given execution traces, with an ad-hoc offline runtime verification algorithm-based verifier, or for a C source code. Since CASTT is based on Frama-C, it benefits from existing Frama-C verification plug-ins. We have evaluated our tool on two use cases, at both model and code levels. CASTT is able to successfully verify the valid examples and detect the invalid ones. We have also evaluated our tool on large traces and large code. CASTT is able to handle traces with $1,000,000$ events in less than 4s, and adds a small overhead during the verification process using the Frama-C verification-based tool even on code with more than $100,000$ function calls. The current version of CASTT translates CSpeL for C code. A similar translation could be defined towards other mainstream programming languages for which an ACSL-like specification language exists, such as Java with JML annotations, or towards models (targetting for instance IAT [23], a tool for verifying executions of distributed systems). Another research direction consists in extending CSpeL and CASTT for specifying and verifying other consent and privacy properties such as consent evolution, or storage limitation.

Acknowledgments. We are grateful to André Maroneze for his english corrections and his help improving the artefacts. We would also like to thank the anonymous reviewers for their helpful comments. This work was partly funded by the "France 2030" government investment plan managed by the French National Research Agency, under the reference "ANR-22-PECY-0005", project SECUREVAL.

References

1. Abrial, J.R.: The B-Book, Assigning Programs to Meaning. Cambridge University Press (1996)
2. Ahmadian, A.: Model-Based Privacy by Design. Phd thesis, Universität Koblenz-Landau (2020)
3. Barati, M., Rana, O., Petri, I., Theodorakopoulos, G.: GDPR compliance verification in internet of things. IEEE Access (2020)
4. Baudin, P., et al.: The dogged pursuit of bug-free c programs: the frama-c software analysis platform. Commun. ACM (2021)
5. Baudin, P., Filliâtre, J.C., Marché, C., Monate, B., Moy, Y., Prevosto, V.: ACSL: ANSI/ISO C Specification Language. Tech. rep.
6. Bavendiek, K., et al.: Automatically proving purpose limitation in software architectures. In: Dhillon, G., Karlsson, F., Hedström, K., Zúquete, A. (eds.) SEC 2019. IAICT, vol. 562, pp. 345–358. Springer, Cham (2019). https://doi.org/10.1007/978-3-030-22312-0_24
7. Bernhard, D., Cortier, V., Galindo, D., Pereira, O., Warinschi, B.: Sok: A comprehensive analysis of game-based ballot privacy definitions. In: 2015 IEEE Symposium on Security and Privacy, pp. 499–516. IEEE (2015)

8. Blanchard, A.: Introduction to C program proof with Frama-C and its WP plugin. Tutorial (2020)
9. Blazy, S., Bühler, D., Yakobowski, B.: Structuring abstract interpreters through state and value abstractions. In: Bouajjani, A., Monniaux, D. (eds.) VMCAI 2017. LNCS, vol. 10145, pp. 112–130. Springer, Cham (2017). https://doi.org/10.1007/978-3-319-52234-0_7
10. Chinosi, M., Trombetta, A.: BPMN: an introduction to the standard. Comput. Stand. Interfaces (2012)
11. Clarke, L., Rosenblum, D.: A historical perspective on runtime assertion checking in software development. SIGSOFT Softw. Eng. Notes (2006)
12. Clouet, M., Antignac, T., Arnaud, M., Pedroza, G., Signoles, J.: A new generic representation for modeling privacy. In: International Workshop on Privacy Engineering (IWPE2022) (2022)
13. Conchon, S., Coquereau, A., Iguernlala, M., Mebsout, A.: Alt-Ergo 2.2. In: SMT Workshop: International Workshop on Satisfiability Modulo Theories (2018)
14. Dufay, G., Felty, A., Matwin, S.: Privacy-sensitive information flow with JML. In: International Conference on Automated Deduction (2005)
15. European Commission: Regulation (EU) 2016/679 (General Data Protection Regulation). Tech. rep. (2016). https://eur-lex.europa.eu/legal-content/EN/TXT/PDF/?uri=CELEX:32016R0679
16. Falcone, Y., Havelund, K., Reger, G.: A tutorial on runtime verification. Eng. Depend. Softw. Syst. 141–175 (2013)
17. Filliâtre, J.-C., Gondelman, L., Paskevich, A.: The spirit of ghost code. Formal Methods Syst. Design **48**(3), 152–174 (2016). https://doi.org/10.1007/s10703-016-0243-x
18. Greenaway, D., Andronick, J., Klein, G.: Bridging the gap: automatic verified abstraction of C (2012)
19. Grünewald, E., Wille, P., Pallas, F., Borges, M., Ulbricht, M.: Tira: an openapi extension and toolbox for GDPR transparency in restful architectures. arXiv preprint arXiv:2106.06001 (2021)
20. Hähnle, R., Huisman, M.: Deductive software verification: from pen-and-paper proofs to industrial tools. In: Steffen, B., Woeginger, G. (eds.) Computing and Software Science. LNCS, vol. 10000, pp. 345–373. Springer, Cham (2019). https://doi.org/10.1007/978-3-319-91908-9_18
21. Hayati, K., Abadi, M.: Language-based enforcement of privacy policies. In: International Workshop on Privacy Enhancing Technologies (2004)
22. Huth, M., Ryan, M.: Logic in Computer Science: Modelling and Reasoning about Systems, 2nd edn. Cambridge University Press (2004)
23. Mahe, E.: An operational semantics of interactions for verifying partially observed executions of distributed systems. Phd thesis, Université Paris-Saclay (2021)
24. de Montety, C., Antignac, T., Slim, C.: GDPR modelling for log-based compliance checking. In: Meng, W., Cofta, P., Jensen, C., Grandison, T. (eds.) Trust Management XIII (2019)
25. Nauman, M., Khan, S., Zhang, X.: Apex: extending android permission model and enforcement with user-defined runtime constraints. In: Proceedings of the 5th ACM Symposium on Information, Computer and Communications Security (2010)
26. Petkovic, M., Prandi, D., Zannone, N.: Purpose control: Did you process the data for the intended purpose? In: Workshop on Secure Data Management (2011)
27. Rival, X., Yi, K.: Introduction to Static Analysis: An Abstract Interpretation Perspective. MIT Press (2020)

28. Signoles, J., Kosmatov, N., Vorobyov, K.: E-ACSL, a runtime verification tool for safety and security of C programs. Tool Paper. In: International Workshop on Competitions, Usability, Benchmarks, Evaluation, and Standardisation for Runtime Verification Tools (RV-CuBES) (2017)

29. Smyth, B., Bernhard, D.: Ballot secrecy and ballot independence coincide. In: Crampton, J., Jajodia, S., Mayes, K. (eds.) ESORICS 2013. LNCS, vol. 8134, pp. 463–480. Springer, Heidelberg (2013). https://doi.org/10.1007/978-3-642-40203-6_26

30. Solove, D.: A Taxonomy of Privacy (2005)

31. Ta, V., Eiza, M.: Dataprove: fully automated conformance verification between data protection policies and system architectures. In: Proceedings on Privacy Enhancing Technologies (2022)

32. Tokas, S., Owe, O., Ramezanifarkhani, T.: Language-based mechanisms for privacy-by-design. In: IFIP International Summer School on Privacy and Identity Management (2019)

33. Tschantz, M.C., Wing, J.M.: Formal methods for privacy. In: International Symposium on Formal Methods (2009)

Appendix

This appendix provides optional additional materials for the reader. Section A displays a file generated by CASTT. Section B proves our claims in Example 3. Section C presents the CSpeL specification for the running example at code level.

A   Example of generated file

Figure 11 shows an example of a C file generated by CASTT, from a context specification written in CSpeL and a C source file. For simplicity, some pieces of code generated by Frama-C and not directly related to our translation have been replaced by "...".

B   Proof of Properties of Example 3

This section proves purpose compliance for the traces of Example 3 (or purpose non-compliance, depending on traces). For each trace t, and according to Definition 3, we need to check that at least one of the purposes of some process p used in t is granted before a personal data is handled by p.

B.1   Traces at Model Level

We would like to prove that the trace $Handle(P1, EPR); \epsilon$ is purpose compliant, while the trace $Handle(P2, EPR); \epsilon$ is not purpose compliant for the first context

```
...
#include "stdio.h"
enum _Purposes {RESEARCH = 0,TREATMENT = 1};
typedef enum _Purposes Purposes;
enum _PersonalData {TRIALDATA = 0,PATIENT = 1};
typedef enum _PersonalData PersonalData;
/*@ ghost int \ghost Consent[2][2]; */

struct __anonstruct_Dos_1 {char date[20] ;char medicine[20] ;};
typedef struct __anonstruct_Dos_1 Dos;
struct __anonstruct_Patient_2 {
  int id ;char name[20] ;char lastname[20] ;char birthdate[20] ;
  char address[20] ;char sexe[20] ;Dos dosList[20] ;};
typedef struct __anonstruct_Patient_2 Patient;
struct __anonstruct_TrialData_3 {
  char birthdateList[20][20] ;
  char sexeList[20][20] ;Dos dosList[20] ;};
typedef struct __anonstruct_TrialData_3 TrialData;

Patient makePrescr(Dos newd, Patient p_makePrescr)
{
  /*@ assert Need[MAKEPRESCR][PATIENT] ≡1; */
  /*@ assert Consent[PATIENT][TREATMENT] ≡1; */
  return p_makePrescr;
}

TrialData getData(Patient patientList[3])
{
  /*@ assert Need[GETDATA][PATIENT] ≡1; */
  /*@ assert Consent[PATIENT][RESEARCH] ≡1; */
  Patient p_getData = *(patientList + 0);
  /*@ assert Need[GETDATA][TRIALDATA] ≡1; */
  /*@ assert Consent[TRIALDATA][RESEARCH] ≡1; */
  TrialData d = {.birthdateList = {...}, .genderList = {...},
                 .dosList = {...}};
  /*@ assert Need[GETDATA][TRIALDATA] ≡1; */
  /*@ assert Consent[TRIALDATA][RESEARCH] ≡1; */
  return d;
}

int computeStats(TrialData data)
{
  ...
  return __retres;
}

int main(void)
{
  int __retres;
  /*@ ghost Consent[PATIENT][RESEARCH] = 0; */
  /*@ ghost Consent[PATIENT][TREATMENT] = 1; */
  /*@ ghost Consent[TRIALDATA][RESEARCH] = 0; */
  /*@ ghost Consent[TRIALDATA][TREATMENT] = 1; */
  /*@ ghost Need[MAKEPRESCR][TRIALDATA] = 0; */
  /*@ ghost Need[MAKEPRESCR][PATIENT] = 1; */
  /*@ ghost Need[GETDATA][TRIALDATA] = 1; */
  /*@ ghost Need[GETDATA][PATIENT] = 1; */
  /*@ ghost Need[COMPUTESTATS][TRIALDATA] = 1; */
  /*@ ghost Need[COMPUTESTATS][PATIENT] = 0; */
    Patient patient =
    {.id = 0,
     .name = {(char)'J', (char)'o', (char)'h', (char)'n', (char)'\000'},
     .lastname = {(char)'D', (char)'o', (char)'e', (char)'\000'},
     .birthdate = {(char)0, ..., (char)0},
     .address = {(char)0, ..., (char)0},
     .sexe = {(char)0, ..., (char)0},
     .dosList = {...}};
  Dos newdos =
    {.date = {(char)'0',...,(char)'\000'},
     .medicine = {(char)'T',...,(char)'\000'}};
  patient = makePrescr(newdos,patient);
  __retres = 0;
  return __retres;
}
```

Fig. 11. Example of generated file.

$\mathcal{C} = (S, D, P, \gamma, \pi, \nu)$ of Example 1, defined by:

$$S \triangleq \{P1; P2\};$$
$$D \triangleq \{EPR\};$$
$$P \triangleq \{Treatment; Research\};$$
$$\gamma \triangleq \begin{cases} (EPR, Treatment) \mapsto \top \\ (EPR, Research) \quad \mapsto \bot; \end{cases}$$
$$\pi \triangleq \begin{cases} P1 \mapsto \{Treatment\} \\ P2 \mapsto \{Research\}; \end{cases}$$
$$\nu \triangleq \begin{cases} P1 \mapsto \{EPR\} \\ P2 \mapsto \{EPR\}. \end{cases}$$

Let us prove that the first trace is purpose compliant, i.e.:

$$\mathcal{C} \vdash Handle(P1, EPR); \epsilon.$$

1. According to the second inference rule of Fig. 5, this property holds if and only both $\mathcal{C} \vdash Handle(P1, EPR)$ and $\mathcal{C} \vdash \epsilon$ holds.
2. The latter case (empty trace) is the axiom of the inference system, so it holds. Let us demonstrate the former.
3. By definition of purpose compliance, $\mathcal{C} \vdash Handle(P1, EPR)$ holds if and only if either $EPR \notin D$, or $\gamma(EPR, p) = \top$ for some purpose p in $\pi(P1)$. We prove the right part of the disjunction.
4. Consider $p = Treatment$. Since, $Treatment \in \pi(P1)$ and $\gamma(EPR, Treatment) = \top$, the property holds.

Therefore the first trace is purpose compliant in the context $\mathcal{C}$. Let us now prove that the second trace is not purpose compliant, i.e.:

$$\mathcal{C} \nvdash Handle(P2, EPR); \epsilon.$$

We prove this property by contradiction, so let us assume that this trace is purpose compliant, i.e.:

$$\mathcal{C} \vdash Handle(P2, EPR); \epsilon.$$

1. From this property and according to the second inference rule of Fig. 5, $\mathcal{C} \vdash Handle(P2, EPR)$ holds.
2. Therefore, by definition of purpose compliance, either $EPR \notin D$ or $\gamma(EPR, p) = \top$ for some purpose p in $\pi(P2)$.
3. The former case contradicts the definition of D: EPR is a personal data in $\mathcal{C}$.
4. Consider the latter case. By definition of π, $Research$ is the only purpose of $P2$. However, $\gamma(EPR, Research) = \bot$, which contradicts $\gamma(EPR, Research) = \top$.
5. Each case leads to a contradiction, so the initial hypothesis. $\mathcal{C} \vdash Handle(P2, EPR); \epsilon$ does not hold.

Therefore the second trace is not purpose compliant in the context $\mathcal{C}$.

B.2   Traces at Program Level

We would like to prove that the trace $Handle(P1, EPR); \epsilon$ is purpose compliant, while the trace $Handle(P2, EPR); \epsilon$ is not purpose compliant for the second context $\mathcal{C} = (S, D, P, \gamma, \pi, \nu)$ of Example 1, defined by:

$$S \triangleq \{\texttt{makePrescr}; \texttt{getData}; \texttt{computeStats}\};$$

$$D \triangleq \{Patient, TrialData\};$$

$$P \triangleq \{Treatment, Research\};$$

$$\gamma \triangleq \begin{cases} (Patient, Treatment) & \mapsto \top \\ (Patient, Research) & \mapsto \bot \\ (TrialData, Treatment) & \mapsto \bot; \\ (TrialData, Research) & \mapsto \bot; \end{cases}$$

$$\pi \triangleq \begin{cases} \texttt{makePrescr} & \mapsto \{Treatment\} \\ \texttt{getData} & \mapsto \{Research\} \\ \texttt{computeStats} & \mapsto \{Research\}; \end{cases}$$

$$\nu \triangleq \begin{cases} \texttt{makePrescr} & \mapsto \{Patient\} \\ \texttt{getData} & \mapsto \{Patient, TrialData\} \\ \texttt{computeStats} & \mapsto \{TrialData\}. \end{cases}$$

Let us prove that the first trace is purpose compliant, i.e.:

$$\mathcal{C} \vdash Handle(\texttt{makePrescr}, Patient); Handle(\texttt{makePrescr}, Dos); \epsilon.$$

1. According to the second inference rule of Fig. 5, this property holds if and only both $\mathcal{C} \vdash Handle(\texttt{makePrescr}, Patient)$ and $\mathcal{C} \vdash Handle(\texttt{makePrescr}, Dos); \epsilon$ holds.
   Let us prove first the left-hand side of this conjunction.
2. By definition of purpose compliance, $\mathcal{C} \vdash Handle(\texttt{makePrescr}, Patient)$ holds if and only if either $Patient \notin D$, or $\gamma(Patient, p) = \top$ for some purpose p in $\pi(\texttt{makePrescr})$. We prove the right part of the disjunction.
3. Consider $p = Treatment$. Since, $Treatment \in \pi(\texttt{makePrescr})$ and $\gamma(Patient, Treatment) = \top$, the property holds.
4. Let us now prove the right-hand side of the conjunction at item 1., which is $\mathcal{C} \vdash Handle(\texttt{makePrescr}, Dos); \epsilon$ holds. According to the second inference rule of Fig. 5, this property holds if and only both $\mathcal{C} \vdash Handle(\texttt{makePrescr}, Dos)$ and $\mathcal{C} \vdash \epsilon$ holds.
5. The latter case (empty trace) is the axiom of the inference system, so it holds. Let us demonstrate the former.
6. By definition of purpose compliance, $\mathcal{C} \vdash Handle(\texttt{makePrescr}, Dos)$ holds if and only if either $Dos) \notin D$, or $\gamma(Dos), p) = \top$ for some purpose p in $\pi(\texttt{makePrescr})$. The former case corresponds to the definition of D: Dos is not a personal data in $\mathcal{C}$.

Therefore the first trace is purpose compliant in the context $\mathcal{C}$.

Let us now prove that the second trace is not purpose compliant, i.e.:

$$\mathcal{C} \nvdash Handle(\texttt{getData}, Patient); Handle(\texttt{getData}, TrialData);$$
$$Handle(\texttt{computeStats}, TrialData); \epsilon.$$

We prove this property by contradiction, so let us assume that this trace is purpose compliant, i.e.:

$$\mathcal{C} \vdash Handle(\texttt{getData}, Patient); Handle(\texttt{getData}, TrialData);$$
$$Handle(\texttt{computeStats}, TrialData); \epsilon.$$

1. From this property and according to the second inference rule of Fig. 5, $\mathcal{C} \vdash Handle(\texttt{getData}, Patient)$ holds.
2. Therefore, by definition of purpose compliance, either $Patient \notin D$ or $\gamma(Patient, p) = \top$ for some purpose p in $\pi(\texttt{getData})$.
3. The former case contradicts the definition of D: $Patient$ is a personal data in $\mathcal{C}$.
4. Consider the latter case. By definition of π, $Research$ is the only purpose of $\texttt{getData}$. However, $\gamma(Patient, Research) = \bot$, which contradicts $\gamma(Patient, Research) = \top$.
5. Each case leads to a contradiction, so the initial hypothesis

$$\mathcal{C} \vdash Handle(\texttt{getData}, Patient); Handle(\texttt{getData}, TrialData);$$
$$Handle(\texttt{computeStats}, TrialData); \epsilon$$

does not hold.

Therefore the second trace is not purpose compliant in the context $\mathcal{C}$.

C   Instantiations using CSpeL

This section presents the CSpeL's specification for the running example at code level. The corresponding context, which is the second context of Example 1, can be specified as follows.

```
\context {
  \process      { makePrescr; getData; computeStats },
  \personalData { Patient, TrialData },
  \purposes     { Treatment, Research },
  \isGranted    { (Patient: Treatment) },
  \hasPurposes  { (makePrescr: { Treatment }),
                  (getData: { Research }),
                  (computeStats: { Research })
                },
```

```
\needData      { (makePrescr: { Patient }),
                 (getData: {Patient, TrialData }),
                 (computeStats: {TrialData })
               },
}
```

Additionnally, we can write in CSpeL the code level's traces of Example 2 as follows.

– For the first trace:

```
\trace {
  \handle(makePrescr, Patient);
  \handle(makePrescr, Dos);
  VOID
}
```

– For the second trace:

```
\trace {
  \handle(getData, Patient);
  \handle(getData, TrialData);
  \handle(computeStats, TrialData);
  VOID
}
```

Model-Based Test Generation

Proving Properties of Operation Contracts with Test Scenarios

Martin Gogolla[1(⊠)] and Lars Hamann[2]

[1] University of Bremen, Bremen, Germany
`gogolla@uni-bremen.de`
[2] Hamburg University of Applied Sciences, Hamburg, Germany
`lars.hamann@haw-hamburg.de`

Abstract. This contribution studies structural and behavioral models by applying (a) UML classes, associations, attributes, generalization and OCL invariants for *structural* model features and (b) UML operations and OCL contracts, i.e., pre- and postconditions, for *behavioral* features. For detecting and assuring model properties that are not explicitly present, but valid in the considered model suitable test cases are constructed. Inspected model properties are: (a) the consistency between the invariants and the contracts, including the consistency between operation calls by checking whether the postcondition of one operation is compatible with the precondition of a following operation, and (b) the reachability of particular model states defined by invariant-like OCL formulas gained through an operation call chain. Thus, by constructing *test* cases we *prove* model consistency and property reachability for behavioral models.

Keywords: UML and OCL model · Operation contract · Invariant · Model consistency · Property reachability

1 Introduction

Testing and proving are essential techniques for advancing software and system reliability. We use these skills for UML [23] and OCL [26] models and build *test* cases with operation calls to *prove* model properties that are valid, but only implicitly present, e.g., as consequences of the model. Our approach relies on constructing examples [17,25] and can be used for a large variety of properties.

We apply the tool[1] USE [12] that supports structural and behavioral UML and OCL models and that in particular allows a developer to automatically build object diagrams for a given class diagram. We use this option here and automatically build object diagrams for so-called filmstrip models. Filmstrip models express dynamic changes through operations by taking snapshots at crucial points in time and aggregate the considered snapshots and operation transitions into a single object diagram. Filmstrip object diagrams represent operation call

---

[1] Access tool version used here at: https://sourceforge.net/projects/useocl/.

© The Author(s), under exclusive license to Springer Nature Switzerland AG 2023
V. Prevosto and C. Seceleanu (Eds.): TAP 2023, LNCS 14066, pp. 97–107, 2023.
https://doi.org/10.1007/978-3-031-38828-6_6

chains and correspond to automatically constructed behavioral test cases that
allow the developer to prove particular model properties. The models, examples,
techniques, tests and proofs shown here are realized in the tool USE as presented.
More details of the models can be found in [10].

2   The Basic Idea Through a Prototypical Example

Figure 1 shows two class diagrams and one object diagram: We call the left class
diagram an application model and the right class diagram a filmstrip model; the
lower object diagram builds an instantiation of the filmstrip class diagram. The
purpose of filmstripping is to express an operation call chain from the application
model in form of a filmstrip object diagram. Our used tool is able to handle
object diagrams in a forceful way. The filmstrip class diagram has been obtained
through an automatic transformation of the application model.

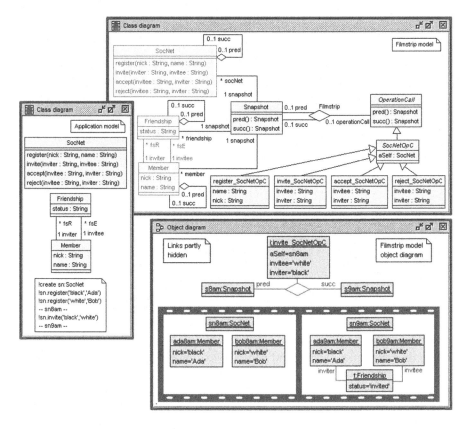

Fig. 1. Application and filmstrip model.

Application Model: The application model describes a social network in which
members (having a unique **nick** name and a further attribute **name**) can establish

Friendships represented by objects and links. Friendships are first in status invited and can then become either accepted or rejected. In the class SocNet, the intention of the operation register is to establish a new Member object, invite is designed for creating a new Friendship object and for linking this object to the respective Member objects (when being called with parameters inviter and invitee), accept changes the Friendship status to accepted (when being called with parameters invitee and inviter, with opposite parameter order compared to invite), and reject changes the Friendship status to rejected. The comment shows a short model usage in form of an operation call chain: A social network is created, two members are registered and a friendship invitation between them is stated. Basically, the resulting application model object diagrams before and after the invite call are pictured on the filmstrip object diagram in the left and right filmstrip snapshot.

Filmstrip Model: The application model is completely included in the filmstrip model, as indicated in the light gray part. The filmstrip model introduces additional classes and associations: A class Snapshot for describing single application model object diagrams, a ternary association Filmstrip for catching transitions between object diagrams by operations calls in the application model, and for each application model operation a class for describing an operation call of the respective operation. Furthermore, associations allow to link snapshots to application model elements (e.g., between Snapshot and Member) or to link application model objects to later incarnations (e.g., the self association on Member with roles 0..1 pred and 0..1 succ). Objects at different points in time are formally different objects, i.e., different incarnations as one might call them.

Object Model: The filmstrip object model gives just a rough overview on how the invite operation call in the left application model would be represented, as a number of details are hidden, in particular not all links are shown. The object diagram represents the two snapshots (here named s8am and s9am) before and after the invite call and the call itself through the object i : invite_SocNetOpC. Roughly speaking, the left snapshot includes the members ada and bob and the right snapshot apart from ada and bob includes a newly created Friendship object f linked to ada and bob in their respective roles. However, in formal terms there are two ada incarnations, namely ada8am and ada9am, analogously for bob. To formally express that one object is a later incarnation of another object, there exists a PredSucc link from the self association on Member that we have not displayed in order to make the filmstrip diagram simple. You see such a PredSucc link in Fig. 2, e.g., in the 4th row between Friendship objects f5 and f2, where the friendship changes from invited to accepted.

Model behavior is expressed in the application model by OCL operation pre- and postconditions and is further restricted by OCL class invariants. These formal restrictions are checked in our filmstrip approach when a filmstrip object diagram is constructed, as pre- and postconditions are represented in form of filmstrip invariants. Thus, in a filmstrip object diagram like the one in Fig. 1, contracts and invariants evaluate to true. Such a filmstrip object diagram, i.e., a test case, proves the executability of an operation as in the pred snapshot

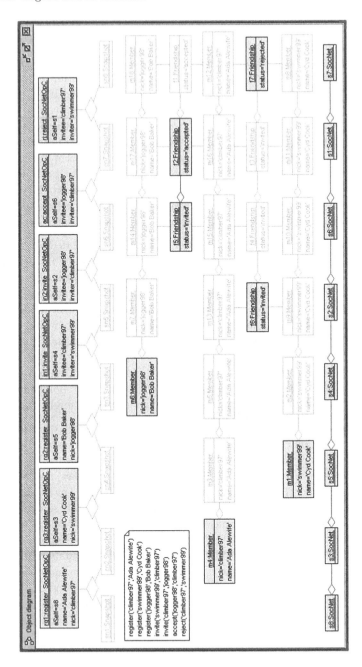

Fig. 2. Test case proving invariant and contract consistency.

the preconditions and invariants and in the `succ` snapshot the postconditons and invariants are valid. In Fig. 1 we demonstrate that at least one valid `invite` operation occurrence exists.

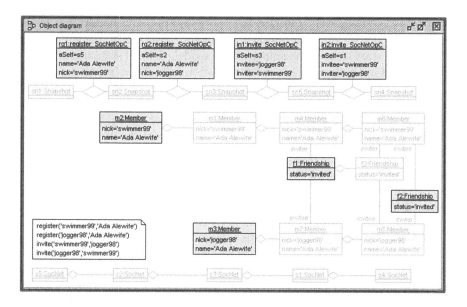

Fig. 3. Test case proving property reachability.

We have already shown the application and filmstrip model class diagrams and will later see in Fig. 4 part of an example contract. The application model contains as postconditions for operations so-called frame conditions. These specify items unchanged by an operation, e.g., for the `register` operation, which is creating a new `Member`, a postcondition requires that existing `Friendship` objects remain unchanged. We have worked out a systematic development method for frame conditions [2] that can be supported by tools. All details of the example and one further demonstration of our approach are available in [10].

3   Consistency and Property Reachability

We now turn to the interplay between contracts and invariants. By considering logical structures in that contracts and invariants are treated uniformly on the same level of abstraction (in our case filmstrip object diagrams), we have the option to study properties that do not treat only contracts or only invariants, but properties that can deal with features of contracts and invariants altogether. We consider (a) consistency of the contracts with the invariants as well as contract consistency by considering how postconditions and preconditions fit together and (b) reachability of properties that are achieved by executing operations, typically gained by starting in the empty system state.

3.1   General Discussion

Consistency: For proving consistency of contracts and invariants, the constructed test cases, i.e., the operation call chains, should cover all operations at least once, so that every precondition, postcondition and invariant is evaluated at least once, in order to obtain a reasonable coverage of model elements. Typically, the start state is the empty object model, the end state has a handful of objects, and in between there are few operation calls. When referring to 'proving consistency', we mean that we construct operation call chains involving all operations, and that in the chains all pre- and postconditions and the invariants evaluate to true at respective spots. Thus we show, that among the collection of all possible operation call chains, there is a collection of chains that altogether satisfy all formally specified invariants and contracts.

Reachability: For proving reachabilty of a particular property through a test case, i.e., an operation call chain, an invariant-like OCL formula is added as an additional invariant to the model, such that the added formula describes the desired state to be reached. The aim is to construct an operation call chain leading from the empty start state to a state satisfying the particular added invariant-like formula and having legal operation calls between valid intermediate states. Thus, a legal operation call chain is constructed that generates a valid state with the desired property. A found *good* state assures the developer in the taken design decisions or, in case of a *bad* state, may indicate that model refactoring is needed in order to rule out the state.

3.2   Example-Specific Discussion

In order to better understand the following details, let us first show in Fig. 4 (part of) a contract example from the application model and its transformed version from the filmstrip model. As the filmstrip model uses invariants to represent contracts, the context of the transformed invariants is the respective operation, represented as a class. The original existential `allInstances` quantification is transformed into a quantification (a) on the `Member` objects `OpCALL.pred().member` in the predecessor snapshot in case of the precondition and (b) in the successor snapshot over `OpCALL.succ().member` in case of the postcondition.

```
SocNet::register(nick:String,name:String)         -- Application model
  pre freshMember:
    not Member.allInstances->exists(m | m.nick=nick)
  post existsMember:
    Member.allInstances->exists(m | m.nick=nick and m.name=name)

context register_SocNetOpC inv pre_freshMember:        -- Filmstrip model
  not self.pred().member->exists(m | m.nick=nick)
context register_SocNetOpC inv post_existsMember:
  self.succ().member->exists(m | m.nick=nick and m.name=name)
```

Fig. 4. (Excerpts from a) Contract example in application and filmstrip model.

Consistency: In Fig. 2, one operation call chain with 7 operation calls is shown that uses all operations at least once. Starting from the empty snapshot, it introduces `Member` and `Friendship` objects and respective links and sets the attribute `status`. This filmstrip object diagram has been built automatically with the USE model validator [12], the USE component for automatically building object diagrams. The applied configuration bounds are displayed in the left column of Fig. 5, i.e., the minimal and maximal number of objects and links per class and association as well as attribute values are specified. The construction takes about 90 s. The bounds have been planned as indicated in Fig. 6. We emphasize that the filmstrip model is a moderately complex UML and OCL model, specifically with about 30 partly complex invariants [10]. This operation call chain proves consistency of the invariants and contracts, as (a) all snapshots are valid w.r.t. invariants, (b) the preconditions are legal in the operation `pred` snapshot and (c) the postconditions are legal in the operation `succ` snapshot.

	Consistency	Reachability	
Snapshot	8..8	5..5	Filmstrip
register	3..3	2..2	model
invite	2..2	2..2	
accept	1..1	0..0	
reject	1..1	0..0	
SocNet	8..8	5..5	Application
Member	18..18	2..7	model
nick	'jogger98','swimmer99','climber97'	'jogger98','swimmer99'	
name	'Ada Alewife','Bob Baker','Cyd Cook'	'Ada Alewife','Bob Baker'	
Friendship	7..7	1..3	
status	'invited','accepted','rejected'	'invited','accepted','rejected'	
/associations/	0..*	0..*	
Solving time	90 sec	1 sec	

Fig. 5. Model validator configurations for consistency and reachability.

	reg	reg	reg	inv	inv	acc	rej	
s	s	s	s	s	s	s	s	s8
	m	m	m	m	m	m	m	m18
		m	m	m	m	m	m	
			m	m	m	m	m	
				f	f	f	f	f7
					f	f	f	

Fig. 6. Planing the configuration for consistency.

Reachability: In Fig. 3, an operation call chain has been constructed after the invariant-like OCL formula from Fig. 7 has been added: It requires that two friendships between two members are present such that the roles are inverted; both members play an `inviter` role *and* an `invitee` role to each other. This is a potential danger of irregularity as this could lead to one `accepted` and to another `rejected` friendship between two members. One probably wants a clear friendship setting so that this situation is avoided. The constructed reachable state is not desired, and the underlying OCL formula should never become true. As for the other constructed filmstrip object diagram, the used configuration is shown in Fig. 5. The construction takes about 1 s, as the number of potential objects and attribute values is much smaller than in the first configuration.

Achieving consistency of the model by seeing that all contracts and invariants are satisfiable increases confidence in the development. Reaching a particular state can strengthen the developer's trust in the model, or it can be a source for refactoring the model, if undesired model features are detected.

```
context Snapshot inv twoMembersWithTwoFriendships:
  Snapshot.allInstances->exists(s|
    s.friendship->exists(f,g| f<>g and
      f.inviter=g.invitee and f.invitee=g.inviter))
```

Fig. 7. Added invariant requiring two members with two, inversed friendships.

4   Related Work

Our short discussion on related work is restrained by space limitation. Invariants and contracts are rarely discussed jointly. If both are treated, the work is not done in the UML and OCL context, but with a different focus as in our modeling perspective (discussion by publication year order): The context of [1] is VDM and B, [24] treats invariants and contracts from an application angle, [7,8] concentrate on loop invariants and contracts, [22] compares auto-generated and user-defined contracts, [18] derives invariants from preconditions, [6] synthesizes invariants and contracts, [21] handles invariants and contracts in C programs, [19] proposes a learning approach for contract invariants, [20] detects invariants in blockchains, and [5] concentrates on loop invariant verification.

We have studied the filmstripping approach previously in [3,4,9,11,13–16]. But in that papers we did not handle the relationship between invariants and contracts and did not study any formal properties in the interplay between invariants and contracts as we do here.

5   Conclusion and Future Work

This contribution has exploited the UML and OCL modeling tool USE that supports structural and behavioral modeling for analyzing behavioral models. USE especially encourages the application of OCL. By automatically constructing test cases, we have proven for behavioral models (a) consistency between class invariants and operation contracts and (b) reachability of a particular property characterized by an OCL formula. We have taken advantage of a filmstrip approach that expresses dynamic changes of operations by taking snapshots at crucial points in time and aggregates the snapshots and operation calls into a single object model.

Future work will use more applications of the USE component that automatically constructs object diagrams, e.g., for proving implications from the model. The tool can also be applied for checking conformance of operation implementations against contracts and invariants. Another option would be to systematically check all possible pairs of operation calls and thus test whether the postconditions of one operation are compatible with the preconditions of another operation. The approach can also be used (a) to detect which operations are callable in the empty state and which are not, as well as (b) for determining which operations are callable in a state characterized by a particular OCL formula. For a comprehensive validation, case studies from real projects have to give feedback on the applicability and quality of the proposal for further improvement.

References

1. Bicarregui, J., Ritchie, B.: Invariants, frames, and postconditions: a comparison of the VDM and B notations. IEEE Trans. Softw. Eng. **21**(2), 79–89 (1995)
2. Desai, N., Gogolla, M.: Developing comprehensive postconditions through a model transformation Chain. J. Object Technol. AITO, DE **18**(3), 5:1–18 (2019)
3. Desai, N., Gogolla, M., Frank, H.: Executing models by filmstripping: enhancing validation by filmstrip templates and transformation alternatives. In: Burgueno, L., et al. (eds.) Proceedings Workshop Executable Modeling (EXE 2017), pp. 88–94. CEUR Proceedings 2019 (2017)
4. Doan, K.-H., Gogolla, M., Hilken, F.: Towards a developer-oriented process for verifying behavioral properties in UML and OCL models. In: Milazzo, P., Varró, D., Wimmer, M. (eds.) STAF 2016. LNCS, vol. 9946, pp. 207–220. Springer, Cham (2016). https://doi.org/10.1007/978-3-319-50230-4_15
5. Ernst, G.: Loop verification with invariants and contracts. In: Finkbeiner, B., Wies, T. (eds.) VMCAI 2022. LNCS, vol. 13182, pp. 69–92. Springer, Cham (2022). https://doi.org/10.1007/978-3-030-94583-1_4
6. Ezudheen, P., Neider, D., D'Souza, D., Garg, P., Madhusudan, P.: Horn-ice learning for synthesizing invariants and contracts. Proc. ACM Program. Lang. **2**(OOPSLA), 131:1–131:25 (2018)
7. Furia, C.A., Meyer, B.: Inferring loop invariants using postconditions. In: Blass, A., Dershowitz, N., Reisig, W. (eds.) Fields of Logic and Computation. LNCS, vol. 6300, pp. 277–300. Springer, Heidelberg (2010). https://doi.org/10.1007/978-3-642-15025-8_15
8. Gladisch, C.: Could we have chosen a better loop invariant or method contract? In: Dubois, C. (ed.) TAP 2009. LNCS, vol. 5668, pp. 74–89. Springer, Heidelberg (2009). https://doi.org/10.1007/978-3-642-02949-3_7

9. Gogolla, M., Desai, N., Doan, K.H.: Developing user and recording interfaces for design time and runtime models. In: Bruneliere, H., Eramo, R., Gomez, A. (eds.) Proc. STAF 2019 Workshops, 2nd Workshop Model-Driven Engineering for Design-Runtime Interaction in Complex Systems (DeRun 2019), pp. 39–48. CEUR Proceedings 2405 (2019)

10. Gogolla, M., Hamann, L.: Addition to 'Proving Properties of Operation Contracts with Test Scenarios'. University of Bremen (2023). https://tinyurl.com/26964sck

11. Gogolla, M., Hamann, L., Hilken, F., Kuhlmann, M., France, R.B.: From application models to filmstrip models: an approach to automatic validation of model dynamics. In: Fill, H., Karagiannis, D., Reimer, U. (eds.) Proceedings of the Modellierung (MODELLIERUNG 2014), pp. 273–288. GI, LNI 225 (2014)

12. Gogolla, M., Hilken, F., Doan, K.H.: Achieving model quality through model validation, verification and exploration. J. Comput. Lang. Syst. Struct. Elsevier, NL 54, pp. 474–511 (2018)

13. Gogolla, M., Hilken, F., Doan, K.-H., Desai, N.: Checking UML and OCL model behavior with filmstripping and classifying terms. In: Gabmeyer, S., Johnsen, E.B. (eds.) TAP 2017. LNCS, vol. 10375, pp. 119–128. Springer, Cham (2017). https://doi.org/10.1007/978-3-319-61467-0_7

14. Hilken, F., Gogolla, M.: Verifying linear temporal logic properties in UML/OCL class diagrams using filmstripping. In: Kitsos, P. (ed.) Proceedings of the Digital System Design (DSD 2016), pp. 708–713. IEEE (2016)

15. Hilken, F., Hamann, L., Gogolla, M.: Transformation of UML and OCL models into filmstrip models. In: Di Ruscio, D., Varró, D. (eds.) ICMT 2014. LNCS, vol. 8568, pp. 170–185. Springer, Cham (2014). https://doi.org/10.1007/978-3-319-08789-4_13

16. Hilken, F.., Niemann, P., Gogolla, M., Wille, R.: Filmstripping and unrolling: a comparison of verification approaches for UML and OCL behavioral models. In: Seidl, M., Tillmann, N. (eds.) TAP 2014. LNCS, vol. 8570, pp. 99–116. Springer, Cham (2014). https://doi.org/10.1007/978-3-319-09099-3_8

17. Jackson, D.: Alloy: a lightweight object modelling notation. ACM Trans. Softw. Eng. Methodol. 11(2), 256–290 (2002)

18. Karpenkov, E.G., Monniaux, D.: Formula slicing: inductive invariants from preconditions. In: Bloem, R., Arbel, E. (eds.) HVC 2016. LNCS, vol. 10028, pp. 169–185. Springer, Cham (2016). https://doi.org/10.1007/978-3-319-49052-6_11

19. Liu, J., Chen, Y., Tan, B., Dillig, I., Feng, Y.: Learning contract invariants using reinforcement learning. In: 37th IEEE/ACM Int. Conf. Automated Software Engineering, ASE, pp. 63:1–63:11. ACM (2022)

20. Liu, Y., Li, Y.: Invcon: a dynamic invariant detector for ethereum smart contracts. In: 37th IEEE/ACM Int. Con. Automated Software Engineering, ASE 2022, Rochester, 10–14 October 2022, pp. 160:1–160:4. ACM (2022)

21. Lu, H., Wang, C., Gui, J., Huang, H.: Pblinv: postcondition-based loop invariant learning for C programs. In: 20th IEEE International Conference on Software Quality, Reliability and Security, QRS 2020, pp. 1–12. IEEE (2020)

22. Rahman, F., Labiche, Y.: A comparative study of invariants generated by daikon and user-defined design contracts. In: 2014 14th International Conference on Quality Software, pp. 174–183. IEEE (2014)

23. Rumbaugh, J., Jacobson, I., Booch, G.: The Unified Modeling Language Reference Manual, 2nd Edn. Addison-Wesley (2004)

24. Savidis, A.: Application invariants: design by contract augmented with deployment correctness logic. Softw. Pract. Exp. 36(3), 255–282 (2006)

25. Steel, G.: The importance of non-theorems and counterexamples in program verification. In: Meyer, B., Woodcock, J. (eds.) VSTTE 2005. LNCS, vol. 4171, pp.
491–495. Springer, Heidelberg (2008). https://doi.org/10.1007/978-3-540-69149-
5_53
26. Warmer, J., Kleppe, A.: The Object Constraint Language: Getting Your Models
Ready for MDA, 2nd edn. Addison-Wesley (2004)

Testing Languages with a Languages-as-Databases Approach

Matteo Cimini[✉]

University of Massachusetts Lowell, Lowell, MA 01854, USA
`matteo_cimini@uml.edu`

Abstract. Language testing is an important element in the cycle of a programming language development. A part of these tests aim at determining features such as what type of binders the language has, whether evaluation takes place underneath a binder, as well as other features.

In prior work, we have proposed languages-as-databases, an approach that is based on storing languages as databases, which then can be interrogated with declarative queries.

This paper illustrates a number of language tests on various aspects of programming languages. We also formulate tests that establish whether the language at hand conforms to the GSOS rule format.

Our tests show that languages-as-databases provides a lightweight approach to language testing.

Keywords: Language testing · Domain-specific languages · SQL

1 Introduction

After designing a programming language, the work of a language designer is not finished yet. Ideally, the language designer would engage in an effort to determine whether the newly created language meets the expectations that were intended at the time of design. This effort may range from extensive endeavors such as establishing type safety with mechanized proofs to more lightweight approaches based on tests, that is, *language testing*.

This paper focuses on automated testing approaches on parametrized languages, that is, the language definition is given as input. Prior work in this area has focused on generating a test suite of randomized programs from the description of languages [8,18,32,34]. Well-known instances of this approach are adopted in language semantics tools such as the $\mathbb{K}$ framework [35], PLT Redex [17], and MPS[1], to name a few. A notable work by Klein et al. [23] showed bugs in a handful of systems using PLT Redex features. (A good part of those bugs have been found thanks to randomized tests).

In this paper, we follow a different approach. Rather than testing the language from its programs, that is, in some sense, by its *products*, we test the language

---

[1] http://www.jetbrains.com/mps/.

V. Prevosto and C. Seceleanu (Eds.): TAP 2023, LNCS 14066, pp. 108–126, 2023.
https://doi.org/10.1007/978-3-031-38828-6_7

based on its *qualities*. In much the same way that (static) program analysis examines the text of a program without executing it, here we analyze the text of the language definition at hand in order to test its language design features. For example, is evaluation taking place underneath a binder? Perhaps, it was not intended. Is some type covariant when it should be invariant for the sake of type safety? These and similar tests go a long way to help debug languages.

Lang-SQL. In prior work, we have developed *languages-as-databases* [13], an approach based on storing languages as database tables. The approach starts from the perspective that interrogating language definitions should be akin to interrogating databases, where queries are separate from application code, and are also concise, declarative and mostly readable. To this aim, [13] has also developed LANG-SQL, a SQL-style domain-specific language for retrieving information from grammars, reduction rules, and other components of languages. That paper shows some queries to retrieve the canonical forms and the elimination forms of a language given as input, and also uses LANG-SQL to reimplement a good part of a tool called LANG-N-CHECK, which can establish type safety for a limited class of functional languages. [13] reports doing so in 23 lines of LANG-SQL code when its corresponding part in LANG-N-CHECK is over 1200 lines of OCaml code.

Language Testing with Lang-SQL. This paper demonstrates the use of LANG-SQL in language testing. We augment LANG-SQL with syntactic constructs for expressing tests, and with convenient macros, as well. Our tests can check that the table produced by a query contains some data, is a subset of another table, or its rows are all distinct, among other tests. We have introduced macros to quickly access P in the formula $P \longrightarrow P'$ with the name `stepSource`, and similar others. These macros improve the readability of our tests greatly.

We show the language testing features of LANG-SQL with the following tests:

- Test that the language does not evaluate underneath a binder,
- Test that errors are typed at any type (to ensure type preservation).
- Test that references are invariant in the presence of subtyping.
- Test that there are no types that bind expressions (such as dependent types).

Our tests are concise and declarative. As language design is a variegated endeavor, it is difficult to identify a series of language tests that can be regarded as representative. We believe that our tests touch on diverse aspects of programming languages such as binders, evaluation contexts, variance, and typing.

A GSOS Validator in Lang-SQL. Results on rule formats [28] say that if the inference rules of a language definition conform to some syntactic template then some property is guaranteed to hold. Rule formats have been applied to process algebras to derive the congruence of bisimilarity [10,20,37] and to establish algebraic laws of operators modulo bisimilarity [3,4,16,29], among other properties. The GSOS rule format is one of the most popular formats [10], and can establish the congruence of bisimilarity for a wide range of process algebras.

In this paper, we use LANG-SQL to write a full validator for the GSOS format. That is, we formulate the syntactic constraints of the GSOS format as LANG-SQL tests. This is an example of *"tests that prove"*: Although our tests do not provide a proof certificate, the results of [10] guarantee that they are sufficient to formally derive that bisimilarity is a congruence.

We have used our LANG-SQL tests against several process algebras. We have evaluated our tool against the repo of GSOS-Validator [14], which includes common concurrency operators such as the choice operator of CCS [24], the disrupt operator, and the priority operator [7]. This repo contains 18 process algebras that our tool validates as adhering to the GSOS format. (Each of these process algebras are already known to be compliant to the GSOS format.) All our tests are carefully reported [12].

Our GSOS validator is concise and amounts to 14 lines of code, and expresses the GSOS format declaratively. Overall, this paper gives evidence that languages-as-databases is an effective and lightweight approach to language testing.

Relation with [13] *and Structure of the Paper.* [13] introduced the languages-as-databases approach. This paper extends that approach with syntactic constructs for tests and suitable macros, and demonstrates the approach to language testing. Also, [13] provides only the example queries for canonical forms, elimination forms, and for counting the number of typing rules, before diving into rewriting a specific tool (LANG-N-CHECK). These examples do not sufficiently demonstrate languages-as-databases. We believe that combining the examples of this paper with those of [13] helps demonstrate languages-as-databases more substantially.

The paper is organized as follows. The next section reviews how languages-as-databases stores languages. Section 3 reviews LANG-SQL and describes our extensions to it (tests and macros). Section 4 provides examples of language tests. Section 5 presents our GSOS validator. Section 6 discusses our evaluation. Section 7 discusses related work and Sect. 8 concludes the paper.

2   Language Definitions in Lang-SQL

We review the languages-as-databases approach from [13]. The approach has been proposed for operational semantics. Our running example is fpl, a λ-calculus with integers, floating points, functions and references. fpl also features subtyping. Figure 1 shows the grammar of fpl. (Operations on integers and floating are not important here, and so we have omitted them for brevity.) This grammar is stored as database tables. For the sake of a uniform notation, the terms that are used in grammars, which we range over t, are in abstract syntax, that is, they have a top-level constructor applied to a list of terms. The notation $(X).t$ denotes unary binding [11] (X is bound in t). For example, $(e\ e)$ is stored as $app\ e\ e$, and $\lambda x : T.e$ is stored as $abs\ T\ (x)e$. Notation $t[t/X]$ also denotes the capture-avoiding substitution.

The tables grammar-info and grammar store grammars. The former table, grammar-info, records for each category its name in the attribute category, its metavariable in meta-var, and its object variable (like x in $\lambda x : T.e$) in obj-var.

Warning: We did not intend to evaluate underneath λ, i.e., $\boxed{\lambda x : T.E}$ is an oversight.

Type	T	$::=$ Int $\mid$ Float $\mid$ $T \to T$ $\mid$ Ref T
Expression	e	$::= n \mid f \mid x \mid \lambda x : T.e \mid e\,e \mid l \mid$ ref $e \mid$ $!e \mid e := e \mid$ error e
Value	v	$::= n \mid f \mid x : T.e \mid l$
EvalCtx	E	$::= \Box \mid E\,e \mid v\,E \mid \boxed{\lambda x : T.E} \mid$ ref $E \mid$ $!E \mid E := e \mid v := E \mid$ error E
Error	er	$::=$ error v
TypeEnv	Γ	$::= \emptyset \mid \Gamma, x : T$
Heap	μ	$::= \emptyset \mid \mu, (l \mapsto v)$
LocEnv	Σ	$::= \emptyset \mid \Sigma, (l \mapsto T)$

Fig. 1. Grammar of fpl

(When some categories do not have a object level variable we use an unused variable _.) Table grammar stores, for each category, its name in category and its grammar productions, one production per row, in term. Figure 2 shows a part of these tables for fpl. Notice that our approach has primitive maps declared with, for example, *map l v* (a map from labels to values), and operations such as *lookup*, as well as others.

grammar-info

category	meta-var	obj-var
Type	T	$-$
Expression	e	x
Value	v	$-$
Heap	μ	$-$
$\ldots$	$\ldots$	$\ldots$

grammar

category	term
Type	*int*
Type	*arrow T T*
$\ldots$	$\ldots$
Expression	*abs T $(x)e$*
Expression	*app e e*
$\ldots$	$\ldots$
Heap	*map l v*

Fig. 2. Table grammar-info and grammar of fpl (some rows)

Figure 3 shows the inference rules of fpl. These rules define the typing, subtyping, and reduction relation of fpl. Table rule stores inference rules. Each row of rule contains the name of the rule in rulename, a formula in predname and args (which we explain shortly), and whether the formula is a premise (PREM) or the conclusion (CONCL) in the attribute role. A formula has a predicate name in predname, and the list of its arguments in args. Figure 4 shows a part of the table rule for fpl.

Warning: References should be invariant, and error *should be typed at any type.*

$$\Sigma \mid \Gamma \vdash n : \texttt{Int} \qquad \Sigma \mid \Gamma \vdash f : \texttt{Float} \qquad \Sigma \mid \Gamma, x : T \vdash x : T \qquad \frac{lookup(\Sigma, l) = T}{\Sigma \mid \Gamma \vdash l : T}$$

$$\frac{\Sigma \mid \Gamma, x : T_1 \vdash e : T_2}{\Sigma \mid \Gamma \vdash \lambda x : T_1.e : T_1 \to T_2} \qquad \frac{(\text{T-APP})}{\begin{array}{c} \Sigma \mid \Gamma \vdash e_1 : T_1 \to T_2 \\ \Sigma \mid \Gamma \vdash e_2 : T_3 \\ T_3 <: T_1 \\ \hline \Sigma \mid \Gamma \vdash e_1 \, e_2 : T_2 \end{array}} \qquad \frac{(\text{T-ERROR})}{\begin{array}{c} \Sigma \mid \Gamma \vdash e : \boxed{T} \\ \hline \Sigma \mid \Gamma \vdash \texttt{error} \, e : \boxed{T} \end{array}}$$

$$\frac{\Sigma \mid \Gamma \vdash e : T}{\Sigma \mid \Gamma \vdash \texttt{ref} \, e : \texttt{Ref} \, T} \qquad \frac{\Sigma \mid \Gamma \vdash e : \texttt{Ref} \, T}{\Sigma \mid \Gamma \vdash !e : T} \qquad \frac{\begin{array}{c} \Sigma \mid \Gamma \vdash e_1 : \texttt{Ref} \, T \\ \Sigma \mid \Gamma \vdash e_2 : T \end{array}}{\Sigma \mid \Gamma \vdash e_1 := e_2 : T}$$

$$\begin{array}{c} (\text{S-BASE}) \\ \texttt{Int} <: \texttt{Int} \\ \texttt{Float} <: \texttt{Float} \\ \texttt{Int} <: \texttt{Float} \end{array} \qquad \frac{(\text{S-ARROW})}{\frac{T_1' <: T_1 \qquad T_2 <: T_2'}{T_1 \to T_2 <: T_1' \to T_2'}} \qquad \frac{(\text{S-REF})}{\frac{\boxed{T <: T'}}{\texttt{Ref} \, T <: \texttt{Ref} \, T'}}$$

$$\begin{array}{c} (\lambda x : T.e) \, v; \mu \longrightarrow e[v/x]; \mu \qquad (\text{BETA}) \\ !l; \mu \longrightarrow \mu(l); \mu \qquad (\text{R-DEREF}) \\ l := v; \mu \longrightarrow v; \mu, (l \mapsto v) \end{array}$$

$$\frac{newLabel(\mu) = l}{\texttt{ref} \, v; \mu \longrightarrow l; \mu, (l \mapsto v)} \qquad \frac{e; \mu \longrightarrow e'; \mu'}{E[e] \longrightarrow E[e']; \mu'} \qquad E[er]; \mu \longrightarrow er; \mu$$

Fig. 3. Typing, subtyping, and reduction rules of fpl

rule

rulename	predname	args	role
(T-APP)	$\vdash$	$[\Sigma; \Gamma; e_1; T_1 \to T_2]$	PREM
(T-APP)	$\vdash$	$[\Sigma; \Gamma; e_2; T_1]$	PREM
(T-APP)	$\vdash$	$[\Sigma; \Gamma; app \, e_1 \, e_2; T_2]$	CONCL
(BETA)	$\longrightarrow$	$[app \, (abs \, T \, (x)e) \, v; \mu; e[v/x]; \mu]$	CONCL
(R-DEREF)	$lookup$	$[\mu; l; v]$	PREM
(R-DEREF)	$\longrightarrow$	$[deref \, l; \mu; v; \mu]$	CONCL
$\ldots$	$\ldots$	$\ldots$	$\ldots$

Fig. 4. Table rule of fpl (some rows)

The language-as-databases approach makes use of other tables that store the signature of relations and constructors. As they do not play a role in this paper, we do not cover them here and refer the reader to [13].

Issues of `fpl`. The language definition of `fpl` has some issues: 1) We did not intend to allow evaluation to occur underneath a λ-binder. That is, the presence of the evaluation context $\lambda x : T.E$ is an oversight. 2) To prove type preservation, (`error` e) must be typed at any type because it can appear in any context through small-step evaluation. For example !(`ref` (`error` 0)) $\longrightarrow$!(`error` 0), where the target is ill-typed because ! is applied to an expression of type `Int` rather than a reference. We can fix this by assigning a new fresh variable to the type of `error` in (T-ERROR). 3) To ensure type safety in the presence of subtyping, the reference type must be invariant. Instead, `fpl` uses covariant references, which is unsafe [31, Sect. 15.5].

It would be desirable if we could quickly write tests to catch these issues. In this paper, we show that we can use the languages-as-databases approach to concisely write this type of tests.

3   The Lang-SQL Query Language

The languages-as-databases approach has been equipped with a SQL-like language called LANG-SQL, which is tailored for interrogating operational semantics. Figure 5 presents a subset of the syntax of LANG-SQL from [13]. We show only the operations that are relevant to this paper.

The queries of LANG-SQL have a typical **SELECT** statement, which behaves as that of ordinary SQL. Queries return a table such as those that we have seen in the previous section. As SQL, queries can also be combined by union. LANG-SQL can refer to the tables of Sect. 2, and to the names of grammar categories. The latter instance produces a table with attribute **term** that has a row for each of the productions of the category. For example, for `fpl` we have that *Type* denotes the table with one column **term** with rows *int, float, bool, arrow T T*, and *ref T*.

Expressions can be terms, attributes, names (of constructors, categories, predicates, and rules), **CONCL**, and **PREM**. LANG-SQL includes lists and $\text{NTH}(l, n)$ for retrieving the n-th element of the list l. $\text{GET-VARS}(t)$ returns a list with all the variables in t. For example, $\text{GET-VARS}(arrow \ T_1 \ T_2)$ returns $[T_1; T_2]$. $\text{GET-OPNAME}(opname \ t_1 \cdots \ t_n)$ returns $opname$. $\text{GET-ARGS}(opname \ t_1 \cdots \ t_n)$ returns the list $[t_1; \cdots ; t_n]$. The expression $\text{GET-BOUND-TERM}((X).t)$ returns t. $\text{GET-BOUND-VAR}((X).t)$ returns X.

Formulae can use syntactic equality $=$. The formula X IS *cname* VAR is true when X is a metavariable of the category *cname*, e.g., e_3 IS *Expression* VAR is true. t IS BOUND is true when t is of the form $(X)t'$, for some t'. The formula t IS CONSTANT is true when t is a constant such as *int* and *float* above. We say that a term t is a *skeleton* of the grammar category *cname* whenever t is of the form ($opname \ X_1 \cdots \ X_n$) (notice that the arguments are all variables). Skeletons are pervasive in operational semantics, for example the conclusions of all the typing *attr* is an attribute name.

Table	τ	$::=$ **grammar** $\|$ **grammar-info** $\|$ **rule** $\|$ **declaration** $\|$ *name*
Expression	e	$::= t \| attr \| name \|$ **CONCL** $\|$ **PREM** $\| [e; e \cdots ; e] \|$ **NTH**$(e, e) \|$ **GET-VARS**(e)
		$\|$ **GET-OPNAME**$(e) \|$ **GET-ARGS**(e)
		$\|$ **GET-BOUND-TERM**$(e) \|$ **GET-BOUND-VAR**(e)
Formula	f	$::= e = e \| e$ **IS** e **VAR** $\| e$ **IS BOUND** $\| e$ **IS CONSTANT** $\| e$ **IS** e **SKELETON**
		$\| f$ **AND** $f \| f$ **OR** $f \|$ **NOT** f
Select Item	e^*	$::= \star \| \overline{e \text{ \textbf{AS} (\textbf{ROWS}}^\star) \ attr}$
Query	q	$::=$ **SELECT** (**DISTINCT**) e^* **FROM** $\bar{q}$ **WHERE** $f \| \tau \| q$ **UNION** q

Fig. 5. Syntax of LANG-SQL from [13]. The notation $\bar{\ }$ denotes finite sequences.

rules in Fig. 3 are skeletons of *Expression*. The formula t IS *cname* SKELETON is true when t is a skeleton of *cname*. Formulae can also use AND, OR, and NOT.

LANG-SQL can store an entire list as attribute. Sometimes it is convenient to expand that list so that the table contained one row for each element of the list. LANG-SQL does that with the keywords "AS ROWS*" on an attribute that contains a list. Our examples in Sect. 4 will exemplify the use of AS ROWS*.

Adding Tests and Macros. Notice that formulae act on expressions. Our aim is, rather, to perform tests over the tables produced by queries. Therefore, we extend LANG-SQL with *tests* with the following syntax.

TestPreamble	$tp ::=$	**TEST** ϕ
Test	$\phi ::=$	$q = q \| q$ **CONTAINS** $q \| q$ **DISJOINT** $q \| q$ **IS EMPTY**
		$\| q$ **DISTINCT ROWS** $\| \phi$ **AND** $\phi \| \phi$ **OR** $\phi \|$ **NOT** ϕ

We can test whether two queries produce the same table with $q_1 = q_2$. We can test whether a table contains all the rows of another table with q_1 CONTAINS q_2, and whether two tables do not have any row in common with q_1 DISJOINT q_2. We can also test whether a query produces an empty table with q IS EMPTY, and whether the rows of a table are all distinct with q DISTINCT ROWS. To help debugging, LANG-SQL displays the query (or queries) of a test when the test fails. That is, q is displayed when q IS EMPTY and q DISTINCT ROWS fail, and both q_1 and q_2 are displayed when $q_1 = q_2$, q_1 CONTAINS q_2, and q_1 DISJOINT q_2 fail. We can also combine tests with AND, OR, and NOT. When they fail, LANG-SQL displays the query or queries of the formula that failed.

Our queries often need to extract the components of formulae. For example, when LANG-SQL operates on the row of a formula $e \longrightarrow e'$ in **rule**, we can extract e with NTH(**args**, 0) and e' with NTH(**args**, 1). However, to improve readability, we define some macros to extract these components. We do the same for typing and subtyping formulae, as well as for labeled steps of the form $P \longrightarrow^l P'$, which we encounter in Sect. 5.

We define the following macros. (The notation $\bar{\cdot}$ denotes finite sequences.)

$$\text{stepSource} \triangleq \text{subtypeLeft} \triangleq \text{lstepSource} \triangleq \text{NTH}(\text{args}, 0)$$
$$\text{stepTarget} \triangleq \text{subtypeRight} \triangleq \text{typeExp} \triangleq \text{lstepLabel} \triangleq \text{NTH}(\text{args}, 1)$$
$$\text{typeOutput} \triangleq \text{lstepTarget} \triangleq \text{NTH}(\text{args}, 2)$$
$$\text{premises} \triangleq \text{SELECT} * \text{FROM rule WHERE role} = \text{PREM}$$
$$\text{conclusions} \triangleq \text{SELECT} * \text{FROM rule WHERE role} = \text{CONCL}$$
$$\text{ROW } \overline{attr = e} \triangleq \text{SELECT } \overline{e \text{ AS } attr}$$

The prefix step denotes a macro for a reduction formula $e \longrightarrow e'$. The prefix lstep is for labeled step formulae. The prefix subtype denotes a macro for subtyping formulae $T <: T'$, and the prefix type is for typing formulae $\Gamma \vdash e : T$. We use premises and conclusions to retrieve all the conclusions and all the premises of rules. The last line also provides a linguistically more intuitive way to produce a table with one row: For example, ROW $attr = value$ rather than SELECT $value$ AS $attr$.

4   Examples of Language Tests

We provide a series of tests that showcase the testing features of languages-as-databases. *Test (a)*, *(b)*, and *(c)*, address the issues of fpl that we have identified in Sect. 2. We also show an additional example, *Test (d)*, that makes sure that types do not bind expressions (as in dependent types).

Test (a): *Evaluation in the Context of Binders.* Let us consider the following query and test.

```
1  whereEvalUnderBinders ≜
2  SELECT * FROM
3                 (SELECT GET-OPNAME(term) AS opname,
4                  GET-ARGS(term) AS ROWS* arg
5                  FROM EvalCtx)
6  WHERE arg IS BOUND AND GET-BOUND-TERM(arg) = E
7
8  TEST whereEvalUnderBinders IS EMPTY
```

Recall that *EvalCtx* refers to a table with the grammar production of that syntactic category, depicted in Fig. 6 for fpl. SELECT at Line 3–5 creates a table where, for each grammar production of *EvalCtx*, the top-level constructor of this term (obtained with GET-OPNAME(term)) has a row with each of its arguments, expanded with AS ROWS*. This query produces the table in Fig. 6 in the middle.

SELECT at Line 2 then selects those rows where the argument in *arg* has a bound term and where the metavariable E of evaluation contexts is under a binder (Line 6). In our example, *whereEvalUnderBinders* produces a table with only the second row of the table computed at Line 3–5. Figure 6 shows the table produced by *whereEvalUnderBinders*. As we do not intend to evaluate underneath binders, the test at Line 7 checks whether this table is empty. This test

EvalCtx

term
$abs\,[T;(x)E]$
$app\,[E;e]$
$app\,[v;E]$
$\cdots$

SELECT at Line 3-5

opname	arg
abs	T
abs	$(x)E$
app	E
app	e
$\cdots$	$\cdots$

$whereEvalUnderBinders$

opname	arg
abs	$(x)E$

Fig. 6. Tables of *Test (a)*

fails for `fpl`, so the language designer is warned about this issue. Furthermore, LANG-SQL displays *whereEvalUnderBinders* so that the language designer have a chance to debug the language definition.

Test (b): Errors Should Be Typed at Any Type. A typical way to ensure that errors can be typed at any type is to have their typing rules assign a fresh variable as output type. We address this test in two parts. The first test checks that errors are typed with a variable. The second test checks that the variable does not come from the premises. The following is the first test.

```
1   errOutputVars ≜
2   SELECT GET-OPNAME(term) AS err, rulename AS rname,
3          typeOutput AS var
4   FROM Error, rule
5   WHERE predname = ⊢ AND role = CONCL
6          AND GET-OPNAME(term) = GET-OPNAME(typeExp)
7
8   TEST errOutputVars = SELECT * FROM errOutputVars WHERE var IS VAR
```

Line 4–6 seek the conclusion of typing rules whose expression being typed (`GET-OPNAME(typeExp)`) is an error (`GET-OPNAME(term)` of *Error*). *errOutputVars* produces a table that records an error constructor, the name of a typing rule, and the output type of such rule (`typeOutput`). As `fpl` has only one error, *errOutputVars* produces the table on the left in Fig. 7.

Our test at Line 8 keeps the rows of *errOutputVars* whose output type, recorded in the attribute *var*, is a variable. If they are all variables then this latter table is equal to *errOutputVars*. When this test fails, LANG-SQL displays *errOutputVars* for debugging.

$errOutputVars$

err	rname	var
error	(T-ERROR)	T

$errPremisesVars$

err	rname	var
error	(T-ERROR)	T

Fig. 7. Tables of *Test (b)*

The following test addresses the second part.

```
1  errPremisesVars ≜
2  SELECT err, rulename, GET-VARS(typeOutput) AS ROWS* var
3  FROM errOutputVars, rule WHERE rulename = rname AND role = PREM
4
5  TEST errOutputVars DISJOINT errPremisesVars
```

errPremisesVars finds the typing rules of errors thanks to their names being stored in *errOutputVars*. *errPremisesVars* selects the premises of such rules and stores a row for each variable in `typeOutput`. *errPremisesVars* produces the table on the right in Fig. 7 for `fpl`. Our test checks that *errPremisesVars* and *errOutputVars* are disjoint. Were not to be the case, the type of some error receives its value from some premises, which may jeopardizes type preservation, as explained in Sect. 2. LANG-SQL displays *errOutputVars* in such a case.

Test (c): References Should Be Invariant. Let us consider the following.

```
1  invariantTypes ≜ SELECT GET-OPNAME(subtypeLeft) AS type FROM rule
2                    WHERE predname = <: AND role = CONCL
3                    AND subtypeLeft = subtypeRight
4                    AND (NOT (subtypeLeft IS CONSTANT))
5
6  TEST invariantTypes CONTAINS ROW type = ref
7       AND Types CONTAINS ROW term = ref T
```

invariantTypes seeks the conclusions of subtyping rules, such as $T_1 \to T_2 <: T'_1 \to T'_2$ of (S-ARROW) and $\text{Ref } T <: \text{Ref } T'$ of (S-REF). Next, it selects a rule when the left and right arguments of $<:$ are equal. Line 5 also checks that the type is not a constant so that `Int` may not be classified as invariant from $\text{Int} <: \text{Int}$. Of the subtyping rules so selected, we record the top-level type constructors that these rules handle (`GET-OPNAME(subtypeLeft)`). *invariantTypes* produces an empty table for `fpl`. Our test checks that *ref* is in *invariantTypes* whenever references are types of the language. This test fails for `fpl`, and LANG-SQL displays *invariantTypes*. If references were invariant in `fpl`, *invariantTypes* would be a one-row table with attribute *type = ref*.

Test (d): Types Do Not Bind Expressions. Dependent and refinement types bind expressions, they have a notoriously complicated meta-theory, and are hard to implement. It is desirable then to test languages for the presence of such features. Let us consider a language with dependent types with constructor Π, and

SELECT at Line 3-5

opname	arg
Π	$(x)T$
$\forall$	$(X)T$
arrow	T
arrow	T
...	...

grammar-info

category	meta-var	obj-var
Type	T	X
Expression	e	x
...	...	...

boundByTypes

category
Expression
Type

Fig. 8. Tables of *Test (d)*

universal types with constructor $\forall$, and hence grammar Type $T ::= \text{Int} \mid \ldots \mid \Pi x.T \mid \forall X.T$, where X is the object variable for types (type variable), and the dots are the other types of the language. (Although our test will not reject universal types, they provide another example of binding in types and so we include them.) Let us consider the following test.

```
1   boundByTypes ≜
2   SELECT category
3   FROM (SELECT GET-OPNAME(term) AS opname,
4         GET-ARGS(term) AS ROWS* arg
5         FROM Type),
6         grammar-info
7   WHERE arg IS BOUND AND GET-BOUND-VAR(arg) = obj-var
8
9   TEST (NOT (boundByTypes CONTAINS ROW category = Expression))
```

SELECT at Line 3–5 creates the table on the left in Fig. 8 from *Type*. SELECT at Line 1 works on this table and on grammar-info. Line 7 finds those *arg* that use a binder and extracts their bound variable. For $(x)T$, this would be x, and for $(X)T$ it would be X. Then, *boundByTypes* searches these variables among the obj-var values in grammar-info, and selects their corresponding grammar category in category. Our test at Line 9 checks that *Expression* is not in *boundByTypes*, as it would mean that some type is a binder for expressions.

5   A GSOS Validator with Language Tests

In this section we focus on the GSOS rule format [10], which applies to process algebras. Figure 9 shows an example of a process algebra, which we call pa. Processes P perform labeled transitions $P \longrightarrow^l P'$, where l can be an action a, b, or c (GSOS imposes a finite set of actions). We have the terminated process $\mathbf{0}$, the prefix operator $l.P$, which performs a transition with label l and executes P, the priority operator $\theta(P)$, which always prefers to take an action a from P, if

$$a. P \longrightarrow^a P$$
$$b. P \longrightarrow^b P$$
$$c. P \longrightarrow^c P$$

$$\frac{P \longrightarrow^a P'}{\theta(P) \longrightarrow^a \theta(P')}$$

$$\frac{P \longrightarrow^b P' \quad P \not\longrightarrow^a}{\theta(P) \longrightarrow^b \theta(P')}$$

$$\frac{P \longrightarrow^c P' \quad P \not\longrightarrow^a}{\theta(P) \longrightarrow^c \theta(P')}$$

rulename	predname	args	role
(PREFIX-a)	$\longrightarrow$	$[prefix\ a\ P; a; P]$	CONCL
(PRIORITY-a)	$\longrightarrow$	$[P; a; P']$	PREM
(PRIORITY-a)	$\longrightarrow$	$[priority\ P; a; priority\ P']$	CONCL
(PRIORITY-b)	$\longrightarrow$	$[P; b; P']$	PREM
(PRIORITY-b)	$\not\longrightarrow$	$[P; a]$	PREM
(PRIORITY-b)	$\longrightarrow$	$[priority\ P; b; priority\ P']$	CONCL
$\dots$	$\dots$	$\dots$	$\dots$

Fig. 9. Process algebra pa, and a subset of rule for pa

available [7]. The rules of pa use negative transition formulae of the form $P \not\longrightarrow^l$, which means that P does not perform an l-labeled transition. The languages-as-databases can accommodate pa and other process algebras. Figure 9 shows some rows of rule only, as it is the most relevant table.

We recall the GSOS format [10]. The template for rules s the following.

$$\{x_i \longrightarrow^{l_{ij}} y_{ij} \mid i \in I, 1 \leq j \leq m_i\}$$
$$\cup$$
$$\frac{\{x_j \not\longrightarrow^{l'_{jk}} \mid j \in J, 1 \leq k \leq n_j\}}{(op\ x_1 \dots x_h) \longrightarrow^l t}$$

Here, xs and ys must all be distinct, and I and J are subsets of $\{1, \dots, h\}$. This means that xs in the premises come from the conclusion and each x can be used zero or more times as the source of positive premises and as the source of negative premises. The metavariables that appear in the target of the conclusion of the rule (t) can only come from xs and ys. Labels ls must be constants (hence the three prefix rules in Fig. 9 rather than a single rule $l.P \longrightarrow^l P$).

The following is a classic result in operational semantics [10]: If all the rules of the language conform to these restrictions then bisimilarity is a congruence for the language. GSOS is expressive enough to prove that bisimilarity is a congruence for many process algebras. For example, pa adheres to the format.

In the rest of this section, we write a GSOS validator in LANG-SQL. Our validator consists of 5 tests, which are meant to be applied sequentially.

Test 1: Conclusions Are of the Form $(op \cdots) \longrightarrow^l t$. Test 1 is the following.

validConclusions ≜
```
SELECT * FROM rule WHERE role = CONCL AND predname = ⟶
        AND 1stepSource IS Process SKELETON
        AND 1stepLabel IS CONSTANT
TEST validConclusions = conclusions
```

validConclusions produces a table with the rows of `rule` that contains conclusions of rules with the following characteristics. The source of the step is a skeleton, that is, $(opname \cdots)$ applied to variables (which Test 4 will check that they are distinct), and the label of the step is a constant. The test succeeds when this table is exactly the table with all conclusions.

Test 2: Premises Are of the Form $x \longrightarrow^l y$ *or* $x \not\longrightarrow^l$. Test 2 is the following.

validPositivePrems ≜
```
SELECT * FROM rule WHERE role = PREM AND predname = ⟶
        AND 1stepSource IS Process VAR
        AND 1stepLabel IS CONSTANT
        AND 1stepTarget IS Process VAR
```
validNegativePrems ≜
```
SELECT * FROM rule WHERE role = PREM AND predname = ↛
        AND 1stepSource IS Process VAR
        AND 1stepLabel IS CONSTANT
TEST (validPositivePrems UNION validNegativePrems) = premises    ʼ
```

This follows similar lines as the previous test, though we check the shape of premises rather than conclusions. The test succeeds if the valid positive premises together with the valid negative premises form the full table of premises.

Test 3: xs in Premises Come from the Conclusion. Test 3 is the following.

xs ≜
```
SELECT rulename, GET-VARS(1stepSource) AS ROWS* var
FROM conclusions
```
xsInPremises ≜ `SELECT rulename, 1stepSource AS var FROM premises`
`TEST xs CONTAINS xsInPremises`

xs produces a table where each row contains a rule name and a variable from the source of the conclusion. Each row of *xsInPremises* contains a rule name and the source of a step premise. (When Test 2 is successful, this source is a variable.) Our test checks that *xsInPremises* are all from *xs*.

Test 4: xs and ys Are All Distinct. Test 4 is the following.

ys ≜ `SELECT rulename, 1stepTarget AS var FROM premises`
`TEST (xs UNION ys) DISTINCT ROWS`

ys follows the same lines as *xs* above, though it selects the targets of the steps in premises. (When Test 2 is successful, all these targets are variables.) Our test checks that the union of *xs* and *ys* is made of distinct rows.

Test 5: Variables of Conclusion Targets Are xs or ys. Test 5 is the following.

$$varsInTarget \triangleq \texttt{SELECT rulename, GET-VARS(1stepTarget) AS ROWS}^\star \; var$$
$$\texttt{FROM conclusions}$$
$$\texttt{TEST } (xs \texttt{ UNION } ys) \texttt{ CONTAINS } varsInTarget$$

varsInTarget contains rule name and variable for each variable in the target of the conclusion. Our test checks that the union of *xs* and *ys* contains *varsInTarget*.

6 Evaluation

We have extended the implementation of Lang-Sql with the new elements (tests and macros) described in Sect. 3. To recall from [13], Lang-Sql accepts a textual representation of language definitions similar to Ott [36]. (See .lan files at [12]). The tool compiles these languages into the tables grammar, rule, and the rest, and applies the queries and tests on them. The output is a table and, after our extension, an error message when some test fails.

Evaluation of the Examples of Language Tests. We have run *Test (a)*, *(b)*, and *(c)* of Sect. 4 on fpl, and we confirm that they fail. We have sequentially fixed fpl. We have first removed the evaluation context $\lambda x : T.E$: we confirm that *Test (a)* succeeds while the others still fail. We have then changed the output type of (T-ERROR) into a fresh new variable T': *Test (b)* succeeds while *Test (c)* fails. Finally, we have updated the subtyping rule (S-REF) into Ref T <: Ref T: all tests succeed. *Test (d)* also succeeds on fpl, as there are no dependent types.

The repo of [13] contains several variants of the λ-calculus with integers, booleans, pairs, lists, sums, tuples, fix, let, letrec, universal types, recursive types, option types, exceptions, operations such as append, map, mapi, filter, filteri, range, length, reverse. These are correct language definitions with no expression-binding types, and we confirm that all tests *(a)* to *(d)* succeed on them.

The repo of [13] also contains a handful of λ-calculi where reduction takes place underneath the binders of λ-abstraction, let-declarations, let rec, and a type annotated let rec. We confirm that *Test (a)* fails on these languages.

The repo of [13] also contains a language with dependent types. We confirm that *Test (d)* fails on that.

Evaluation of the GSOS Validator. We have applied the tests of Sect. 5 to the repo of process algebras of GSOS-Validator [14]. To recall from [14], this repo contains 18 languages that adhere to the GSOS format. Each contains the prefix operator $l.P$ and adds a concurrency operator among, to repeat from [14], the interleaving parallel operator of CCS [24], the full parallel operator of CCS, the synchronous parallel composition from CSP [21], the external choice of CCS, the internal choice of CSP, projection of ACP [9], hiding of CSP, left merge of ACP, renaming of CCS, restriction of CCS, the "hourglass" operator from [1], signaling [6], the disrupt operator, the interrupt operator, the sequence operator, priority θ [7] (that is, pa), and a process algebra with a while-loop operator.

We confirm that our tests successfully pass on all these process algebras and therefore establish that they are compliant to the GSOS format. We have also run tests on languages that do not satisfy the format, for example for using xs variables among ys or using complex terms (rather than variables) as the source of premises. The tests of our GSOS validator fail on these cases.

Our GSOS validator is concise and amounts to 14 lines of code. (Section 5 uses new lines for readability). We also believe that the syntactic constraints of the format are expressed declaratively.

Limitations. LANG-SQL presents some limitations in testing languages. For example, [13] reports being able to capture only a part of LANG-N-CHECK, a tool that checks for the type soundness of a limited class of functional languages. The reason is that recursion is prohibited (as in standard SQL). LANG-SQL then cannot type check programs and therefore cannot verify type preservation. For the same reason, LANG-SQL cannot establish the absence of circular dependencies among evaluation contexts. (Circular evaluation contexts may jeopardize the progress theorem.) To establish that, we need a topological sort of such dependencies, which is a recursive function and cannot be expressed with LANG-SQL. Similarly, some information-flow analyses build a dependency graph between variables, which entails a reachability process that is recursive (and without an a priori fixed bound). We then foresee problems in testing languages regarding their information-flow security properties.

7 Related Work

We did not use (plain) SQL because it does not naturally store terms with binding and because LANG-SQL needs operations such as deriving a term from a grammar (which we have not used here, but it has been used in [13]), and it is unclear whether SQL can achieve that for grammars given as input.

Language-parametrized testing has focused on testing the programs of the languages at hand. The work of Kats et al. [22] and Wu [38] aims at generating editor services (error marking, completion, among others) from the language definition, which are specific to help (manually) write tests. Many language semantics tools (K, PLT Redex, MPS, to name a few) offer the automatic generation of randomized test programs [8,18,32,34]. Whether tests are manually written or randomly generated, our approach differs in that we analyze the language definition in a style that resembles static analysis. For example, to detect covariant references, that specific test would have to be randomly generated and checked for type preservation. Our approach, instead, quickly takes a look at the language definition. Moreover, we offer a declarative DSL to quickly write this type of tests. We stress that test programs are remarkably effective, and we simply offer our approach as a complement to them.

Language-parametrized verification has focused on automatically proving type safety [5,15,19,30,33]. These works differ from LANG-SQL in that they do formally prove a property. Language testing cannot do so unless a theoretical result guarantees that certain tests are sufficient. However, these works offer a large analysis on *one* property, while our approach has the flexibility to test a wide range of lightweight questions on programming languages.

PREG Axiomatizer [2] offers a GSOS validator in around four hundred lines of Maude code (including code for parsing). The GSOS validator of Mousavi and Reniers [27] uses the introspective reflective features of Maude to examine the Maude rewriting rules that are used to specify process algebras, which is a difficult style of programming for both code writing and reading. Neither tools provide a declarative approach to the GSOS format. On the contrary, our tests express the constraints of GSOS declaratively.

GSOS-Validator [14] uses a DSL called LANG-N-CHANGE [25, 26] that is tailored for manipulating operational semantics. GSOS-Validator is concise (6 lines) and declarative. However, LANG-N-CHANGE is not tailored for selecting multiple rules, and there are LANG-SQL queries that it cannot express.

8 Conclusion

Prior work [13] has proposed languages-as-databases, and has developed a query language called LANG-SQL to interrogate language definitions. In this paper, we have augmented that approach with tests and convenient macros, and we have used it to write language tests on diverse aspects of programming languages such as binders, evaluation contexts, variance, and typing. We have also used LANG-SQL to write a full GSOS validator with only 14 lines of code. Overall, our language tests are declarative and concise. We believe that this work shows that languages-as-databases can be a lightweight approach to language testing.

In the future, we would like to continue formulating tests about various aspects of programming languages. We also would like to address the limitations described in Sect. 6. Despite those limitations, we believe that LANG-SQL may have the potential to help develop and automate a systematic methodology for language testing. We will explore this research venue in the future, as well. We also would like to embed LANG-SQL into mainstream programming languages and language semantics tools such as $\mathbb{K}$, PLT Redex, Ott, and others.

LANG-SQL, our GSOS validator, and all our tests are publicly available [12].

References

1. Aceto, L., Bloom, B., Vaandrager, F.: Turning SOS rules into equations. Inf. Comput. **111**(1), 1–52 (1994). https://doi.org/10.1006/inco.1994.1040
2. Aceto, L., Caltais, G., Goriac, E.-I., Ingolfsdottir, A.: PREG axiomatizer – a ground bisimilarity checker for GSOS with predicates. In: Corradini, A., Klin, B., Cîrstea, C. (eds.) CALCO 2011. LNCS, vol. 6859, pp. 378–385. Springer, Heidelberg (2011). https://doi.org/10.1007/978-3-642-22944-2_27
3. Aceto, L., Cimini, M., Ingólfsdóttir, A., Mousavi, M.R., Reniers, M.A.: SOS rule formats for zero and unit elements. Theoret. Comput. Sci. **412**(28), 3045–3071 (2011). https://doi.org/10.1016/j.tcs.2011.01.024

4. Aceto, L., Cimini, M., Ingolfsdottir, A., Mousavi, M., Reniers, M.A.: Rule formats for distributivity. Theoret. Comput. Sci. **458**, 1–28 (2012). https://doi.org/10.1016/j.tcs.2012.07.036

5. Bach Poulsen, C., Rouvoet, A., Tolmach, A., Krebbers, R., Visser, E.: Intrinsically-typed definitional interpreters for imperative languages. Proc. ACM Program. Lang. (PACMPL) **2**(POPL), 1–34 (2017). https://doi.org/10.1145/3158104

6. Baeten, J.C.M., Bergstra, J.A.: Process algebra with signals and conditions. In: Broy, M. (ed.) Programming and Mathematical Method, pp. 273–323. Springer, Heidelberg (1992). https://doi.org/10.1007/978-3-642-77572-7_13

7. Baeten, J.C.M., Bergstra, J.A., Klop, J.W.: Syntax and defining equations for an interrupt mechanism in process algebra. Fund. Inform. **9**(2), 127–167 (1986). https://doi.org/10.3233/FI-1986-9202

8. Berghofer, S., Nipkow, T.: Random testing in Isabelle/HOL. In: Proceedings of the 2nd International Conference on Software Engineering and Formal Methods, pp. 230–239, SEFM 2004. IEEE Computer Society, USA (2004). https://doi.org/10.1109/SEFM.2004.10049

9. Bergstra, J., Klop, J.: Process algebra for synchronous communication. Inf. Control **60**(1), 109–137 (1984). https://doi.org/10.1016/S0019-9958(84)80025-X

10. Bloom, B., Istrail, S., Meyer, A.R.: Bisimulation can't be traced. J. ACM **42**(1), 232–268 (1995). https://doi.org/10.1145/200836.200876

11. Cheney, J.: Toward a general theory of names: binding and scope. In: Proceedings of the 3rd ACM SIGPLAN Workshop on Mechanized Reasoning about Languages with Variable Binding, MERLIN 2005, pp. 33–40. Association for Computing Machinery, New York, NY, USA (2005). https://doi.org/10.1145/1088454.1088459

12. Cimini, M.: Lang-SQL (2022). https://github.com/mcimini/lang-sql

13. Cimini, M.: A query language for language analysis. In: Schlingloff, B.H., Chai, M. (eds.) Software Engineering and Formal Methods - 20th International Conference, SEFM 2022, Berlin, Germany, 26–30 September 2022, Proceedings, vol. 13550, pp. 57–73. Springer, Cham (2022). https://doi.org/10.1007/978-3-031-17108-6_4

14. Cimini, M.: A declarative validator for GSOS languages. In: Proceedings of the 14th International Workshop on Programming Language Approaches to Concurrency- and Communication-cEntric Software (PLACES 2023), vol. 378, pp. 14–25. Open Publishing Association (2023). https://doi.org/10.4204/EPTCS.378.2

15. Cimini, M., Miller, D., Siek, J.G.: Extrinsically typed operational semantics for functional languages. In: Proceedings of the 13th ACM SIGPLAN International Conference on Software Language Engineering, SLE 2020, Virtual Event, USA, 16–17 November 2020, pp. 108–125 (2020). https://doi.org/10.1145/3426425.3426936

16. Cranen, S., Mousavi, M., Reniers, M.A.: A rule format for associativity. In: van Breugel, F., Chechik, M. (eds.) CONCUR 2008 - Concurrency Theory, pp. 447–461. Springer, Heidelberg (2008). https://doi.org/10.1007/978-3-540-85361-9_35

17. Felleisen, M., Findler, R.B., Flatt, M.: Semantics Engineering with PLT Redex, 1st edn. The MIT Press (2009)

18. Fetscher, B., Claessen, K., Pałka, M., Hughes, J., Findler, R.B.: Making random judgments: automatically generating well-typed terms from the definition of a type-system. In: Vitek, J. (ed.) European Symposium on Programming Languages and Systems (ESOP 2015), pp. 383–405. Springer, Heidelberg (2015). https://doi.org/10.1007/978-3-662-46669-8_16

19. Grewe, S., Erdweg, S., Wittmann, P., Mezini, M.: Type systems for the masses: deriving soundness proofs and efficient checkers. In: 2015 ACM International Symposium on New Ideas, New Paradigms, and Reflections on Programming and Software (Onward!), pp. 137–150. Onward! 2015. ACM, New York, NY, USA (2015). https://doi.org/10.1145/2814228.2814239

20. Groote, J.F., Vaandrager, F.: Structured operational semantics and bisimulation as a congruence. Inf. Comput. **100**(2), 202–260 (1992). https://doi.org/10.1016/0890-5401(92)90013-6

21. Hoare, C.A.R.: Communicating sequential processes. Commun. ACM **21**(8), 666–677 (1978). https://doi.org/10.1145/359576.359585

22. Kats, L.C., Vermaas, R., Visser, E.: Integrated language definition testing: enabling test-driven language development. In: Proceedings of the 2011 ACM International Conference on Object Oriented Programming Systems Languages and Applications, OOPSLA 2011, pp. 139–154. Association for Computing Machinery, New York, NY, USA (2011). https://doi.org/10.1145/2048066.2048080

23. Klein, C., et al.: Run your research: on the effectiveness of lightweight mechanization. In: Proceedings of the 39th Annual ACM SIGPLAN-SIGACT Symposium on Principles of Programming Languages, POPL 2012, pp. 285–296. Association for Computing Machinery, New York, NY, USA (2012). https://doi.org/10.1145/2103656.2103691

24. Milner, R. (ed.): A Calculus of Communicating Systems. LNCS, vol. 92. Springer, Heidelberg (1980). https://doi.org/10.1007/3-540-10235-3

25. Mourad, B., Cimini, M.: A calculus for language transformations. In: Chatzigeorgiou, A., et al. (eds.) SOFSEM 2020. LNCS, vol. 12011, pp. 547–555. Springer, Cham (2020). https://doi.org/10.1007/978-3-030-38919-2_44

26. Mourad, B., Cimini, M.: System description: Lang-n-Change - a tool for transforming languages. In: Nakano, K., Sagonas, K. (eds.) FLOPS 2020. LNCS, vol. 12073, pp. 198–214. Springer, Cham (2020). https://doi.org/10.1007/978-3-030-59025-3_12

27. Mousavi, M.R., Reniers, M.A.: Prototyping SOS meta-theory in Maude. Electron. Notes Theoret. Comput. Sci. **156**(1), 135–150 (2006). https://doi.org/10.1016/j.entcs.2005.09.030, Proceedings of the Second Workshop on Structural Operational Semantics (SOS 2005)

28. Mousavi, M.R., Reniers, M.A., Groote, J.F.: SOS formats and meta-theory: 20 years after. Theoret. Comput. Sci. **373**(3), 238–272 (2007). https://doi.org/10.1016/j.tcs.2006.12.019

29. Mousavi, M., Reniers, M., Groote, J.F.: A syntactic commutativity format for SOS. Inf. Process. Lett. **93**(5), 217–223 (2005). https://doi.org/10.1016/j.ipl.2004.11.007

30. Pfenning, F., Schürmann, C.: System description: Twelf — a meta-logical framework for deductive systems. In: CADE 1999. LNCS (LNAI), vol. 1632, pp. 202–206. Springer, Heidelberg (1999). https://doi.org/10.1007/3-540-48660-7_14

31. Pierce, B.C.: Types and Programming Languages. MIT Press (2002)

32. Ratiu, D., Voelter, M.: Automated testing of DSL implementations: experiences from building mbeddr. In: Proceedings of the 11th International Workshop on Automation of Software Test, AST 2016, pp. 15–21. Association for Computing Machinery, New York, NY, USA (2016). https://doi.org/10.1145/2896921.2896922

33. van der Rest, C., Poulsen, C.B., Rouvoet, A., Visser, E., Mosses, P.: Intrinsically-typed definitional interpreters à la carte. Proc. ACM Program. Lang. **6**(OOPSLA2), 1903–1932 (2022). https://doi.org/10.1145/3563355

34. Roberson, M., Harries, M., Darga, P.T., Boyapati, C.: Efficient software model checking of soundness of type systems. In: Harris, G.E. (ed.) Proceedings of the 23rd ACM SIGPLAN Conference on Object-Oriented Programming Systems Languages and Applications, OOPSLA 2008, pp. 493–504. Association for Computing Machinery, New York, NY, USA (2008). https://doi.org/10.1145/1449764.1449803
35. Rosu, G., Şerbănuţă, T.F.: An overview of the K semantic framework. J. Logic Algebraic Program. **79**(6), 397–434 (2010). https://doi.org/10.1016/j.jlap.2010.03.012
36. Sewell, P.: Ott: effective tool support for the working semanticist. J. Funct. Program. **20**(1), 71–122 (2010). https://doi.org/10.1017/S0956796809990293
37. Verhoef, C.: A congruence theorem for structured operational semantics with predicates and negative premises. In: Jonsson, B., Parrow, J. (eds.) CONCUR 1994. LNCS, vol. 836, pp. 433–448. Springer, Heidelberg (1994). https://doi.org/10.1007/978-3-540-48654-1_32
38. Wu, H.: Grammar-driven generation of domain-specific language tools. In: Companion to the 21st ACM SIGPLAN Symposium on Object-Oriented Programming Systems, Languages, and Applications, OOPSLA 2006, pp. 772–773. Association for Computing Machinery, New York, NY, USA (2006). https://doi.org/10.1145/1176617.1176718

Symbolic Observation Graph-Based Generation of Test Paths

Kais Klai[1] , Mohamed Taha Bennani[2] , Jaime Arias[1]([✉]) , Jörg Desel[3],
and Hanen Ochi[4]

[1] Université Sorbonne Paris Nord, LIPN UMR CNRS 7030, Villetaneuse, France
{kais.klai,jaime.arias}@lipn.univ-paris13.fr
[2] Faculty of Sciences of Tunis, University of Tunis El Manar, Tunis, Tunisia
taha.bennani@fst.utm.tn
[3] Fern Universität in Hagen, Hagen, Germany
joerg.desel@fernuni-hagen.de
[4] EFREI Paris, EFREI Research Lab, Villejuif, France
hanen.ochi@efrei.fr

Abstract. The paper introduces a theoretical foundation for generating abstract test paths related to Petri net specifications. Based on the structure of the Petri net model of the system, we first define the notion of *unobservable* transition. Unless such a transition is unreachable, we prove that its firing is necessarily ensured by the firing of another transition (namely *observable* transition) of the Petri net. We show that the set of *observable* transitions is the smallest set that guarantees the *coverage* of all the transitions of the Petri net model, i.e., any set of firing sequences of the model, namely *observable traces*, involving all the *observable* transitions passes eventually through the *unobservable* transitions as well. If some unobservable transitions are mandatory to trigger the execution of a test sub-sequence, observable traces are completed with such transitions to enhance the controllability of the test scenario. In addition to structurally identifying observable (and unobservable) transitions, we mainly propose two algorithms: the first allows to generate a set of observable paths ensuring full coverage of all the system transitions. It is based on an on-the-fly construction of a hybrid graph called the *symbolic observation graph*. The second algorithm completes the observable paths in order to explicitly cover the whole set of system's transitions. The approach is implemented within an available prototype, and the preliminary experiments are promising.

Keywords: Model-based testing · transition coverage · Petri nets

1 Introduction

Model-based testing automates a set of processes, namely the generation of test cases from models, the derivation of executable scripts, and the execution of test cases or test scripts [45]. The cornerstone of model-based testing is the generation of test inputs from the behavioural model of the system under test. Several techniques have been introduced for test inputs generation, such as solvers [34], constrained logic programming [32], search-based algorithms [38] and model checking [19]. Except for some educational systems, the number of input data is often infinite. Therefore, testing cannot be exhaustive. Thus, these techniques seek to reduce the number of test inputs by modelling sets of similar behaviours through coverage criteria. As a result, an abstract test path would characterize a sequence of actions or events a system must perform to achieve a certain behaviour, represented by a set of requirements of a coverage criterion.

Test inputs generation satisfying structural or behaviour coverage criteria suffers from the well known state space explosion problem [41]. Several approaches have offered solutions to cope with this problem such as symmetry reduction [17], live variable reduction [18], cone of influence [13], slicing [11], transition merging [50], partial order reduction [42], τ-confluence [33], and simultaneous reachability analysis [44]. *Symbolic Observation Graph* (SOG) [20,25] represents an efficient technique to reduce the state space graph based on the observation of the pertinent atomic propositions of a temporal formula to be verified. In this paper, we adopt the SOG technique for the input generation perspective.

Given a finite system modelled with a Petri net [37], our goal is to generate a set of firing sequences that ensure the coverage of the whole set of the model transitions. A Petri net structure-based solution to identify the set of significant transitions, which we call *observable*, is first proposed. We show that the choice of the test inputs that allow the system behaviour to cover this set of transitions guarantees the coverage of all the model transitions of the system to be tested. *Unobservable* transitions are then guaranteed to be covered by observable transitions unless they belong to an unobservable cycle in the model (i.e., cycles with unobservable transitions only), in which case the transitions of such a cycle are proven to be dead. Such cycles can be detected and removed by a simple browsing of the Petri net model. This discrimination allows us to build, on-the-fly, the SOG w.r.t. the observable transitions, reducing considerably the state space to be traversed to cover all the transitions of the system. During the construction of the SOG, we aim to find paths that cover all the observable transitions. As soon as this goal is reached, the construction of the SOG is stopped. If necessary, the obtained paths can be completed by backtracking with unobservable transitions to obtain *complete abstract* sequences involving all the transitions of the system.

The rest of this paper is organized as follows: in Sect. 2, required concepts and formalisms are presented. Section 3 and Sect. 4 are the core of the paper, where the proposed approach is presented. In the former, we show how to use the structure of the Petri net model to partition the transitions into two subsets: observable and unobservable transitions, and we establish underlying theoretical results. In the latter, we show how to check the coverage of all Petri net model's transitions by exploiting the SOG. The different algorithms were implemented in a software tool, and the obtained results of our experiments are reported in Sect. 5. Before concluding and presenting directions for future work in Sect. 7, we discuss related work and give their pros and cons in Sect. 6.

2 Preliminaries

2.1 Labelled Transition Systems (LTS)

Definition 1 (Labelled Transition Systems). *A labelled transition system (LTS for short) T is a 4-tuple $(S, Act, \rightarrow, s_0)$ where:*

- *S is a (finite) set of states;*
- *Act is a (finite) set of actions;*
- *$\rightarrow \in S \times Act \times S$ is a transition relation; and*
- *s_0 is the initial state.*

The set of actions of an *LTS* could be divided into two disjoint subsets of observable (namely *Obs*) and unobservable transitions (namely *UnObs*). Determining which transitions are observable, and which ones are not, depends on the approach/objective/domain. In our approach, the precise (unique) definition of unobservable/observable transitions is presented in Sect. 3. For instance, Fig. 1 shows an *LTS* where transitions t_7, t_8, t_{10} and t_{11} (coloured) are observable.

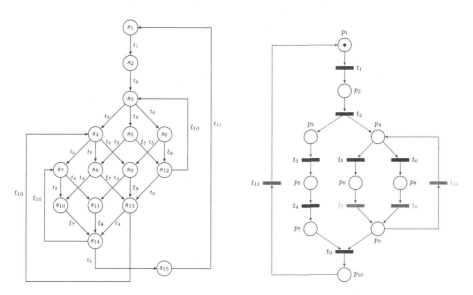

Fig. 1. An *LTS*   **Fig. 2.** A Petri net

2.2 Petri Nets

Definition 2 (Syntax). *A Petri net is a tuple $\mathcal{N} = (P, T, F, W)$, where:*

- *P is a finite set of places;*
- *T is a finite set of transitions;*
- *$F \subseteq (P \times T) \cup (T \times P)$ is a set of arcs (as one-way arrows) connecting places to transitions and transitions to places; and*
- *$W : (P \times T) \cup (T \times P) \rightarrow \mathbb{N}$ represents arcs' weight.*

For the sake of simplicity and without loss of generality, we assume, in this paper, that the weight of the edges are all equal to 1. A marking of a Petri net $\mathcal{N}$ is a function $m : P \rightarrow \mathbb{N}$ assigning a number of tokens to each place. A Petri net model is generally associated with an initial marking, denoted by m_0, that represents the initial state of the underlying system. Figure 2 illustrates a Petri net example where the places are represented by circles and transitions by rectangles. The initial marking is such that place p_1 contains one token and all the other places are empty. Each node $x \in P \cup T$ of the net has a pre-set and a post-set defined respectively as follows: $^\bullet x = \{y \in P \cup T \mid (y,x) \in F\}$, and $x^\bullet = \{y \in P \cup T \mid (x,y) \in F\}$. Adjacent nodes are then denoted by $^\bullet x^\bullet = {}^\bullet x \cup x^\bullet$.

Semantics and Notation A transition t is said to be enabled by a marking m (denoted by $m \xrightarrow{t}$) iff $\forall p \in {}^\bullet t$, $W(p,t) \leq m(p)$. If a transition t is enabled by a marking m, then its firing leads to a new marking m' (denoted by $m \xrightarrow{t} m'$) s.t. $\forall p \in P : m'(p) = m(p) - W(p,t) + W(t,p)$. For a finite sequence of transitions $\sigma = t_1 \ldots t_n \in T^*$, $m_0 \xrightarrow{\sigma}$ denotes the fact that σ is enabled by m_0, i.e., $\exists m_0, \ldots m_n$ s.t., $m_0 \xrightarrow{t_1} m_1 \xrightarrow{t_2} \ldots \xrightarrow{t_n} m_n$. $m \xrightarrow{\sigma} m'$ denotes the fact that the firing of σ from marking m leads to marking m'. $\bar{\sigma}$ denotes the set of transitions occurring in σ.

The language of finite firing sequences associated with a marked Petri net $(\mathcal{N}, m_0)$ is then defined as $L((\mathcal{N}, m_0)) = \{\sigma \in T^* \mid m_0 \xrightarrow{\sigma}\}$. Given a set of markings S, we denote by $Enable(S)$ the set of transitions enabled by elements of S. The set of markings reachable from a marking m in $\mathcal{N}$ is denoted by $R(\mathcal{N}, m)$. A transition t is said to be a *dead* transition in $(\mathcal{N}, m_0)$ if it is enabled in no marking in $R(\mathcal{N}, m_0)$. The set of markings reachable from a marking m, by firing transitions of a subset T' only, is denoted by $Sat(m, T')$. By extension, given a set of markings S and a set of transitions T', $Sat(S, T') = \bigcup_{m \in S} Sat(m, T')$. The graph of reachable markings of a marked Petri net $(\mathcal{N}, m_0)$, denoted $G(\mathcal{N}, m_0)$, is an LTS whose nodes S are the set of markings $R(\mathcal{N}, m_0)$, and the arcs are labelled with the transitions of $\mathcal{N}$. The initial node is the initial marking m_0, and a node (marking) m' is the successor of a node m iff $\exists t \in T$ s.t. $m \xrightarrow{t} m'$. The previous notations on markings of a Petri net are extended (and used in the rest of the paper) for states of an LTS. The LTS of Fig. 1 represents the reachability graph corresponding to the Petri net of Fig. 2.

2.3   Symbolic Observation Graph (SOG)

The SOG induced by a given LTS with transitions partitioned into observable and unobservable ones is defined as an *LTS* where nodes, called *aggregates*, are sets of single states connected by unobservable transitions, and compactly encoded by decision diagram techniques (e.g., BDDs [22]). The edges of the SOG are however labelled with observable transitions only.

Definition 3 (Aggregate). *Let $\mathcal{T} = (S, Act, \rightarrow, s_0)$ be an LTS, where $Act = Obs \cup UnObs$ (with $Obs \cap UnObs = \emptyset$). An* aggregate *a is a non-empty subset of S satisfying $s \in a \Leftrightarrow Sat(s, UnObs) \subseteq a$.*

Definition 4 (Symbolic Observation Graph (SOG)). *A symbolic obser-vation graph associated with an LTS $T = (S, Act, \rightarrow, s_0)$ is an LTS $G = (S', Act', \rightarrow', a_0)$ such that:*

- *S' is a finite set of aggregates satisfying:*
  - ⋆ *$\forall a \in S', \forall t \in Act', \exists (s, s') \in a \times S \colon s \xrightarrow{t} s' \Leftrightarrow \exists a' \in S' \colon a' = Sat(\{s' \in S \mid \exists s \in a \wedge s \xrightarrow{t} s'\}, UnObs) \wedge (a, t, a') \in \rightarrow';$*
- *$Act' = Obs$;*
- *$\rightarrow' \subseteq S' \times Act' \times S'$ is the transition relation, obtained by applying ⋆; and*
- *a_0 is the initial aggregate s.t. $a_0 = Sat(s_0, UnObs)$.*

Point ⋆ of the previous definition deserves explanation. By Definition 3, an aggregate contains the maximal set (fix-point computation with *Sat* function) of states linked by unobservable transitions. An arc (a, t', a'), connecting an aggregate a to an aggregate a', labelled with an observable transition t', must exist in the SOG iff the set of states in a enabling t' is not empty, and any state that is reachable by any sequence $t'.\sigma$, where $\sigma \in UnObs^*$, is necessarily in a'.

The SOG construction algorithm is presented in [20]. Despite the exponential theoretical complexity of its construction (a single state could belong to different aggregates), the SOG has in practice a rather moderate size comparing to the explicit representation of the corresponding *LTS* (see [20,25,26] for experimental results). Figure 3 shows the SOG related to the *LTS* example of Fig. 1 based on the observation of transitions t_7, t_8, t_{10} and t_{11}. Notice that, in this figure, the aggregate internal sub-graphs as well as the connection between explicit states belonging to different aggregates, are showed for the readability purpose. The internal set of states is represented by a binary decision diagram (BDD) [22], while for observable transition labels, only one solid edge connects two aggregates.

2.4 Test Coverage Criteria

Since the evaluation of all system's inputs values is not possible, testers must rely on measurements' features to argue the trust they can place in the system under test. Coverage criteria define test objectives or requirements that test entries (deduced from test cases) strive to satisfy. Therefore, if the test inputs meet the test objectives, the confidence placed by a tester in the system will match the exigency of the coverage criterion.

Several coverage criteria related to Petri nets are defined in [40], e.g., Structural and Behavioural Analysis Coverage (SBAC), and Concurrent Session Behaviour Coverage Criteria (CSBCC). This paper deals with the transition coverage criterion. That is, a test suite (i.e., a set of firing sequences) that covers this criterion must fire any transition of a Petri net at least once.

Definition 5 (Transition Coverage). *Let $N = (P, T, F, W)$ be a Petri net, and $T_s = \{\sigma_1, \sigma_2, \ldots, \sigma_n\}$ be a test suite. T_s satisfies transition coverage criterion iff $\forall t \in T, \exists \sigma \in T_s, t \in \bar{\sigma}$.*

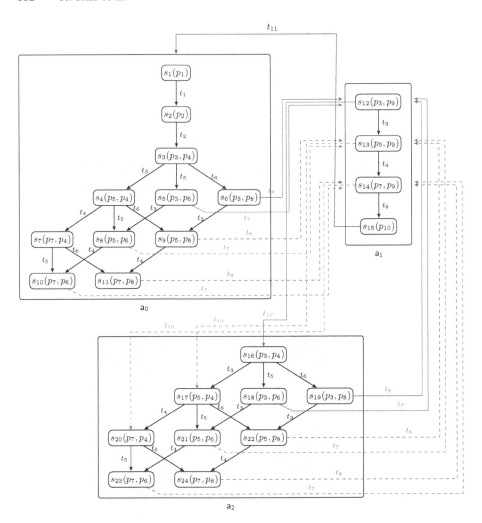

Fig. 3. SOG related to the *LTS* of Fig. 1 under the observation of $\{t_7, t_8, t_{10}, t_{11}\}$

3 Structure-Based Coverage Relation for Petri Nets

In this section, we illustrate how covering a reduced set of transitions can lead to the coverage of all the system's transitions. To reach this goal, we propose an original approach based on the identification of a specific structural pattern in a Petri net model. Such a pattern allows to deduce behavioural information related to the firing of the transitions of the model.

Definition 6. *The coverage relation, denoted by ▷ is the transitive relation defined as follows:* ▷ : $T \to T$ *s.t.* $\forall t' \in T$, $t' \triangleright t$ *implies that any firing sequence containing t' contains necessarily t.*

In the following, we define *unobservable* transitions.

Definition 7. *A transition t in a marked Petri net* $(\mathcal{N}, m_0)$ *is said to be **unobservable*** $\Longleftrightarrow \exists\, p \in t^\bullet,\ {}^\bullet p = \{t\} \wedge p^\bullet \neq \emptyset \wedge m_0(p) = 0$. *For a given transition t, the set of such places is denoted by* $t^\sim$.

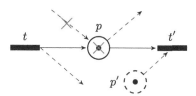

Fig. 4. Unobservable transition t

Informally (see Fig. 4), an unobservable transition t is a transition having, at least, one unmarked output place p such that no other transition can produce tokens in p (${}^\bullet p = \{t\}$). Thus, p being initially unmarked, the firing of any output transition of p is impossible before firing t. For this reason, any firing sequence containing any transition $t' \in p^\bullet$ contains necessarily t (i.e., $t' \rhd t$).

Example 1. Consider the marked Petri net of Fig. 2. The set of unobservable transitions is $\{t_1, t_2, t_3, t_4, t_5, t_6, t_9\}$. Transitions t_7, t_8, t_{10} and t_{11} are not. Indeed, each of the transitions t_7, t_8 and t_{10} has a single output place that has another input transition, while t_{11} is not unobservable since place p_1 is initially marked.

In the rest of the paper, each transition that is not *unobservable* is said to be *observable*. Given a marked Petri net $(\mathcal{N}, m_0)$, the set T of its transitions can then be divided into the two disjoint subsets *Obs* and *UnObs* that represent the observable and the unobservable transitions, respectively.

Next, we establish some theoretical results about the fireability of a transition depending on its type (observable or unobservable). The proof is in Appendix A.

Lemma 1. *Given a marked Petri net* $(\mathcal{N}, m_0)$ *and a transition* t, $t \in UnObs \implies \forall p \in t^\sim,\ \forall t' \in p^\bullet,\ t' \rhd t$.

Corollary 1. *Given a marked Petri net* $(\mathcal{N}, m_0)$ *and a transition* $t \in UnObs$. *Then, t is dead* $\implies \forall p \in t^\sim,\ \forall t' \in p^\bullet,\ t'$ *is dead.*

The proof of the previous corollary is immediate from Lemma 1. In fact, if an unobservable transition t is dead (i.e., there is no firing sequence $\sigma.t$ from the initial marking m_0), none of the output places in $t^\sim$ will be marked, preventing to fire their output transitions. In the following lemma, an *unobservable cycle* denotes a cycle in the Petri net model that contains unobserved transitions only. The proof is presented in Appendix B.

Lemma 2. *Let $(\mathcal{N}, m_0)$ be a marked Petri net. Then, $\forall t \in UnObs$, $\exists t' \in Obs$: $t' \rhd t$, or t belongs to an unobservable cycle.*

Our ultimate goal is to generate a set of traces that cover all the transitions of the system (represented by a Petri net). Instead of considering all the transitions of the system, we consider only the observable transitions (Obs) and look for sequences that cover these transitions. In general, covering observable transitions implies the covering of the unobservable ones. However, as established in the previous lemma, this does not hold when the Petri net model contains unobservable cycles. In this case, all the transitions of an unobservable cycle are dead. The proof is presented in Appendix C.

Lemma 3. *Given a marked Petri net $(\mathcal{N}, m_0)$, all the transitions belonging to an unobservable cycle are dead.*

Next, we present the main result of our approach: if there exists a set of firing sequences $\sigma_1 \ldots \sigma_n$ covering Obs, then all the transitions of the Petri net are covered by these sequences except those belonging to unobservable cycles.

Theorem 1. *Let $(\mathcal{N}, m_0)$ be a marked Petri net. Let Obs be the set of observable transitions (i.e. any transition not satisfying Definition 7). If $\exists \sigma_1 \ldots \sigma_n \in L((\mathcal{N}, m_0))$ s.t. $Obs \subseteq \bigcup_{i=1}^{n} \bar{\sigma}_i$, then $\forall t \in T$ one of the two following holds:*

1. *$\exists i \in \{1 \ldots n\}$ s.t. $t \in \bar{\sigma}_i$.*
2. *t belongs to an unobservable cycle.*

Proof. The proof is trivial using Lemma 2.

In the following theorem, we state that the set of observable transitions Obs is the smallest set ensuring the coverage of all the transitions of a Petri net (except those belonging to an unobservable cycle whose transitions are necessarily dead). The proof is presented in Appendix D.

Theorem 2. *$\forall Obs' \subseteq Obs$, Obs' satisfies Theorem 1 $\implies Obs' = Obs$.*

Limit Cases: It is worth noting that there are two limit cases to our approach:

1. *$Obs = \emptyset$.* This happens when the whole set of transitions of the Petri net is involved in a dead cycle.
2. *$Obs = T$* (i.e., all the transitions are observable). This happens, for instance, when none of the places has one input transition only. Such a case is obviously not favourable to our approach.

4   Test Specification Computation

The main theoretical result of the previous section is that covering the structurally computed observable transitions ensures the coverability of the whole set of system's transitions. It is then sufficient to find a collection of firing sequences with all observable transitions to cover all system's transitions. In this section, we propose a SOG-based approach to generate traces of the system that pass through the observable transitions. Such traces are first generated as the projection of full traces of the system on observable transitions only (called *observable traces/paths*). The construction of the SOG is revisited in our work in order to generate these observable traces on-the-fly (i.e., the construction is stopped as soon as all the observable transitions are covered). Once the observable traces are generated, the full traces (called *abstract paths*) are generated using a symbolic algorithm (BDD-based operations) based on a backward traversal of the SOG's nodes involved by these observable traces. Without loss of generality, we assume in this section that the system has no unobservable cycles. Indeed, one can detect (and remove) them using a structural analysis of the Petri net model.

4.1   On-the-Fly SOG-Based Generation of Observable Traces

The purpose of Algorithm 1 is to extract the observable traces during the construction of the SOG. Given the system model and the set of observable transitions, the goal of the algorithm is to collect a test suite $T_s = \{\sigma_1, \sigma_2, \ldots, \sigma_n\}$ such that, for any observable transition o, there exists an observable trace σ_i containing an occurrence of o.

Algorithm 1 is based on a depth-first search (DFS) traversal during the construction of the SOG. It takes as input the Petri net $\mathcal{N}$, its initial marking m_0, and the set of observable transitions Obs. The main used data structures are: (1) a stack "st" containing the aggregates "a" not yet completely treated, associated with the not yet treated observable transitions fireable from "a" and computed with the function EnableObs; (2) a set of sequences T_s to be calculated (the output of the algorithm); (3) the current trace $curT$; and (4) the set of covered observable transitions Cov. The initialization step of the algorithm (lines 4-6) computes the SOG's first aggregate using function InitialAggregate. It also initializes stack "st" with the first aggregate, and its fireable observable transitions are identified with function EnableObs. An iteration of the main loop (lines 7-28) picks and processes an item (a, f) from the stack. The algorithm ends in two cases: (1) the set of observable transitions Obs is fully covered, and (2) the stack is empty i.e., the SOG is completely built without covering the dead observable transitions. At each step of the main loop, we pick up the top couple (a, f). If the set of enabled transitions is not empty (line 9), then we choose (and remove from f) a transition to fire using the function chooseTransition that favours transitions that have not been covered yet, if any . Such a function could be more sophisticated to rely on some objective function (e.g., the length and/or the number of generated observable traces). If the selected transition o is the last observable transition to be covered, we save the current trace in T_s before leaving the loop (lines 13-15). Then, we push back the couple (a, f) to the stack and compute the successor a' of a by transition o (lines 16-17). If the successor already exists (lines 18-20), we add the current trace to T_s and then remove the last transition from the current path. In fact, we just finished traversing a path

---

Algorithm 1: Generation_of_observable_traces

Data: $\mathcal{N}$, m_0, Obs

Result: $\mathcal{T}_s$

1 Stack<aggregate, set<transition>> st; Set of traces $\mathcal{T}_s$; aggregate a, a';
2 Current observable trace $curT$; Set of covered observable transitions Cov;
3 **begin**
4 | $Cov \leftarrow \emptyset$;
5 | $a \leftarrow$ InitialAggregate$((\mathcal{N}, m_0))$;
6 | st.push$(a$, EnableObs$(a))$;
7 | **while** $(st \neq \emptyset \wedge Cov \subset Obs)$ **do**
8 | | st.pop(a,f);
9 | | **if** $(f \neq \emptyset)$ **then**
10 | | | $o \leftarrow$ chooseTransition(f, Cov);
11 | | | $Cov = Cov \cup \{o\}$;
12 | | | $curT \leftarrow curT.o$;
13 | | | **if** $(Cov == Obs)$ **then**
14 | | | | $\mathcal{T}_s \leftarrow \mathcal{T}_s \cup \{curT\}$
15 | | | **end**
16 | | | st.push(a,f);
17 | | | $a' \leftarrow Succ(a, o)$;
18 | | | **if** *(a' already exist)* **then**
19 | | | | $\mathcal{T}_s \leftarrow \mathcal{T}_s \cup \{curT\}$
20 | | | | $curT \leftarrow curT - curT.last$;
21 | | | **else**
22 | | | | st.push$(a'$, EnableObs$(a'))$;
23 | | | **end**
24 | | **else**
25 | | | $\mathcal{T}_s \leftarrow \mathcal{T}_s \cup \{curT\}$
26 | | | $curT \leftarrow curT - curT.last$;
27 | | **end**
28 | **end**
29 **end**

---

leading to a' where the last transition is o (such a trace has to be saved in $\mathcal{T}_s$), and we are going in the next iteration to come back to aggregate a to explore another path (o must be removed from the current trace). In case the aggregate a' is a new aggregate, we push it on the stack with the corresponding set of enabled observable transitions (line 22). Finally, in case the picked aggregate is completely treated (lines 24-26), we add the current trace to $\mathcal{T}_s$ and then remove the last transition from the current path. The reason is the same as when the compute successor aggregate exists. Notice that the current trace $curT$ is added to $\mathcal{T}_s$ only if there exists at least one transition in $curT$ that is newly covered.

Example 2. When Algorithm 1 gets the Petri net of Fig. 2 as a first parameter $\mathcal{N}$, an initial marking m_0 where only p_1 contains a token, and a set of observed transitions $Obs = \{t_7, t_8, t_{10}, t_{11}\}$, the initialization operation (line 5) generates the aggregate a_0 of Fig. 3. As there are two outgoing transitions, t_7 and t_8, identified by `EnableObs` (line 6), when the algorithm picks one of them in line 10, the statement of line 17 will create a_1. Aggregate a_1 has two outgoing transitions: t_{10} and t_{11}, where the former conducts to a_2. The last created aggregate leads to a previously created one a_1 through t_7 or t_8. At this step, line 19 inserts the variable $curT$ containing $< t_8, t_{10}, t_7 >$ into the set of observed traces identified by the variable T_s. Using the backtracking mechanism implemented in lines 20 and 26, the algorithm goes back to the aggregate a_1 to explore the last uncovered transition t_{11} leading to a previously explored aggregate a_0. Therefore, line 19 generates a new observed trace $< t_8, t_{11} >$. In this final iteration, the stack st is empty, and all transitions are covered.

4.2   Extracting Abstract Traces

The set of observable traces could be important to trigger particular executions of the system. However, in case we need to have complete executions involving the totality of the system transitions, we can extract such traces from the observable ones. Therefore, we will insert a sequence of unobserved transitions between two observed ones generated by the previous algorithm, starting from the initial marking state. Several criteria could be used to choose the unobserved sequence, such as test feasibility, balanced combinations, and sequence length. In our case, we aim to minimize the sequence's length traversing an aggregate.

Algorithm 2: Generation_of_abstract_path

Data: obsPath, SOG, UnObs

Result: abs_path

1 sequence<transition> abs_path, path_agr; aggregate agr; Set exitpts source;
2 transition trans; Pair<aggregate, Set entrypts> arg_entry;
3 Stack<pair<aggregate, Set entrypts>> entry_points; Set entrypts target;
4 **begin**
5   trans=obsPath.pop();
6   entry_points = **research_entry_points**(obsPath, SOG);
7   abs_path=Null ;   /*entry marking of next aggregate*/
8   **while** *(entry_points not empty)* **do**
9   agr_entry = entry_points.pop();
10   target = agr_entry.second;
11   agr = agr_entry.first;
12   source = **FirableObs**(agr, trans);   /*exit points of agr*/
13   path_agr = **sub_path_aggregate**(source, target, agr, UnObs);
14   abs_path = path_agr + trans + abs_path;
15   trans = obsPath.pop();
16   **end**
17 **end**

Algorithm 2 takes as input the observable path `obsPath`, the SOG built earlier `SOG`, and the set of unobservable transitions `UnObs`, and it returns the abstract path `abs_path`. During the first phase (lines 5-7), the algorithm extracts the observed path's last transition, identifies the aggregates' entry points set, and initializes the abstract path. The function `research_entry_points` calculates and stores in the stack ($entry\_points$) the list of aggregates traversed along the observable path `obsPath`, each associated with the set of its input states (i.e., the set of states reached by the previous observable transition in the trace starting from the previous aggregate). As long as there are items in the stack (aggregates and their entry points), the second phase (lines 8-16) uses a backtracking traversal of the current aggregate (at the top of the stack) in order to build a trace of unobservable transitions linking the *source* set of states (i.e., the ending points in an aggregate that will lead to the next aggregate while traversing the path) to the *target* set of states (i.e. entry points of the same aggregate). The above process is done by the function `sub_path_aggregate`. The last function uses a BFS strategy to provide the shortest unoboservable path linking the entry and exit points of the aggregate.

Example 3. To apply Algorithm 2 to our illustrative example, the first parameter $obsPath$ contains one of the two observed paths provided by the previous algorithm: $< t_8, t_{10}, t_7 >$ and $< t_8, t_{11} >$. If the second parameter is described by Fig. 3, the third one, called $UnObs$, contains all transitions of the Petri net of Fig. 2, except the observed transitions t_7, t_8, t_{10}, and t_{11}. For the first unobserved path $< t_8, t_{10}, t_7 >$, the variable $trans$ stores t_7, and line 6 computes the entry points of the aggregates a_0, a_1, and a_2, that is, $\{s_1\}$, $\{s_{12}, s_{13}, s_{14}\}$, and $\{s_{16}, s_{17}, s_{20}\}$, respectively. The $entry\_points$ stack holds three couples, where $(a_2, \{s_{16}, s_{17}, s_{20}\})$ is on the top. After removing the pair from the stack, lines (10-11) isolate the set of entry points and the aggregate. The former is stored in the $target$ variable, and the latter in the agr variable. Then, line 12 computes the states' set in the aggregate a_2 that can fire the transition t_7. For our example, $source$ variable contains $\{s_{18}, s_{21}, s_{23}\}$. Before extracting the next unobserved transition t_{10} and proceeding to the next iteration, line 13 identifies the path from the entry point of the aggregate a_2 to the observed transition t_7. The generated path is extended, in line 14, by adding the transition t_7 and an empty abstract path, as we are at the first iteration. In this case, we have three different alternatives: $< t_5, t_7 >$, $< t_3, t_5, t_7 >$, or $< t_3, t_4, t_5, t_7 >$. Our function `sub_path_aggregate` chooses the first state that can fire t_7. The actual implementation generates the first abstract path. After two iterations successively processing t_{10} and t_8 and the aggregates a_1 and a_0, respectively, the algorithm returns the abstract path $< t_1, t_2, t_6, t_8, t_{10}, t_5, t_7 >$.

5   Experiments

In this section, we compare the performance of our approach with that of two state-of-the-art tools: `MISTA`[1] and `NModel`[2]. This choice is based on the tools

---

[1] https://github.com/dianxiangxu/MISTA.

[2] https://github.com/juhan/NModel.

presented in the reviews [8,35,43,46]. We selected those that are (1) open-source, (2) available and maintained, (3) take as input either an FMS or a Petri net, (4) support the transition coverage criteria, and (5) generate all the paths.

Our approach has been implemented in the open-source tool sogMBT [3], that is written in C++ and has been integrated to the user-friendly web platform CosyVerif[3]. A total of 8 models from the Model Checking Contest[4] were used in our experiments: *Philosophers* (philo), *Referendum* (referendum), *SafeBus* (sbus), *ServersAndClients* (servers), *SharedMemory* (smemory), *Sudoku* (sudoku), *CircularTrains* (train), and *TokenRing* (tring). The biggest model in terms of state space size is philo20 (3.49E+09 reachable states). We were limited in our choice to Place-Transition 1-safe Petri nets because generalized Petri nets are not supported by MISTA. We ran all the experiments on a Dell Precision Tower 3430 with a processor Intel Xeon E-2136 6-cores @ 3.3GHz, 64 GiB memory, and Ubuntu 20.04. We used a timeout of 1 h. The reader can find in the repository [24] all the files needed to reproduce the benchmarks and the figures.

Table 1 summarizes our results. For each model, we indicate the number of transitions (column 3), the number of observable transitions obtained by our

Table 1. Experimental results (timeout 1 hr)

model	instance	# trans.	# obs. trans.	# paths			Average size of paths			Time (ms)		
				T1	T2	T3	T1	T2	T3	T1	T2	T3
example	example	11	4	2	3	4	8.00	7.00	9.00	0.95	1.0	100.0
philo	philo10	50	30	14	2	TO	39.07	73.00	TO	1344.970	1668.0	TO
	philo20	100	TO	TO	TO	TO	TO	TO	TO	TO	MO	TO
	philo5	25	15	9	2	150	12.44	33.50	8.77	7.57	6.0	337.0
referendum	referendum10	21	20	19	10	TO	10.53	11.00	TO	2622.98	1785.0	TO
	referendum15	31	TO	TO	TO	TO	TO	TO	TO	TO	MO	TO
sbus	sbus3	91	85	20	24	415	267.70	97.67	80.82	314.93	179.0	23522.0
	sbus6	451	TO	TO	TO	TO	TO	TO	TO	TO	MO	TO
servers	servers100-20	4200	2100	2000	2000	1	3.05	3.05	8000.00	335988.00	1640.0	34303.0
	servers100-40	8200	4100	4000	4000	TO	3.03	3.03	TO	1300630.00	6054.0	TO
	servers100-80	16200	TO	TO	TO	TO	TO	TO	TO	TO	MO	TO
smemory	smemory10	210	100	100	100	TO	8.75	45.20	TO	11475.00	269.0	TO
	smemory20	820	TO	TO	TO	TO	TO	TO	TO	TO	MO	TO
	smemory5	55	25	25	15	193	5.56	99.67	71.75	38.49	72.0	4271.0
sudoku	sudokuA-1	1	1	1	1	1	1.00	1.00	1.00	0.68	9.0	85.0
	sudokuA-2	8	8	4	3	32	3.00	3.00	3.00	0.919	0.0	113.000
	sudokuA-3	27	27	17	11	19494	7.26	5.73	6.06	197.47	416.0	52540.0
	sudokuA-4	64	TO	TO	TO	TO	TO	TO	TO	TO	MO	TO
train	train12	12	4	1	1	21	12.00	17.00	29.52	2.40	16.0	215.0
	train24	24	8	1	TO	TO	24.00	TO	TO	330.64	MO	TO
	train48	48	TO	TO	TO	TO	TO	TO	TO	TO	MO	TO
tring	tring10	1111	1111	106	46	TO	18.36	142.54	TO	68507.90	9743.0	TO
	tring15	3616	TO	TO	TO	TO	TO	TO	TO	TO	MO	TO
	tring5	156	156	11	11	100	10.18	59.27	6.87	9.89	5.0	261.0

T1: sogMBT; T2: MISTA; T3: NModel

[3] https://cosyverif.lipn.univ-paris13.fr/.
[4] https://mcc.lip6.fr.

structural analysis of the model (column 4), the number of obtained covering firing sequences (column 5) and their average size (column 6), and the execution time of the three tested tools (column 7) where T1, T2 and T3 refer to our approach (namely sogMBT), MISTA and NModel, respectively. It is clear that NModel could not compete with the other two tools. Amongst the 24 situations, MISTA outperformed sogMBT in 9 cases, while the reverse was true 7 times. It is worth noting that we do not expect our approach to be efficient when the number of observable transitions is high. This is the case for three out of 8 of the selected models: referendum (all the transitions, except one, are observable), and both sudoku and tring models where all the transitions are observable. If we focus on the testing effort that we can deduce from the two penultimate columns, which can be measured by the product of the number of paths and the average path size, we see that amongst 16 situations, the testing effort related to sogMBT is lower in 7 (resp. MISTA in 6) while three cases show perfect equality. MISTA uses a DFS strategy, leading to an average size of the generated paths longer than the computed by our approach.

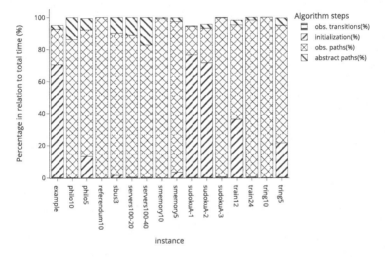

Fig. 5. Times for each step in the computation of observable traces. Some bars do not reach the 100% because some times are very small, thus accumulating precision errors.

Figure 5 is given in order to have a detailed analysis of the distribution of the execution time of sogMBT among the different phases of our approach: (1) initialization of data structure (BDD staff); (2) computation of the observable transitions; (3) computation of observable paths; and (4) extraction of abstract paths from observable ones. It is clear that for small models, the initialization time is prevailing while for medium to large models, the generation time of the observed paths is more important since the construction of the aggregates is realized during the exploration. The last phase is not very time-consuming.

To summarize these preliminary results, the sogMBT, as a proof of concept prototype, is competitive w.r.t. existing tools. This is promising, and the approach can be improved from different perspectives. For instance, more sophisticated heuristics can be elaborated to decide which path to follow during the DFS-based construction/exploration of the SOG, in order to cover the observable transitions with less effort. Another improvement would be to parallelize the initialization phase (e.g., following [23]), among others.

6 Related Work

Given the widespread use of Petri nets in the specification of critical systems, several works have aimed at developing approaches for generating test inputs from models described with them. Many research projects have combined the reachability graph and standard search algorithms from graph theory to produce test inputs [29]. Other approaches have used the same structure to build a transition tree representing the test inputs. This transition tree is rooted in the initial state of the marking graph, and each path leading to a leaf is a sequence of firing transitions from the Petri net [47]. Dianxiang et al. [49] have shown that this data structure is helpful to have provided a strategy for robustness testing. Dianxiang [48] published an integrated development environment for automated test generation and execution two years earlier.

Identifying the change related to a specification modification has been the subject of two research projects on regression testing [1,16]. Their main goal was to identify test inputs which are no longer relevant due to the removal of some transitions. Besides, they propose new entries or modify old ones to cover the new transitions added to the model. The test quality measurement of the interactions between agents was introduced by Miller et al. [36]. Authors have modified an existing debugging tool to measure the coverage rate of various protocol-based criteria related expressed using Petri nets. Several coverage criteria have been formalized for high-level Petri nets [30,51]. The work of [14] uses the cause-effect network's concept for the generation of test inputs, while [15] uses the execution potential of the model by the simulation to measure the coverage rate of the generated test inputs. Most of these approaches face the problem of state space explosion when aiming to test systems with a marking graph containing thousands of states. From the work of Chusho [12], which introduces the notion of the essential branch, to that of Bardin et al. [6], which defines a unified framework to identify essential test objectives, several works and theories have emerged to address this problem. They rely on graph theory, dynamic symbolic execution, weakest calculus, model-checking, proof, constraint-based techniques, and value analysis. Based on the notion of the decision-to-decision path (dd-path) [21], Chusho [12] introduced the essential branch measure, which represents the cornerstone to transform a control flow graph (CFG), representing the target code, into a reduced graph called an inheritor-reduced graph. Following this reduction, covering essential branches implies the coverage of all branches. In the same vein, Bertolino and Marré [9] have used the relations of dominance and implication among the arcs of a *ddgraph*, which allowed the deduction of unconstrained arcs. The deduced set constitutes a minimal set of the ddgraph's arcs such that the paths which cover them are a path cover. These approaches cannot identify infeasible structural objectives without human assistance to tune the selection strategy. Also, these approaches are suitable to handle CFG but do not scale up to handle large systems with thousands of nodes. A broader perspective of our work includes the generation of test paths such as those proposed by Li et al. [28]. They have used search-based approaches, whereas the one proposed by Hallé revolves around Cayley graph and triaging function. The latter defines a unified method to handle different coverage criteria, and the Cayley graph gathers the test paths into equivalence classes. As a result, this approach reduces the number of test paths. However, it does not offer a solution to identify the unfeasible objectives and the subsumed elementary components (transitions).

Offutt and Pan [39] encode the test objectives under constraints that are extracted from the program under test. Unresolved constraints represent infeasible objectives. By associating properties to the structural test objects, the use of model-checking [10] verifies whether the test object is verifiable or not. If the first approach shows limits when the constraints are non-linear [2] or when the program uses aliases [27], model-checking faces the problem of scaling.

Other techniques use the weakest precondition to remedy the scaling problem. This technique allows [7] to identify infeasible instructions while [4] determines infeasible branches. Since these first two criteria are the most basic, Bardin et al. [5] use the weakest precondition to address more advanced structural test objectives. Marcozzi et al. [31] unfold this technique to identify polluting test targets that do not stop at infeasible targets. Blending the identification of infeasible test objectives with symbolic or even concolic execution accelerates the generation of test inputs and refines the coverage measures.

7   Conclusion

Unlike verification, which can show that software is fault-free, testing discloses the presence of faults in the software only. Although researchers are not unanimous about the ability of test inputs that meet the coverage criteria to expose flaws, these criteria can help to evaluate the quality of the tests generated. We have formalized the separation of a Petri net's transitions into two disjoint sets: *Obs* and *UnObs*. We have shown that an *UnObs* transition is either unreachable or subsumed by another transition. Also, we have shown that the coverage of all the *Obs* transitions meets the transition coverage criterion of a given Petri net. Then, we have proposed a structural manner to extract the set of observable transitions from a Petri net. The construction of the *Obs* test paths was presented through an algorithm based on the partial building of a SOG. Yet, we have introduced the final algorithm, which builds abstract test paths from *Obs* tests. Since it is not mandatory to build the whole SOG's aggregates, our approach shows potential signs to improve the performance of test path generation. This has been confirmed by our preliminary experimental results. As future work, we plan to use linear programming and machine learning approaches in order to minimize the number and the length of the test sequences during the SOG construction. Also, we aim to extend our approach to other types of coverage criteria related to Petri nets and to evaluate the potential of fault identification using mutation testing.

A   Proof of Lemma 1

Proof. Let t be an unobservable transition, p be a place in $t^\sim$ and $t' \in p^\bullet$. Assume that there exists a firing sequence $\sigma.t'$. Given that place p is not marked initially and that no transition, except t, can produce a token in p, t must be fired before t' to produce the necessary token in p.

B   Proof of Lemma 2

Proof. Let $(\mathcal{N}, m_0)$ be a marked Petri net, $t_0 \in UnObs$ be an unobservable transition, $p \in t_0^\sim$ be an output place of t_0 having t_0 as unique input transition, and $t_1 \in p^\bullet$ be an output transition of p. Then, by Lemma 1, $t_1 \rhd t_0$. If t_1 is observable, then the lemma is proved. Else, by an iterative application of this reasoning, by the transitivity of the coverage relation $\rhd$ and by the fact that the number of transitions in a Petri net is finite, we end on two possible cases: (1) there exists a transition $t_n \in Obs$ s.t. $t_n \rhd t_{n-1} \rhd \cdots \rhd t_0$, or (2) t_0 belongs to an unobservable cycle, which proves the Lemma.

C   Proof of Lemma 3

Proof. Let t be a transition of the cycle, and $p \in {}^\bullet t$ be the input place of t that belongs to the cycle. p is initially empty because the (unique) transition $t' \in {}^\bullet p$ belongs to the cycle and hence is unobservable. Thus, place p will never be marked because t' is dead by a successive application of Corollary 1 from t.

D   Proof of Theorem 2

Proof. Assume that $Obs' \subset Obs$ is the smallest subset of transitions satisfying Theorem 1. Let $t \in Obs \setminus Obs'$, there exists then a transition $t' \in Obs'$ s.t. $t' \rhd t$, i.e., $\forall$ firing sequence $t_1 \ldots t_n.t'$ (for $n \geq 1$), $\exists i \in \{1, \ldots, n\}$ s.t., $t = t_i$. Let $p \in t^\bullet \cap {}^\bullet t'$. Then, by Definition 7, p is necessarily not marked, otherwise the sequence $t_{i+1} \ldots t_n.t'$ is a firing sequence that does not contain t. Also, there exists a transition $t_i' \neq t$ in ${}^\bullet p$, otherwise t is unobservable. If t_i' is observable, then there exists a firing sequence $\beta.t_i'$ which makes the sequence $\beta.t_i'.t_{i+1} \ldots t_n.t'$ a firing sequence not involving t, and that is not possible. If t_i' is unobservable, then, by using Lemma 2, there exists a transition $t_i'' \in Obs$ s.t. $t_i'' \rhd t_i'$. By hypothesis, there exists a sequence $\alpha.t_i'.\gamma.t_i''$. Thus, the sequence $\alpha.t_i'.t_{i+1} \ldots t_n.t'$ covers t' but not t, which is impossible. To conclude, such a transition t could not exist and Obs' is necessarily equal to Obs.

References

1. Ahmad, F., Qaisar, Z.H.: Scenario based functional regression testing using petri net models. In: ICMLA (2), pp. 572–577. IEEE (2013)
2. Anand, S., et al.: An orchestrated survey of methodologies for automated software test case generation. J. Syst. Softw. **86**(8), 1978–2001 (2013)
3. Arias, J., Bennani, M.T., Desel, J., Klai, K., Ochi, H.: sogMBT: Symbolic observation graph-based generator of test paths (2023). https://depot.lipn.univ-paris13.fr/PMC-SOG/sogMBT
4. Baluda, M., Denaro, G., Pezzè, M.: Bidirectional symbolic analysis for effective branch testing. IEEE Trans. Software Eng. **42**(5), 403–426 (2016)
5. Bardin, S., et al.: Sound and quasi-complete detection of infeasible test requirements. In: ICST, pp. 1–10. IEEE Computer Society (2015)
6. Bardin, S., Kosmatov, N., Marcozzi, M., Delahaye, M.: Specify and measure, cover and reveal: A unified framework for automated test generation. Sci. Comput. Program. **207**, 102641 (2021)
7. Beckman, N.E., Nori, A.V., Rajamani, S.K., Simmons, R.J., Tetali, S., Thakur, A.V.: Proofs from tests. IEEE Trans. Software Eng. **36**(4), 495–508 (2010)
8. Bernardino, M., Rodrigues, E.M., Zorzo, A.F., Marchezan, L.: Systematic mapping study on MBT: tools and models. IET Softw. **11**(4), 141–155 (2017)
9. Bertolino, A., Marré, M.: Automatic generation of path covers based on the control flow analysis of computer programs. IEEE Trans. Software Eng. **20**(12), 885–899 (1994)
10. Beyer, D., Chlipala, A., Henzinger, T.A., Jhala, R., Majumdar, R.: Generating tests from counterexamples. In: ICSE, pp. 326–335. IEEE Computer Society (2004)
11. Chariyathitipong, P., Vatanawood, W.: Dynamic slicing of time petri net based on MTL property. IEEE Access **10**, 45207–45218 (2022)
12. Chusho, T.: Test data selection and quality estimation based on the concept of esssential branches for path testing. IEEE Trans. Software Eng. **13**(5), 509–517 (1987)
13. Darvas, D., Fernández Adiego, B., Vörös, A., Bartha, T., Blanco Viñuela, E., González Suárez, V.M.: Formal verification of complex properties on PLC programs. In: Ábrahám, E., Palamidessi, C. (eds.) FORTE 2014. LNCS, vol. 8461, pp. 284–299. Springer, Heidelberg (2014). https://doi.org/10.1007/978-3-662-43613-4_18
14. Desel, J., Oberweis, A., Zimmer, T., Zimmermann, G.: Validation of information system models: Petri nets and test case generation. In: ICSMC, vol. 4, pp. 3401–3406. IEEE (1997)
15. Ding, J., Argote-Garcia, G., Clarke, P.J., He, X.: Evaluating test adequacy coverage of high level petri nets using spin. In: AST, pp. 71–78. ACM (2008)
16. Ding, Z., Jiang, M., Chen, H., Jin, Z., Zhou, M.: Petri net based test case generation for evolved specification. SCIENCE CHINA Inf. Sci. **59**(8), 1–25 (2016). https://doi.org/10.1007/s11432-016-5598-5
17. Emerson, E.A., Wahl, T.: Dynamic symmetry reduction. In: Halbwachs, N., Zuck, L.D. (eds.) TACAS 2005. LNCS, vol. 3440, pp. 382–396. Springer, Heidelberg (2005). https://doi.org/10.1007/978-3-540-31980-1_25
18. Fernandez, J., Bozga, M., Ghirvu, L.: State space reduction based on live variables analysis. Sci. Comput. Program. **47**(2–3), 203–220 (2003)
19. Fraser, G., Wotawa, F., Ammann, P.: Testing with model checkers: a survey. Softw. Test. Verification Reliab. **19**(3), 215–261 (2009)

20. Haddad, S., Ilié, J.-M., Klai, K.: Design and evaluation of a symbolic and abstraction-based model checker. In: Wang, F. (ed.) ATVA 2004. LNCS, vol. 3299, pp. 196–210. Springer, Heidelberg (2004). https://doi.org/10.1007/978-3-540-30476-0_19

21. Huang, J.C.: Error detection through program testing. Current Trends in Program. Methodol. II, 16–43 (1977)

22. Akers, S.B., Jr.: Binary decision diagrams. IEEE Trans. Comput. **27**(6), 509–516 (1978)

23. Klai, K., Abid, C.A., Arias, J., Evangelista, S.: Hybrid parallel model checking of hybrid LTL on hybrid state space representation. In: Nouri, A., Wu, W., Barkaoui, K., Li, Z.W. (eds.) VECoS 2021. LNCS, vol. 13187, pp. 27–42. Springer, Cham (2022). https://doi.org/10.1007/978-3-030-98850-0_3

24. Klai, K., Bennani, M.T., Arias, J., Desel, J., Ochi, H.: sogMBT benchmarks (2023). https://depot.lipn.univ-paris13.fr/PMC-SOG/experiments/test-paths

25. Klai, K., Petrucci, L.: Modular construction of the symbolic observation graph. In: ACSD, pp. 88–97. IEEE (2008)

26. Klai, K., Poitrenaud, D.: MC-SOG: An LTL model checker based on symbolic observation graphs. In: van Hee, K.M., Valk, R. (eds.) PETRI NETS 2008. LNCS, vol. 5062, pp. 288–306. Springer, Heidelberg (2008). https://doi.org/10.1007/978-3-540-68746-7_20

27. Kosmatov, N.: All-paths testgeneration for programs with internal aliases. In: ISSRE, pp. 147–156. IEEE Computer Society (2008)

28. Li, N., Li, F., Offutt, J.: Better algorithms to minimize the cost of test paths. In: ICST, pp. 280–289. IEEE Computer Society (2012)

29. Li, Y., Zhang, X., Zhang, Y., Guo, J., Rao, C.: A test cases generation method for atp. In: RSVT, pp. 21–26. ACM (2021)

30. Liu, Z., Liu, T., Cai, L., Yang, G.: Test coverage for collaborative workflow application based on petri net. In: CSCWD, pp. 213–218. IEEE (2010)

31. Marcozzi, M., Bardin, S., Kosmatov, N., Papadakis, M., Prevosto, V., Correnson, L.: Time to clean your test objectives. In: ICSE, pp. 456–467. ACM (2018)

32. Martin-Lopez, A., Arcuri, A., Segura, S., Ruiz-Cortés, A.: Black-box and white-box test case generation for restful apis: Enemies or allies? In: ISSRE, pp. 231–241. IEEE (2021)

33. Mateescu, R., Wijs, A.: Sequential and distributed on-the-fly computation of weak tau-confluence. Sci. Comput. Program. **77**(10–11), 1075–1094 (2012)

34. Meng, Y., Gay, G.: Understanding the impact of solver choice in model-based test generation. In: ESEM, pp. 22:1–22:11. ACM (2020)

35. Micskei, Z.: Model-based testing (MBT). http://mit.bme.hu/~micskeiz/pages/modelbased_testing.html#tools

36. Miller, T., Padgham, L., Thangarajah, J.: Test coverage criteria for agent interaction testing. In: Weyns, D., Gleizes, M.-P. (eds.) AOSE 2010. LNCS, vol. 6788, pp. 91–105. Springer, Heidelberg (2011). https://doi.org/10.1007/978-3-642-22636-6_6

37. Murata, T.: Petri nets: Properties, analysis and applications. Proc. IEEE **77**(4), 541–580 (1989)

38. Nosrati, M., Haghighi, H., Vahidi-Asl, M.: Test data generation using genetic programming. Inf. Softw. Technol. **130**, 106446 (2021)

39. Offutt, A.J., Pan, J.: Automatically detecting equivalent mutants and infeasible paths. Softw. Test. Verification Reliab. **7**(3), 165–192 (1997)

40. Offutt, J., Thummala, S.: Testing concurrent user behavior of synchronous web applications with petri nets. Softw. Syst. Model. **18**(2), 913–936 (2019)

41. Pelánek, R.: Fighting state space explosion: review and evaluation. In: Cofer, D., Fantechi, A. (eds.) FMICS 2008. LNCS, vol. 5596, pp. 37–52. Springer, Heidelberg (2009). https://doi.org/10.1007/978-3-642-03240-0_7

42. van der Sanden, B., Geilen, M., Reniers, M.A., Basten, T.: Partial-order reduction for supervisory controller synthesis. IEEE Trans. Autom. Control **67**(2), 870–885 (2022)

43. Shafique, M., Labiche, Y.: A systematic review of state-based test tools. Int. J. Softw. Tools Technol. Transf. **17**(1), 59–76 (2015)

44. Teodorov, C., Leroux, L., Drey, Z., Dhaussy, P.: Past-free[ze] reachability analysis: reaching further with dag-directed exhaustive state-space analysis. Softw. Test. Verification Reliab. **26**(7), 516–542 (2016)

45. Utting, M., Legeard, B., Bouquet, F., Fourneret, E., Peureux, F., Vernotte, A.: Recent Advances in Model-Based Testing, vol. 101 (2016)

46. Villalobos-Arias, L., Quesada-López, C., Martínez, A., Jenkins, M.: Model-based testing areas, tools and challenges: A tertiary study. CLEI Electron. J. **22**(1) (2019)

47. Wang, C.C., Pai, W., Chiang, D.J.: Using a petri net model approach to object-oriented class testing. In: ICSMC, vol. 1, pp. 824–828. IEEE (1999)

48. Xu, D.: A tool for automated test code generation from high-level petri nets. In: Kristensen, L.M., Petrucci, L. (eds.) PETRI NETS 2011. LNCS, vol. 6709, pp. 308–317. Springer, Heidelberg (2011). https://doi.org/10.1007/978-3-642-21834-7_17

49. Xu, D., Tu, M., Sanford, M., Thomas, L., Woodraska, D., Xu, W.: Automated security test generation with formal threat models. IEEE Trans. Dependable Secur. Comput. **9**(4), 526–540 (2012)

50. Zhang, J., Zhang, D., Huang, K.: A regular expression matching algorithm using transition merging. In: PRDC, pp. 242–246. IEEE Computer Society (2009)

51. Zhu, H., He, X.: A methodology of testing high-level petri nets. Inf. Softw. Technol. **44**(8), 473–489 (2002)

Abstraction and Refinement

Slow Down, Move Over: A Case Study in Formal Verification, Refinement, and Testing of the Responsibility-Sensitive Safety Model for Self-Driving Cars

Megan Strauss[iD] and Stefan Mitsch[✉][iD]

Computer Science Department, Carnegie Mellon University, Pittsburgh, USA
mstrauss@andrew.cmu.edu, smitsch@cs.cmu.edu

Abstract. Technology advances give us the hope of driving without human error, reducing vehicle emissions and simplifying an everyday task with the future of self-driving cars. Making sure these vehicles are safe is very important to the continuation of this field. In this paper, we formalize the Responsibility-Sensitive Safety model (RSS) for self-driving cars and prove the safety and optimality of this model in the longitudinal direction. We utilize the hybrid systems theorem prover KeYmaera X to formalize RSS as a hybrid system with its nondeterministic control choices and continuous motion model, and prove absence of collisions. We then illustrate the practicality of RSS through refinement proofs that turn the verified nondeterministic control envelopes into deterministic ones and further verified compilation to Python. The refinement and compilation are safety-preserving; as a result, safety proofs of the formal model transfer to the compiled code, while counterexamples discovered in testing the code of an unverified model transfer back. The resulting Python code allows to test the behavior of cars following the motion model of RSS in simulation, to measure agreement between the model and simulation with monitors that are derived from the formal model, and to report counterexamples from simulation back to the formal model.

Keywords: differential dynamic logic · refinement · testing · self-driving cars · collision avoidance · theorem proving

1 Introduction and Motivation

As technology advances, it becomes both more appealing and feasible to automate everyday tasks. In doing this, there is a higher need for robust formal verification and testing strategies to ensure that these automated systems are safe. Formal verification ensures that all situations encountered in a model of physics are safe, while testing provides evidence that the formal model works as expected and can give insight to bugs in a yet-to-be-verified model. To this end, a testing strategy analyzes some (representative) situations that an automated

V. Prevosto and C. Seceleanu (Eds.): TAP 2023, LNCS 14066, pp. 149–167, 2023.
https://doi.org/10.1007/978-3-031-38828-6_9

system may encounter. This paper develops a formal framework to link modeling, offline verification, online monitoring, and testing, sketched in Fig. 1 and illustrated throughout the paper with an example in autonomous driving.

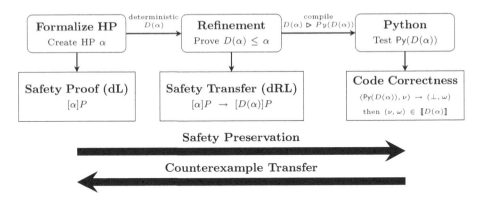

Fig. 1. Verification, refinement, and compilation for safety and counterexample transfer. All steps are accompanied with a correctness proof.

We use hybrid systems to describe the dynamic components of a car, with the goal of creating discrete computer controllers which prevent collisions and other unsafe situations. Analyzing such a system requires two components: a differential equation modeling the cars' motion and a car control algorithm. For the differential equation, we follow [12] and describe the longitudinal motion of a car in response to acceleration/deceleration inputs. For the discrete controller, we follow the Responsibility-Sensitive Safety (RSS) model [23]. Its discrete control choices influence the continuous motion of the car, and are given in terms of a nondeterministic control envelope that allows for many different ways of deterministic control implementation. In the resulting hybrid systems model, we prove the safety (defined by absence of collision) of all possible implementations within the control envelope. This proof step replaces the need to test through simulation whether the model is safe, i.e. checking if cars collide in any implementation of the system, but simulation can help in debugging unverified models. We also want the ability to analyze concrete (deterministic) controller implementations and motion models and determine whether they follow the general verified model. We do this through refinement proofs in differential refinement logic [13] to a deterministic hybrid program followed by a verified compilation to Python which allows us to further analyze the behavior of a system. This way, we can analyze concrete behavior for concrete parameter choices in the formal model, and simulate behavior for analysis in select driving situations. In order to transfer the safety proof to *all encountered situations*, the remaining question after a safety proof is then to detect at runtime when the proof applies and when it does not. We answer this by applying ModelPlex [17] to generate monitors that are able to validate unverified code and motion model alike. We

Table 1. RSS variables and model parameters

Parameter	Description
x_1, x_2	positions in lateral or longitudinal direction of car 1 and 2
v_1, v_2	velocities in lateral or longitudinal direction of car 1 and car 2
a_1, a_2	acceleration in lateral or longitudinal direction of car 1 and car 2
$a_{minBrake}$	minimum deceleration during evasion maneuver
$a_{maxBrake}$	maximum deceleration
$a_{minBrakeCorrect}$	minimum deceleration during evasion maneuver in the correct direction (only used for cars driving in opposite directions)
$a_{maxAccel}$	maximum acceleration (positive constant, used in both directions)
ρ	reaction time for starting evasion maneuver

utilize the same monitors in testing and simulation to measure the robustness of control choices, or in other words, the safety-criticality of test scenarios. The proof, refinement, and compilation framework is set up in such a way that, if a proof step fails, compiling the formal model and analyzing it for counterexamples through testing is still possible.

2 Background

2.1 Responsibility-Sensitive Safety

We briefly summarize Responsibility-Sensitive Safety (RSS, [23]) that we use as a case study throughout this paper. The general purpose of RSS is to describe a safe algorithm for the interaction of (semi-)autonomous cars, with safety being defined as the avoidance of collision. RSS defines a lane-based coordinate system which describes the position of cars with a longitudinal and lateral coordinate relative to the lane they are in on a road. The longitudinal coordinate measures the distance relative to a starting position along the road, which abstracts from road geometry. The lateral position describes the distance from the center of the road. The lane-based coordinate system simplifies the motion model into a linear differential equation system as in [12].

The general idea behind the RSS control envelope is that two cars should maintain a safe distance between them, which is a function of the current speeds of the two cars. If at a safe distance, they are allowed to drive at any acceleration or deceleration within their cars' maximum acceleration and maximum braking bounds. Otherwise, if not at a safe distance, they must respond with a predefined evasion maneuver called *proper response* within a specified reaction time horizon in order to remain safe. The safe distance is specified as a function of (relative) vehicle speed and vehicle parameters, as summarized in Table 1 [23].

2.2 Differential Dynamic Logic and Notation

We use differential dynamic logic (dL) [20] to create models of car control and motion, and to express correctness and optimality properties of RSS. Differential

Table 2. Syntax and informal semantics of hybrid programs

Program	Meaning
$x := \theta$	Assigns the value of θ to x
$x := *$	Assigns any real value to x
$\{x' = \theta \;\&\; Q\}$	Evolves x along θ for any duration $t \geq 0$ while Q is true throughout
$?P$	Tests formula P and continues if true, aborts if false
$\alpha; \beta$	Follows program α and subsequently follows program β
$\alpha \cup \beta$	Follows either program α or program β, nondeterministically
α^*	Repeats program α a nondeterministic $n \geq 0$ number of times

dynamic logic supports modeling hybrid systems complete with support for continuous dynamics expressed using differential equations. Within the RSS model, we utilize discrete dynamics to describe the control options in terms of instantly changing the acceleration or deceleration that the car is following. We use differential equations to model the resulting motion change in speed and position of the cars with respect to this chosen acceleration. dL comes with a proof calculus [20], which is supported in the automated theorem prover KeYmaera X [5]. For the scope of this paper, the following informal understanding, summarized in Table 2 suffices. Assignment of a variable $x := \theta$ instantly assigns the value of θ to x, nondeterministic assignment $x := *$ assigns any real value to x (e.g. choosing an arbitrary acceleration value). Continuous evolution $\{x' = \theta \;\&\; Q\}$ evolves x along the differential equation $x' = \theta$ for an arbitrary duration while Q is true throughout (e.g. change position of cars along kinematic equations, but prevent moving backwards). The test $?P$ checks that formula P is true and continues running if it is, and if not aborts the program (possibly backtracking to other nondeterministic options). Sequential composition $\alpha; \beta$ first runs hybrid program α and subsequently runs hybrid program β from the resulting states of α (e.g. first choose acceleration, then follow motion). A nondeterministic choice of operations allows for the choice of two separate hybrid programs, $\alpha \cup \beta$ (e.g. running α if there is a safe distance between two cars and running emergency braking β otherwise). Nondeterministic repetition α^* repeats hybrid program α some $n \geq 0$ times (e.g. repeatedly running control and motion).

The set of dL formulas is generated by the following grammar, where $\sim \in \{<, \leq, =, \neq, \geq, >\}$ and terms f, g in $+, -, \cdot, /$ are over the reals, contain number literals, variables and n-ary rigid function symbols, plus support interpreted minimum, maximum, absolute value and trigonometric functions [6]:

$$P, Q := f \sim g \mid P \wedge Q \mid P \vee Q \mid P \to Q \mid P \leftrightarrow Q \mid \forall x\, P \mid \exists x\, P \mid [\alpha]\, P \mid \langle \alpha \rangle\, P \,.$$

We use $f \sim g \sim h$ as shorthand for $f \sim g \wedge g \sim h$. Arithmetic operations, comparisons, Boolean connectives, and quantifiers are as usual. Formulas of the form $[\alpha]\, P$ and $\langle \alpha \rangle\, P$ express properties about programs: $[\alpha]\, P$ is true when in all states reachable through transitions of program α the property P is true (used for safety); $\langle \alpha \rangle P$ is true when there exists a state reachable by the program α in which P is true (used for liveness, optimality, and runtime monitoring).

The semantics of dL [20] is a Kripke semantics in which the states of the Kripke model are the states of the hybrid system. A state is a map $\omega : V \to \mathbb{R}$, assigning a real value $\omega(x)$ to each variable $x \in V$ in the set of variables V. We write $[\![P]\!]$ to denote the set of states in which formula P is true, $\omega \in [\![P]\!]$ or equivalently $\omega \models P$ if formula P is true at state ω, $\models P$ for P being valid (true in all states), and $\omega [\![e]\!]$ to denote the real value of term e in state ω. The semantics of hybrid programs is expressed as a transition relation $[\![\alpha]\!] \subseteq S \times S$ of initial and final states in S [20] and we write $(\omega, \nu) \in [\![\alpha]\!]$ to express that program α reaches state ν when starting in state ω. dL is decidable relative to either an oracle for the continuous first-order logic of differential equations or an oracle for the discrete fragment of dL [19, Theorem 11].

2.3 Differential Refinement Logic

Differential refinement logic dRL [13] defines a relationship between two hybrid programs $\alpha \le \beta$ that tells us that all the states reachable from program α are also reachable by operations of β. This allows us to transfer safety properties between programs: safety properties about a hybrid program also hold for all refinements of this program. In this paper, we refine the RSS control envelopes to create deterministic controllers, which are guaranteed to inherit the verified safety properties of the original control envelopes.

2.4 ModelPlex

A proof of $[\alpha] P$ gives us confidence in the safety of the model α. The remaining question is now whether α represents a useful real (driving) behavior, and whether an implementation is faithful to the conditions of the verified model. ModelPlex [17] combines an offline safety proof of the shape $A \to [\alpha] P$ with a runtime monitor checking whether two concrete states ω, ν are connected by a program α, i.e., semantically whether $(\omega, \nu) \in [\![\alpha]\!]$. The safety proof witnesses that, starting from states satisfying A, *all* states reachable by model α satisfy P, while satisfying the runtime monitor witnesses that the two concrete states ω, ν are connected by the program α, and so state ν inherits the safety proof, i.e., $\nu \models P$ if $\omega \models A$. The semantic runtime monitor is equivalently phrased in dL as a monitor specification $\langle \alpha \rangle \bigwedge_{x \in BV(\alpha)} (x = x^+)$ with fresh variables x^+ not occurring in α [17]. The dL monitor specification allows ModelPlex, in contrast to online reachability analysis, to shift computation offline by using theorem proving in order to translate a hybrid systems model into a formula $\phi \in M$ where M is the set of quantifier-free, modality-free formulas over real arithmetic. Note that the dL monitor specification is not provable offline, since it introduces fresh variables x^+. Instead, the proof can be finished at runtime for two concrete states (a state ω providing values for x and a state ν providing values for x^+)

Model 1. Model template for collision avoidance in longitudinal motion $\texttt{longitudinal}(\texttt{safeDist}, \texttt{edc}, \texttt{freeDriving}, \texttt{properResponse})$

init	1	$x_1 \leq x_2 \wedge \texttt{safeDist}(v_1, v_2) \leq x_1 - x_2$
	2	$\wedge\, 0 < a_{minBrake} < a_{maxBrake} \wedge 0 < a_{maxAccel}$
	3	$\wedge\, \rho > 0$
	4	$\wedge\, \texttt{edc}$
	5	$\rightarrow$
	6	$[\,($
ctrl	7	$\big(?\texttt{safeDist}(v_1, v_2) \leq x_2 - x_1;\ (a_1, a_2) := \texttt{freeDriving}$
	8	$\cup$
	9	$?\texttt{safeDist}(v_1, v_2) \geq x_2 - x_1;\ (a_1, a_2) := \texttt{properResponse}\big);$
	10	$t := 0;$
motion	11	$\{x_1' = v_1,\ x_2' = v_2,\ v_1' = a_1,\ v_2' = a_2,\ t' = 1\ \&\ \texttt{edc} \wedge t \leq \rho\}$
safe	12	$\big)^*\,]\,(x_1 \leq x_2)$

by plugging in concrete measurements for all variables of the runtime monitor. When a runtime monitor ϕ is satisfied over states ω, ν, we write $(\omega, \nu) \in [\![\phi]\!]$.

3   Formalization of RSS Safety and Optimality

In this section we begin our case study on RSS. We first formalize the RSS guidelines and verify the safety of the model. We then propose a way to verify that the RSS model drives optimally. The models and proofs [25] are formalized in the KeYmaera X ASCII syntax [15]. After this we create deterministic controllers which we show are refinements of the general verified model and utilize these to illustrate RSS behavior in simulation.

3.1   Formalization and Verification of RSS Safety

Models in the subsequent sections follow the same structure. To capture this common structure, we introduce a safety template in Model 1. All subsequent safety proofs for the longitudinal motion regardless of direction (same or opposite direction of motion), follow this template, but with specific formulas and programs to fill in the placeholders for the safety distance $\texttt{safeDist}$, evolution domain constraint $\texttt{edc}$, free driving program $\texttt{freeDriving}$, and evasion maneuver program $\texttt{properResponse}$.

The template defines preconditions (Line 1–4) under which all runs of the hybrid program in Line 6–11 are expected to establish the safety condition in Line 12. The preconditions $\texttt{init}$ set parameter bounds for acceleration, deceleration, and reaction time ρ, make sure that the cars are oriented correctly (driving in the expected direction and car 1 is closer to the lane origin than car 2), and are at a safe distance initially. The `ctrl` program implements the RSS control envelope by setting the accelerations of the cars based on whether the distance between them is safe: the nondeterministic choice in Line 8 expresses the two options of executing `freeDriving` when at a safe distance and evasion maneuver `properResponse` otherwise (we use notation $(a_1, a_2) := \texttt{prg}$ to emphasize that the program `prg` chooses acceleration values a_1 and a_2). At the boundary, either choice is possible. The `motion` program uses a differential equation to model the continuous dynamics of driving in response to the chosen acceleration, modeled through kinematics. Subsequent sections utilize this template to create specific dL models to prove several aspects of RSS safety. First we start with cars driving in the same longitudinal direction.

3.2   Longitudinal Safety

In the longitudinal direction, two cars may either drive in the same direction (a follower car following at a safe distance behind a lead car), or in opposite directions (a narrow road with two-way traffic, or a lead car backing up). We describe both models as instances of the template Model 1, using the sign of their respective longitudinal velocities to determine driving direction. We analyze these driving situations in isolation, under the assumption that a gear change when fully stopped is necessary to transition between these situations, which also allows for switching between the formal models that guide runtime safety.

Same Longitudinal Direction. For two cars driving in the same longitudinal direction, RSS [23] defines a safe distance between these cars with respect to their velocities: if the cars were to drive with worst-case behavior (rear car with the maximum possible acceleration and lead car with the maximum possible deceleration) for the entire reaction time ρ, there would still be enough space for the rear car to come to a full stop before the stopping point of the lead car, i.e., before colliding, see Eq. (1).

$$\texttt{safeDist}_s \triangleq \max(v_1\rho + \frac{1}{2}a_{\text{maxAccel}} + \frac{(v_1 + \rho a_{\text{maxAccel}})^2}{2a_{\text{minBrake}}} - \frac{v_2^2}{2a_{\text{maxBrake}}}, 0) \quad (1)$$

Whenever the cars are not satisfying the safe distance Eq. (1), the cars must execute the proper response behavior as an evasion maneuver. In a leader and follower setup, the follower car is responsible for not hitting the lead car. As a consequence, the proper response allows the lead car to continue with any acceleration or deceleration that does not exceed maximum braking, but requires the follower car to decelerate at rate at least a_{minBrake} [23]. We will now fill in

Model 1 with formulas and programs Eqs. (2)–(4), which gives [12, Model 1].

$$\texttt{freeDriving}_s \triangleq a_1 := *; ?-a_{\text{maxBrake}} \le a_1 \le a_{\text{maxAccel}};$$
$$a_2 := *; ?-a_{\text{maxBrake}} \le a_2 \le a_{\text{maxAccel}} \tag{2}$$
$$\texttt{properResponse}_s \triangleq \left(a_1 := *; ?a_1 \le -a_{\text{minBrake}} \cup ?v_1 = 0; a_1 := 0\right);$$
$$\left(a_2 := *; ?a_2 \ge a_{\text{maxBrake}} \cup ?v_2 = 0; a_2 := 0\right) \tag{3}$$
$$\texttt{edc}_s \triangleq v_1 \ge 0 \wedge v_2 \ge 0 \tag{4}$$

The definition of `properResponse` includes a choice of $a_{1,2} := 0$ if $v_{1,2} = 0$ in order to allow time to pass in the ODE if one or both cars are stopped.

Theorem 1 (Same Longitudinal Safety). *Model 1 with* `safeDist` *as per Eq. (1),* `freeDriving` *as per Eq. (2),* `properResponse` *as per Eq. (3), and* `edc` *as per Eq. (4) is valid.*

Proof. The key insight to this proof is the loop invariant $J \equiv x_1 \le x_2 \wedge x_1 + \frac{v_1^2}{2a_{\text{minBrake}}} \le x_2 + \frac{v_1^2}{2a_{\text{maxBrake}}}$ for proving inductive safety using the loop invariant (LI) rule.

$$\frac{\Gamma \vdash J, \Delta \quad J \vdash P \quad J \vdash [\alpha]J}{\Gamma \vdash [\alpha*]P, \Delta} LI$$

The loop invariant J summarizes that the cars maintain sufficient distance to stop before colliding. The resulting real arithmetic proof obligations become tractable by relating terms of the safe distance formula to terms in the solution of the differential equations using a series of cuts. The details of this proof are in [24]. □

Opposite Longitudinal Direction. The responsibility for collision avoidance is shared among the cars when they drive towards each other (in opposite longitudinal direction on the same lane). Similar to the same longitudinal direction, the safe distance to be maintained in opposite direction driving considers the worst-case behavior for the full reaction time ρ followed by the collision avoidance proper response. In opposite direction, the worst-case behavior is accelerating towards each other with acceleration of a_{maxAccel} for a_1 and $-a_{\text{maxAccel}}$ for a_2 in the opposing direction. For two cars driving with opposite longitudinal velocity signs, let $v_{1,\rho} = v_1 + \rho a_{\text{maxAccel}}$ and $v_{2,\rho} = |v_2| + \rho a_{\text{maxAccel}}$. Then, [23] defines the safe distance in longitudinal opposite direction as in Eq. (5).

$$\texttt{safeDist}_o = \frac{v_1 + v_{1,\rho}}{2}\rho + \frac{(v_{1,\rho})^2}{2a_{\text{minBrake}}} + \frac{v_2 + v_{2,\rho}}{2}\rho + \frac{(v_{2,\rho})^2}{2a_{\text{minBrake}}} \tag{5}$$

In this case, we assume the cars drive towards each other (car 1 driving "forward", i.e., away from the lane origin, car 2 driving "backward", i.e., towards the lane origin, and want both of them to decelerate in the proper response. This differs from the same longitudinal direction case, where only the follower car reacts. In this case, the car driving forward reacts to imminent collision with deceleration $a_1 \leq -a_{\mathrm{minBrake}}$, and the car driving backward reacts with deceleration $a_2 \geq a_{\mathrm{minBrake}}$, formalized in Eqs. (6)–(8).

$$\mathtt{freeDriving}_o \triangleq a_1 := *; ? - a_{\mathrm{maxBrake}} \leq a_1 \leq a_{\mathrm{maxAccel}};$$
$$a_2 := *; ? - a_{\mathrm{maxAccel}} \leq a_2 \leq a_{\mathrm{maxBrake}} \qquad (6)$$
$$\mathtt{properResponse}_o \triangleq \big((a_1 := *; ?a_1 \leq -a_{\mathrm{minBrake}}) \cup (?v_1 = 0; a_1 := 0)\big);$$
$$\big((a_2 := *; ?a_2 \geq a_{\mathrm{minBrake}}) \cup (?v_2 = 0; a_2 := 0)\big) \qquad (7)$$
$$\mathtt{edc}_o \triangleq v_1 \geq 0 \wedge v_2 \leq 0 \qquad (8)$$

Theorem 2 (Opposite Longitudinal Safety). *Model 1 with* $\mathtt{safeDist}_o$ *Eq. (5),* $\mathtt{freeDriving}_o$ *Eq. (6),* $\mathtt{properResponse}_o$ *Eq. (7), and* $\mathtt{edc}_o$ *Eq. (8) is valid.*

Proof. The proof of this model follows a similar structure to the proof of Theorem 1 in the same longitudinal direction. The key insight again is a loop invariant: $J \equiv x_1 \leq x_2 \wedge x_2 - \frac{v_2^2}{2a_{\mathrm{minBrake}}} \geq x_1 + \frac{v_1^2}{2a_{\mathrm{minBrake}}}$. Details of this proof are in [24]. □

3.3   Formalization and Verification of RSS Optimality

This section analyzes whether the safe distance is the minimal safe distance needed to avoid collision. To this end, we encode the rationale behind $\mathtt{safeDist}_s$ and $\mathtt{safeDist}_o$ as a hybrid program, and ask if we were to follow a smaller safe distance, would there exist collisions (which is a liveness property of the shape $P \rightarrow \langle \alpha \rangle Q$). Recall that in both cases, the safe distance was determined by one iteration of worst-case behavior of duration ρ, followed by executing the proper response until both cars are stopped. Model 2 captures this intuition behind the safe distance formulas in a hybrid program: first, the worst-case behavior in Line 5–7 is executed, followed by any number and duration of proper response in Line 8–9. We show that starting from an initial separation of $\mathtt{safeDist} - \varepsilon$ for any arbitrarily small ε, leads to collisions, i.e., we can reach states in which $x_1 > x_2$.

Theorem 3 (Same Longitudinal Optimality). *Model 2 with* $\mathtt{safeDist}$ *as per Eq. (1),* $\mathtt{freeDriving}$ *as per Eq. (2),* $\mathtt{properResponse}$ *as per Eq. (3), and* $\mathtt{edc}$ *as per Eq. (4) is valid.*

Proof. The proof strategy for this case simulates worst case behavior, choosing $a_1 = a_{\mathrm{maxAccel}}$, $a_2 = -a_{\mathrm{minBrake}}$. Unrolling the loop twice enables both cars to come to a complete stop and stay stopped by picking $a_{1,2} = 0$ once stopped. The choice of accelerations and loop unrolling results in a collision. Note that two iterations are necessary in the case that one car stops before the other one does, in order to allow for the stopped car to change its deceleration to $a_{1,2} = 0$ so that the differential equation can be followed without violating the evolution domain constraint $v_{1,2} \geq 0$ until the second car stops. The proof strategy again simplifies

---

Model 2. Minimum Distance Template

---

init	1	`init` per Model 1
	2	$\wedge\, \varepsilon > 0$
	3	$\wedge\, \texttt{safeDist}(v_1, v_2) - \varepsilon = x2 - x1 \rightarrow$
	4	$\langle\,($
worst case	5	`freeDriving`;
	6	$t := 0;$
	7	$\{x_1{}' = v_1,\ x_2{}' = v_2,\ v_1{}' = a_1,\ v_2{}' = a_2,\ t' = 1\ \&\ t \leq \rho \wedge \texttt{edc}\}$
attempt evade	8	$(\texttt{properResponse};$
	9	$\{x_1{}' = v_1,\ x_2{}' = v_2,\ v_1{}' = a_1,\ v_2{}' = a_2,\ t' = 1\ \&\ \texttt{edc}\})^{*}$
unsafe	10	$)\rangle\,(x_1 > x_2)$

---

arithmetic proof obligations by matching terms in the safe distance formula with terms in the solution of the differential equation. Since the distance between the cars is initially equal to safe distance reduced by an arbitrarily small ε, using Theorem 1 we conclude that the minimum safe distance between the two cars is characterized by Eq. (1). $\qquad\square$

Theorem 4 (Opposite Longitudinal Optimality). *Model 2 with* `safeDist` *as per Eq. (5),* `freeDriving` *as per Eq. (6),* `properResponse` *as per Eq. (7), and* `edc` *as per Eq. (8) is valid.*

Proof. The proof strategy follows Theorem 3: we again choose worst case behaviors of both cars, namely both cars driving toward each other at maximum acceleration. $\qquad\square$

4 Refinement from dL to Python

The previous section proves correctness of control decisions in all situations using dL under an assumed model of car dynamics. Increased model fidelity often comes at the price of higher verification effort. For example, if we wanted to consider tire friction, the dynamical motion model would no longer have symbolic closed-form solutions, but would require advanced differential equation reasoning [21]. In order to determine whether a model is sufficiently realistic, and to test concrete implementation behavior in specific situations (e.g., how abruptly a car would brake when encountering obstacles), we now discuss refinement to deterministic implementation and simulation. This provides a way of showing fidelity evidence for models to complement the safety evidence, and to debug unverified models.

In formal models, nondeterminism is beneficial to model a large variety of concrete implementations at an abstract level: nondeterministic choice of acceleration in the controllers, nondeterministic number of loop iterations, and nondeterministic duration of ODEs within each loop iteration capture variation in total driving time and behavior. For execution and testing purposes, deterministic behavior is beneficial to produce repeatable, predictable, and comprehensible results. In order to generate control code, integrate with testing, and ensure that a simulation of a system follows its formal model, we select a deterministic subset of hybrid programs to introduce an intermediate language that can then be directly compiled to Python. This language, det-HP, supports assignment, deterministic choice (defined from nondeterministic choice and tests), and loops (defined from nondeterministic repetition and tests). The deterministic subset det-HP of hybrid programs is generated by the grammar below, where θ is an arithmetic term in $+, -, \cdot, /$ and P is a quantifier-free formula in real arithmetic:

$$\alpha, \beta := x := \theta \mid \alpha; \beta \mid \underbrace{(?P; \alpha) \cup (?\neg P; \beta)}_{\text{if } P \text{ } \alpha \text{ else } \beta} \mid \underbrace{(?P; \alpha)^*; ?\neg P}_{\text{while } P \text{ } \alpha}$$

Starting from the formal models in Sect. 3, we need a way of resolving the following points of nondeterminism when examining the behavior of these models: First, the nondeterministic choice between free driving and proper response at the boundary of the safe distance region needs to be resolved (e.g., aggressively by favoring freeDriving, or conservatively by favoring properResponse). Second, the nondeterministic choice of acceleration value in both freeDriving and properResponse must be resolved with a deterministic computation of acceleration within the acceleration bounds (e.g., a bang-bang controller implementation will only choose the values of $a_{\text{maxAccel}}, a_{\text{minBrake}}$, and a_{maxBrake}). Third, the nondeterministic duration of differential equations and hence the nondeterministic control cycle time must be resolved (e.g., conservatively by picking the maximum reaction time ρ, but not violating the remaining conditions of the evolution domain constraint). Fourth, the nondeterministic number of repetitions must be resolved (e.g., by picking a test length or a finite amount of time to be followed). Note that the model parameter choices and initial values for variables are not sources of nondeterminism as they are symbolically defined and preset.

We now illustrate det-HP with a deterministic controller freeDriving-det that chooses the same acceleration for every iteration of freeDriving below:

$$\text{freeDriving-det} \triangleq a_1 := a_{\text{maxAccel}}; a_2 := -a_{\text{maxBrake}}$$

In order to inherit Theorem 1, we use dRL to prove that freeDriving-det reaches a subset of the states of freeDriving$_s$ Eq. (2).

Theorem 5 (Refinement). *The deterministic free driving controller refines the RSS free driving control envelope, i.e., freeDriving-det $\leq$ freeDriving$_s$ Eq. (2) is valid under assumptions $\Gamma \equiv a_{maxAccel} > 0 \wedge a_{maxBrake} > 0$.*

Proof. We prove by refinement in dRL. Let $P \equiv -a_{\text{maxBrake}} \leq a_1 \leq a_{\text{maxAccel}}$ and $Q \equiv -a_{\text{maxBrake}} \leq a_2 \leq a_{\text{maxAccel}}$:

$$\cfrac{\mathbf{B1} \quad \cfrac{\cfrac{\cfrac{*}{\Gamma, a_1 = a_{\mathrm{maxAccel}}, a_2 = -a_{\mathrm{maxBrake}} \vdash \top \to P} \; \mathbb{R}}{\Gamma, a_1 = a_{\mathrm{maxAccel}}, a_2 = -a_{\mathrm{maxBrake}} \vdash ?\top \leq P} \; ?}{\Gamma \vdash [a_1 := a_{\mathrm{maxAccel}}; a_2 := -a_{\mathrm{maxBrake}}]?\top \leq P} \; :=}{\Gamma \vdash a_1 := a_{\mathrm{maxAccel}}; a_2 := -a_{\mathrm{maxBrake}} \leq a_1 := *; ?P; a_2 := *; ?Q} \; ;$$

$$\cfrac{\cfrac{\cfrac{*}{\Gamma \vdash a_1 := a_{\mathrm{maxAccel}} \leq a_1 := *} \; * \quad \cfrac{\cfrac{*}{\Gamma, a_1 = a_{\mathrm{maxAccel}} \vdash a_2 := -a_{\mathrm{maxBrake}} \leq a_2 := *}}{\Gamma \vdash [a_1 := a_{\mathrm{maxAccel}}](a_2 := -a_{\mathrm{maxBrake}} \leq a_2 := *)} \; *}{\Gamma \vdash \{a_1 := a_{\mathrm{maxAccel}}; a_2 := -a_{\mathrm{maxBrake}}\} \leq \{a_1 := *; a_2 := *\}} \; :=}{\mathbf{B1}} \; ;$$

In this proof we utilize the test, sequential and assignment rules [13] to show that each step that the deterministic controller takes is within the bounds that the nondeterministic controller sets. The main insight is that deterministic assignments are refinements of unguarded nondeterministic assignments.   □

The intermediate language `det-HP` serves as a stepping stone towards compilation to Python. We introduce the compilation rules in Fig. 2, where we use the following subset of the Python expression and statement syntax [8] (for simplicity, we will ignore the difference between $\mathbb{R}$ and Float, which can be addressed with interval arithmetic [3]):

pexpr := true | false | $z \in \mathbb{Z}$ | $x \in$ Float

$\quad$ | $-$pexpr | pexpr $\circ$ pexpr | pexpr $\bullet$ pexpr

$\quad$ | not pexpr | pexpr and pexpr | pexpr or pexpr

pprg := x=pexpr | if pexpr: pprg else: pprg | while pexpr: pprg | pprg; pprg

The simplified syntax uses arithmetic operators $\circ \in \{\texttt{+}, \texttt{-}, \texttt{*}, \texttt{/}, \texttt{**}\}$ and comparison operators $\bullet \in \{\texttt{<}, \texttt{<=}, \texttt{>=}, \texttt{>}, \texttt{==}, \texttt{!=}\}$. The compilation from deterministic hybrid programs to the restricted Python syntax preserves safety, see Lemmas 1–2 and Theorem 6. We abbreviate arithmetic evaluation [8] as $\mathsf{eval}(\mathsf{Py}(\theta))_\nu \to u$ to real value u and Boolean evaluation as $\nu(\mathsf{bool}\ \mathsf{Py}(\theta)) \to v$ to Boolean value v.

Lemma 1 (Term compilation is correct). *Assuming Float* $= \mathbb{R}$*, terms evaluate equivalently, i.e., if* $\mathsf{eval}(\mathsf{Py}(\theta))_\nu \to u$ *then* $\nu[\![\theta]\!] = u$.

Proof. By structural induction over dL terms, see [24].   □

Lemma 2 (Formula compilation is correct). *Formulas evaluate equivalently, i.e.,* $\nu \models \phi$ *iff* $\nu(\mathsf{bool}\ \mathsf{Py}(\phi)) \to \mathtt{true}$.

Proof. By structural induction over dL formulas, see [24].   □

Theorem 6 (Compilation of `det-HP` to Python is correct). *All states that are reachable with the compiled Python program are also reachable by the source HP program, i.e.* $(\mathsf{Py}(\alpha), \nu) \to (\bot, \omega)$ *then* $(\nu, \omega) \in [\![\alpha]\!]$.

Programs

$$\mathsf{Py}(x := \theta) \rhd \mathsf{Py}(x)\text{=}\mathsf{Py}(\theta)$$
$$\mathsf{Py}(?P; \alpha \cup ?\neg P; \beta) \rhd \texttt{if } \mathsf{Py}(P)\texttt{: } \mathsf{Py}(\alpha) \texttt{ else: } \mathsf{Py}(\beta)$$
$$\mathsf{Py}(\{?P; \alpha\}^*; ?\neg P) \rhd \texttt{while } \mathsf{Py}(P) \texttt{ : } \mathsf{Py}(\alpha) \texttt{ else pass}$$

Arithmetic

$\mathsf{Py}(z) \rhd \texttt{z}$	for number literal z
$\mathsf{Py}(x) \rhd \texttt{x}$	for variable x
$\mathsf{Py}(\theta + \eta) \rhd \mathsf{Py}(\theta)\texttt{+}\mathsf{Py}(\eta)$	
$\mathsf{Py}(\theta - \eta) \rhd \mathsf{Py}(\theta)\texttt{-}\mathsf{Py}(\eta)$	
$\mathsf{Py}(\theta \cdot \eta) \rhd \mathsf{Py}(\theta)\texttt{*}\mathsf{Py}(\eta)$	
$\mathsf{Py}(\frac{\theta}{\eta}) \rhd \mathsf{Py}(\theta)\texttt{/}\mathsf{Py}(\eta)$	
$\mathsf{Py}(\theta^\eta) \rhd \mathsf{Py}(\theta)\texttt{**}\mathsf{Py}(\eta)$	

Boolean

$\mathsf{Py}(\top) \rhd \texttt{True}$	
$\mathsf{Py}(\bot) \rhd \texttt{False}$	
$\mathsf{Py}(\theta < \eta) \rhd \mathsf{Py}(\theta)\texttt{<}\mathsf{Py}(\eta)$	similar for $\leq, =, \neq, \geq, >$
$\mathsf{Py}(\neg P) \rhd \texttt{not } \mathsf{Py}(P)$	
$\mathsf{Py}(P \wedge Q) \rhd \mathsf{Py}(P) \texttt{ and } \mathsf{Py}(Q)$	
$\mathsf{Py}(P \vee Q) \rhd \mathsf{Py}(P) \texttt{ or } \mathsf{Py}(Q)$	

Fig. 2. `det-HP` to Python compilation rules

Proof. By structural induction over hybrid programs, see [24].   □

Theorem 6 ensures that any state reached in a compiled Python program will also be reachable in the source `det-HP` program. Together with the refinement step from our original model, we therefore know that any counterexample found in the compiled simulation will also be a counterexample of the original formal dL model.

5   Testing and Monitoring by Example

The previous sections introduced safety verification and refinement proofs that eliminate the need for correctness testing. These two steps, if completed, assure that the system is safe under all implementations. In this section, we consider testing and simulation as a method to provide insight for correcting the formal model and/or an implementation when either of these steps fails, and as a way to assess the fidelity of the formal model and experiment with model parameter selection once the proofs are completed.

5.1   Monitor Structure

In order to assess whether the simulation and the formal model agree and flag differences, we utilize ModelPlex [17]. ModelPlex monitors are formally verified and derived automatically from a hybrid systems model; they flag whenever states encountered at runtime (e.g., in simulation) disagree with the expectations of the formal model. For this, the monitors collect the relationship between starting and final states along all possible execution paths of the formal model. For example, a monitor derived from the discrete statements of Model 1 as instantiated in Theorem 1 is illustrated below (variables of the initial state are x, y, z, variables of the final state are x^+, y^+, z^+).

$$(\texttt{safeDist}_s(v_1, v_2) \leq x_2 - x_1 \wedge -a_{\text{maxBrake}} \leq a_1^+ \leq a_{\text{maxAccel}}$$
$$\wedge -a_{\text{maxBrake}} \leq a_2^+ \leq a_{\text{maxAccel}} \wedge t^+ = 0 \wedge \texttt{edc}_s)$$
$$\vee (\texttt{safeDist}_s(v_1, v_2) \geq x_2 - x_1 \wedge (a_1^+ \leq -a_{\text{minBrake}} \vee (v_1 = 0 \wedge a_1^+ = 0))$$
$$\wedge (a_2^+ \geq a_{\text{maxBrake}} \vee (v_2 = 0 \wedge a_2^+ = 0)) \wedge t^+ = 0 \wedge \texttt{edc}_s)$$

5.2   Examples of Monitor Usage

Monitoring for Faulty Implementation. Our first example illustrates the use of testing and monitoring when the refinement proof cannot be completed due to an incorrect implementation. With user-defined test scenarios, ModelPlex monitors in simulation highlight the vulnerabilities of the controller implementation as an intermediate step towards finding implementation fixes and completing the refinement proof. In this case, counterexamples found in simulation represent control decisions of the unverified controller implementation that violate the expectations of the formal model. In Fig. 3, a front and a rear car are driving in the same direction, while the rear car follows a faulty controller. The user-defined test scenario is an example of a boundary test by picking worst case behavior where the rear car is accelerating at maximum acceleration whenever allowed

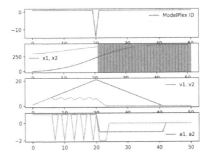

Fig. 3. Leader-follower same direction test scenario, with rear car control implementation violating the conditions of RSS. Plots from top to bottom are: ModelPlex monitor verdict, car positions x_1, x_2, car speeds v_1, v_2, and accelerations a_1, a_2.

by its control guards. The ModelPlex monitor derived from Model 1 with the formulas and programs of Theorem 1 fails at the point of violating RSS: executing the proper response instead of the faulty controller at time time of the monitor alarm would have prevented collision, but following the faulty controller makes the rear car exceed the front car's position (i.e., cause a collision). The monitor verdict ("ModelPlex ID" in Fig. 3) flags the violated condition of the monitor, which directly relates to a path through the formal model: the faulty controller allowed to continue accelerating forward for one more time step when it should have been following the proper response already. In this case, a boundary test reveals the controller implementation flaw, but other implementation bugs are more subtle and require extensive search. For future work, we envision integration of monitors with falsification techniques.

Monitoring for Modeling Flaws. With a setup similar to monitoring for faulty implementations, we address modeling flaws in unverified models. User-defined test scenarios allow us to examine the behavior of the formal model through monitors: the formal model is faulty when finding scenarios that end in collision without a prior ModelPlex monitor alarm. In this case, the insight for fixing the bug is not merely the (missing) monitor alarm itself, but the sequence of control actions that lead up to the collision.

Parameter Selection. The last example we include illustrates how to use tests for parameter selection once the formal model and the refinement to a concrete controller implementation is proved. The concrete choices for the symbolic parameters, such as $a_{maxBrake}$, $a_{minBrake}$, $a_{maxAccel}$, and ρ, heavily influence the specific behavior of the controller implementation. Simulation with specific parameter choices is a useful technique to inspect the expected real-world behavior, and completes the circle of interaction between formal methods and testing. Formal methods guarantee correctness in a model of physics, refinement proofs and correct compilation guarantee correctness of implementations, and simulation and testing allow for inspecting the fidelity of the formal model and the concrete behavior of the implementation under specific parameter choices. In Fig. 4 we

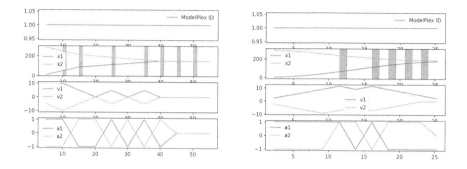

Fig. 4. Car behavior in opposite direction model at $\rho = 1$ (left) and $\rho = 6$ (right).

consider parameter selection and its effect on the behavior of cars in the opposite direction scenario. The controllers of both cars in free driving accelerate towards each other at maximum acceleration and in proper response they both brake at minimum rate. With a "short" response horizon of $\rho = 1$, the final distance between the cars once fully stopped is much lower than when a response $\rho = 6$.

6   Related Work

RSS introduced in [23] has been deployed by the Mobileye research group as the basis for their self-driving car and analyzed extensively from different aspects for its safety and reliablity: [18] considers parameter analysis and concrete behavior of RSS on German highways; [9] extends RSS fidelity by applying Newtonian mechanics to analyze car behavior on slopes and in varying road conditions.

Related work within formal verification of driving models is extensive: [16] utilize a formula equivalent to the same direction safe distance formula introduced by RSS for an adaptive cruise control system, [14] analyze collision avoidance while following Dubin's paths, [4] and [10] formally verify waypoint navigation, [1] verify swerving maneuvers to avoid collision, [22] develops a formally verified motion planner, [2,11] use reachability analysis in highway settings and introduce a toolbox to create simulated driving environments to determine reachable sets, [7] is close to our work in that it uses falsification to find mistakes in motion plans of autonomous vehicles. We complement these approaches by providing proofs of optimality of the RSS safety conditions and proofs of opposite driving direction, combined with refinement proofs and correct compilation to Python for testing.

7   Conclusion and Future Work

In this paper we formalized and proved safety as well as optimality of the Responsibility-Sensitive Safety control envelopes in both longitudinal directions. The safety proofs discover loop invariants, which concisely document design properties of the system. These properties of the longitudinal cases do not transfer to the lateral case in a straightforward way, because velocity direction changes do not require an intermediate stop such as a gear change; formalizing and verifying the lateral case is an area of future research.

To complement the safety guarantees of formal verification with practical tools to test and debug unverified models, as well as to assess the fidelity of verified models in specific driving situations and under specific parameter choices, we introduce refinement proofs and correct compilation from nondeterministic models to deterministic implementations in Python. Formal methods guarantee correctness in a model of physics, refinement proofs and correct compilation guarantee correctness of implementations, and simulation and testing allow for inspecting the fidelity of the formal model and the concrete behavior of the implementation under specific parameter choices. Future research includes combination with falsification methods to provide a systematic automated approach to testing of unverified models in differential dynamic logic.

Acknowledgements. This material is based upon work supported by the National Science Foundation under Grant No. CCF2220311.

References

1. Abhishek, A., Sood, H., Jeannin, J.: Formal verification of swerving maneuvers for car collision avoidance. In: 2020 American Control Conference, ACC 2020, Denver, CO, USA, 1–3 July 2020, pp. 4729–4736 (2020). https://doi.org/10.23919/ACC45564.2020.9147679
2. Althoff, M., Koschi, M., Manzinger, S.: CommonRoad: composable benchmarks for motion planning on roads. In: 2017 IEEE Intelligent Vehicles Symposium (IV), pp. 719–726 (2017). https://doi.org/10.1109/IVS.2017.7995802
3. Bohrer, R., Tan, Y.K., Mitsch, S., Myreen, M.O., Platzer, A.: VeriPhy: verified controller executables from verified cyber-physical system models. In: PLDI, pp. 617–630 (2018). https://doi.org/10.1145/3192366.3192406
4. Bohrer, R., Tan, Y.K., Mitsch, S., Sogokon, A., Platzer, A.: A formal safety net for waypoint-following in ground robots. IEEE Robot. Autom. Lett. **4**(3), 2910–2917 (2019). https://doi.org/10.1109/LRA.2019.2923099
5. Fulton, N., Mitsch, S., Quesel, J., Völp, M., Platzer, A.: KeYmaera X: an axiomatic tactical theorem prover for hybrid systems. In: Proceedings of the 25th International Conference on Automated Deduction, CADE-25, Berlin, Germany, 1–7 August 2015, pp. 527–538 (2015). https://doi.org/10.1007/978-3-319-21401-6_36
6. Gallicchio, J., Tan, Y.K., Mitsch, S., Platzer, A.: Implicit definitions with differential equations for KeYmaera X - (system description). In: Proceedings of the 11th International Joint Conference on Automated Reasoning, IJCAR 2022, Haifa, Israel, 8–10 August 2022, pp. 723–733 (2022). https://doi.org/10.1007/978-3-031-10769-6_42
7. Klischat, M., Althoff, M.: Falsifying motion plans of autonomous vehicles with abstractly specified traffic scenarios. IEEE Trans. Intell. Veh. **8**(2), 1717–1730 (2023). https://doi.org/10.1109/TIV.2022.3191179
8. Köhl, M.A.: An executable structural operational formal semantics for Python. CoRR abs/2109.03139 (2021)
9. Koopman, P., Osyk, B., Weast, J.: Autonomous vehicles meet the physical world: RSS, variability, uncertainty, and proving safety. In: Proceedings of the 38th International Conference on Computer Safety, Reliability, and Security, SAFECOMP 2019, Turku, Finland, 11–13 September 2019, pp. 245–253 (2019). https://doi.org/10.1007/978-3-030-26601-1_17
10. Kopylov, A., Mitsch, S., Nogin, A., Warren, M.: Formally verified safety net for waypoint navigation neural network controllers. In: Proceedings of the 24th International Symposium on Formal Methods, FM 2021, Virtual Event, 20–26 November 2021, pp. 122–141 (2021). https://doi.org/10.1007/978-3-030-90870-6_7
11. Liu, E.I., Würsching, G., Klischat, M., Althoff, M.: CommonRoad-Reach: a toolbox for reachability analysis of automated vehicles. In: 25th IEEE International Conference on Intelligent Transportation Systems, ITSC 2022, Macau, China, 8–12 October 2022, pp. 2313–2320 (2022). https://doi.org/10.1109/ITSC55140.2022.9922232
12. Loos, S.M., Platzer, A.: Safe intersections: at the crossing of hybrid systems and verification. In: 14th International IEEE Conference on Intelligent Transportation Systems, ITSC 2011, Washington, DC, USA, 5–7 October 2011, pp. 1181–1186 (2011). https://doi.org/10.1109/ITSC.2011.6083138

13. Loos, S.M., Platzer, A.: Differential refinement logic. In: Proceedings of the 31st Annual ACM/IEEE Symposium on Logic in Computer Science (2016). https://doi.org/10.1145/2933575.2934555

14. Mitsch, S., Ghorbal, K., Vogelbacher, D., Platzer, A.: Formal verification of obstacle avoidance and navigation of ground robots. Int. J. Robot. Res. **36**(12), 1312–1340 (2017). https://doi.org/10.1177/0278364917733549

15. Mitsch, S., Jin, X., Zhan, B., Wang, S., Zhan, N.: ARCH-COMP21 category report: hybrid systems theorem proving. In: 8th International Workshop on Applied Verification of Continuous and Hybrid Systems (ARCH21), Brussels, Belgium, 9 July 2021, pp. 120–132 (2021). https://doi.org/10.29007/35cf

16. Mitsch, S., Loos, S.M., Platzer, A.: Towards formal verification of freeway traffic control. In: 2012 IEEE/ACM 3rd International Conference on Cyber-Physical Systems, ICCPS 2012, Beijing, China, 17–19 April 2012, pp. 171–180 (2012). https://doi.org/10.1109/ICCPS.2012.25

17. Mitsch, S., Platzer, A.: ModelPlex: verified runtime validation of verified cyber-physical system models. Formal Meth. Syst. Des. **49**(1–2), 33–74 (2016). https://doi.org/10.1007/s10703-016-0241-z

18. Naumann, M., et al.: On responsibility sensitive safety in car-following situations - a parameter analysis on German highways. In: 2021 IEEE Intelligent Vehicles Symposium IV, Nagoya, Japan, 11–17 July 2021, pp. 83–90 (2021). https://doi.org/10.1109/IV48863.2021.9575420

19. Platzer, A.: The complete proof theory of hybrid systems. In: LICS, pp. 541–550. IEEE (2012). https://doi.org/10.1109/LICS.2012.64

20. Platzer, A.: A complete uniform substitution calculus for differential dynamic logic. J. Autom. Reason. **59**(2), 219–265 (2016). https://doi.org/10.1007/s10817-016-9385-1

21. Platzer, A., Tan, Y.K.: Differential equation invariance axiomatization. J. ACM **67**(1), 6:1-6:66 (2020). https://doi.org/10.1145/3380825

22. Rizaldi, A., Immler, F., Schürmann, B., Althoff, M.: A formally verified motion planner for autonomous vehicles. In: Proceedings of the 16th International Symposium on Automated Technology for Verification and Analysis, ATVA 2018, Los Angeles, CA, USA, 7–10 October 2018, pp. 75–90 (2018). https://doi.org/10.1007/978-3-030-01090-4_5

23. Shalev-Shwartz, S., Shammah, S., Shashua, A.: On a formal model of safe and scalable self-driving cars. CoRR abs/1708.06374 (2017)

24. Strauss, M., Mitsch, S.: Slow down, move over: a case study in formal verification, refinement, and testing of the responsibility-sensitive safety model for self-driving cars. CoRR abs/2305.08812 (2023)

25. Strauss, M., Mitsch, S.: Slow down, move over: a case study in formal verification, refinement, and testing of the responsibility-sensitive safety model for self-driving cars (models and proofs) (2023). https://doi.org/10.1184/R1/22825304

Abstract Interpretation of Recursive Logic Definitions for Efficient Runtime Assertion Checking

Thibaut Benajmin[ID] and Julien Signoles[✉][ID]

Université Paris-Saclay, CEA, List, Palaiseau, France
`julien.signoles@cea.fr`

Abstract. Runtime Assertion Checking (RAC) is a lightweight formal method for verifying at runtime code properties written in a formal specification language. One of the main challenge of RAC is to check the properties efficiently, while emitting sound verdicts. In particular, arithmetic properties are only efficiently verified using machine integers, yet soundness can only be achieved by using an exact but slower exact arithmetic library. This paper presents how E-ACSL, a RAC tool for C programs, applies abstract interpretation for efficiently and soundly supporting arithmetic properties. Abstract interpretation provides sound static information regarding the size of terms involved in runtime assertions in order to choose at compile time whether machine integers or exact arithmetic will be used at runtime on a case by case basis. Our specification language includes recursive user-defined logic functions and predicates, for which we rely on fast fixpoint operators based on widening of abstract values.

1 Introduction

Runtime Assertion Checking (RAC) is a lightweigth formal method that consists in checking at runtime formal properties written as code annotations [7]. For this purpose, a RAC tool usually takes a source code (or bytecode) program p as input and generates as output an inline monitor that observes each p's execution. An inline monitor means that the (source, byte or binary) code of the monitor is part of the observed program: the generated chunks of code interleave with pieces of code of the original program [10]. This paper focuses on E-ACSL [20], the RAC tool of Frama-C [1], an analysis framework for code written in C. The formal properties are written in a variant of the ACSL specification language [2], also named E-ACSL and dedicated to runtime checking [9]. The E-ACSL tool takes as input a C program annotated with E-ACSL specifications and generates a new C program in which the formal annotations have been converted to C code.

E-ACSL aims at satisfying four key properties, that are quite usual for RAC tools: *expressivity*, *transparency*, *soundness*, and *efficiency*. *Expressivity* means that the more properties a RAC tool can check the better. *Transparency* means that the inline monitor must not modify the functional behavior of the original

V. Prevosto and C. Seceleanu (Eds.): TAP 2023, LNCS 14066, pp. 168–186, 2023.
https://doi.org/10.1007/978-3-031-38828-6_10

program: when the checked properties are all satisfied, the monitored program must produce the same output as the unmonitored program. Transparency is out-of-scope in this paper. *Soundness* means that the inline monitor must emit correct verdicts when checking properties. *Efficiency* means that the inline monitor must run as efficiently as possible: the time and memory overheads of the monitored program with respect to the unmonitored program must remain as low as possible. It also means that generating the code of the monitor must be efficient enough. In our context, being "efficient enough" for generating the code means being as efficient as standard optimizing compilers.

Regarding expressivity, we focus here on integer properties only. E-ACSL is based on integer arithmetics in $\mathbb{Z}$, the set of mathematical integers, which allows users to specify arithmetic properties without implementation details in mind: assuming x is a C variable of type int and n is an integer constant, x + n can never overflow in a formal property, although it might in C code. The formal properties can also call user-defined possibly-recursive logic functions and predicates. Such definitions allow users to specify once complex parameterized computations and properties and use them several times.

Such an expressivity leads to an issue regarding efficiency and soundness. Indeed, using mathematical integers requires to rely on a dedicated exact arithmetic library, such as GMP[1] in C, for generating correct code, while using machine bounded integers would be much better for efficiency. For taking the best of both worlds and being both correct and efficient, E-ACSL relies on a dedicated static analysis that allows it to use efficient machine bounded integers when it is safe to do so and inefficient-yet-correct exact arithmetics otherwise. The static analysis is itself efficient and thus allows E-ACSL to generate the efficient code efficiently: even if based on abstract interpretation [8], it only uses the simple interval domain and a fast widening operator that scale extremely well, yet is precise enough for our need. Therefore, it reaches the goal of being as efficient as standard optimizing compilers, contrary to most existing abstract interpreters that target proving properties such as absence of bugs. **This paper presents this static analysis in the presence of recursive logic definitions, proves its correctness and shows experimentally how it helps E-ACSL to generate efficient C code.** Although focusing on E-ACSL, our contributions can be applied on other contexts: they can be applied to any runtime system that must deal with mathematical numbers, including other runtime assertion checkers, different kinds of runtime verification tools, or simulators.

This work is the last item of a series of works about formalizing E-ACSL. In particular, it extends the work of Kosmatov et al [13] to logic definitions. To do so, it requires to move from a type-system based setting to an abstract-interpretation based setting to deal with recursive definitions soundly and precisely. This way, we improve a recently published paper [3] that formalizes the E-ACSL's code generator for the very same language fragment, assuming a sound static analysis. Indeed, the static analysis is presented in detail here, while we also prove the assumptions of [3] about soundness of the analysis and push for-

---

[1] http://gmplib.org.

ward the experimental evaluation about efficiency. As far as we know, no other prior work targets recursive logic definitions for runtime assertion checking.

Ly et al. formalized another subset of E-ACSL, targeting memory properties [16,17]. Their works are complementary to ours. Beyond E-ACSL, Cheon [6] was the first to formally study RAC, in the context of JML [14], a formal specification language for Java. He did not focus his work on integer arithmetic since, at that time, the JML's arithmetic was exactly the machine arithmetic. Later, Lehner [15] formalized in Coq a large subset of the JML's semantics. He also formalized a RAC algorithm for the JML's `assignable` clause, which is independent from, but compatible with, our integer properties. More recently, Filliâtre and Pascutto [11] proposed Ortac, a RAC tool for OCaml. It relies on a similar mechanism to ours for generating efficient arithmetic code, but without details nor formalization for that part. They also do not deal with logic definitions. Recently, they formally studied how to optimize referring to the pre-state from the post-state of a function [12]. This work is complementary to ours.

Section 2 presents an overview of our work on a concrete example. Section 3 introduces the programming and specification languages supporting our formalization. Section 4 details our static analysis without considering logic definitions. Section 5 extends it to the whole considered languages and presents our formal results. Section 6 presents our experimental evaluation.

2   Illustrated Overview

Figure 1 shows an example of an annotated program together with a simplified version of the instrumented code generated by E-ACSL. For the sake of simplicity, we assume that the program is executed on an 8-bit architecture, where the type int ranges from -128 to 127, and that there is no machine integer type greater than this. In this example, three assertions are translated. For the first one, the translation is straightforward, as it suffices to replace the assertion with the exact same assertion in C. The second one is more complex: since the addition it involves overflows in the machine integers, we rely on the GMP library, which provides exact integer arithmetic. The last assertion is the most complex since it calls a user-defined recursive function. Its translation generates a C function that specializes this ACSL function, while keeping track of the size of the numbers involved to use either machine integers or GMP. This article presents a static analysis based on abstract interpretation whose purpose is to provide the information required to decide whether a particular term can soundly be translated using machine integer or must rely on inefficient GMP integers.

3   Language Definition

The formal presentation of the paper focuses on a core arithmetic subset of the C language, called mini-C. mini-C programs may contain formal annotations written in a subset of the ACSL specification language [2], called mini-ACSL. Its main feature is the support of user-defined logic functions and predicates, including mutually recursive ones.

```
1 /*@ logic integer f (integer x) = x <= 0 ? 0 : f(x - 1) + 1; */
2 void main () {
3    //@ assert 10 + 20 == 30;
4    //@ assert 120 + 30 == 150;
5    //@ assert f (50) == 50;
6 }                                    (a) Annotated Program
```

```
1  void _f(mpz_t *_res, int x);
2  void main(void) {
3     assert(10 + 20 == 30);
4     { mpz_t _a, _b, _c, _add; int eq;
5       mpz_init_set_si(_a, 120); mpz_init_set_si(_b, 30);
6       mpz_init_set_str(_c,"30"); mpz_init(_add);
7       mpz_add(_add, _a, _b);
8       eq = mpz_cmp(_add, _c);
9       assert (eq == 0);
10      mpz_clear(_a); mpz_clear(_b); mpz_clear(_c); mpz_clear(_add); }
11    { _mpz_t _f_1, _x_1; int eq_2;
12      _f(& _f_1,50);
13      mpz_init_set_si(_x_3,50L);
14      eq_2 = mpz_cmp(_f_1,x_1);
15      assert (eq_2 == 0);
16      mpz_clear(_f_1); mpz_clear(_x_1); }
17 }
18 void _f(_mpz_t *_res, int x) {
19    if (x <= 0) { mpz_init_set_si(*res, 0); }
20    else { mpz_t _f_2, _x;
21      _f(& _f_2,x - 1);
22      mpz_init_set_si(_x,1L); mpz_init(*res);
23      mpz_add(*res,_f_2, _x);
24      mpz_clear(_f_2); mpz_clear(_x); }
25 }
                                       (b) Instrumented Program
```

Fig. 1. Example of an Annotated Program and its Instrumented Version.

3.1   Formal Syntax

Figure 2 presents the syntax of the languages mini-C and mini-ACSL together, as they mutually depend on each other. An annotated mini-C program is a sequence of program variables declarations, followed by a sequence of function definitions, which may be either a mini-C function, or a user-defined logic function or predicate epxressed in the mini-ACSL language. For simplicity, we assume that the only type of mini-C is int, i.e. bounded machine integers: our results can easily be extended to a language with more bounded integer types. The program functions are made of statements that include standard control flow structures, such as loops and conditionals, as well as arithmetic operations. The statements also include logical assertions, expressed in the mini-ACSL specification language. Assertions are propositional predicates over mathematical (unbounded) integer terms. Terms and predicates may include calls to user-defined logic functions and predicates, which can be (mutually) recursive. Syntactically, no restriction is put on the recursion scheme of functions and predicates.

3.2   Program Structure

We assume that all the programs given as inputs are syntactically well-formed and properly typed, even if the type system is omitted here. We denote $\mathcal{V}$ the

$$p ::= d^* \ f^*$$ annotated program
$$d ::= \texttt{int id};$$ program declaration
$$f ::= \texttt{int id}(d^*)\{d^*; s_c\}$$ program function
$$\mid \ /\!*@ \ \texttt{logic} \ \tau \ \texttt{id}(\delta^*) = t \ *\!/$$ logic function
$$\mid \ /\!*@ \ \texttt{predicate id}(\delta^*) = p \ *\!/$$ predicate
$$s_c ::= \texttt{skip};$$ empty statement
$$\mid \ \texttt{id} = e;$$ assignment
$$\mid \ \texttt{id} = \texttt{id}(e^*);$$ function call
$$\mid \ s \ s$$ sequence
$$\mid \ \texttt{if}(e) \ s \ \texttt{else} \ s$$ conditional
$$\mid \ \texttt{while}(e) \ s$$ loop
$$\mid \ \texttt{assert}(e);$$ program assertion
$$\mid \ /\!*@ \ \texttt{assert} \ p \ *\!/$$ logic assertion
$$\mid \ \texttt{return}(e);$$ return statement
$$e ::= z_m$$ machine integer
$$\mid \ \texttt{id}$$ variable access
$$\mid \ e \ \diamond_c \ e$$ $\diamond_c \in \{+; -; *; /\}$
$$\mid \ e \ \lhd_c \ e$$ $\lhd_c \in \{<; <=; >; >=; ==; !=\}$

$$\delta ::= \tau \ \texttt{id}$$ logic declaration
$$p ::= \texttt{\textbackslash true} \mid \texttt{\textbackslash false}$$ truth values
$$\mid \ t \lhd t$$ $\lhd \in \{<; \leq; >; \geq; \overset{?}{=}; \neq\}$
$$\mid \ ! \ t$$ negation
$$\mid \ p \mid\mid p$$ disjunction
$$\mid \ \texttt{id}(\delta^*)$$ predicate call
$$t ::= z$$ integer in $\mathbb{Z}$
$$\mid \ \texttt{id}$$ variable access
$$\mid \ t \diamond t$$ $\diamond \in \{+; -; \times; /\}$
$$\mid \ p \ ? \ t : t$$ conditional term
$$\mid \ \texttt{id}(\delta^*)$$ function call
$$\kappa ::= \texttt{int} \mid \texttt{integer}$$ logic types

Fig. 2. Syntax of mini-C (left) and mini-ACSL (right).

set of program variables and $\mathcal{S}$ the set of statements, as well as $\mathfrak{L}$ the set of logic binders (i.e., the logic variables introduced as parameters of user-defined logic functions and predicates), $\mathfrak{Z}$ the set of logical terms and $\mathfrak{B}$ the set of predicates of the program. For the sake of simplicity, we consider any program function identifier as being a particular program variable, and any logic function and predicate identifier as being a particular logic binder. The partial function $\mathcal{F} : \mathcal{V} \rightharpoonup \mathcal{V}^* \times \mathcal{S}$, associates to each variable denoting a program function, the list of variables corresponding to its parameters together with the statement defining its body. Similarly, we assume two partial functions $\mathfrak{F} : \mathfrak{L} \rightharpoonup \mathfrak{L}^* \times \mathfrak{Z}$ and $\mathfrak{P} : \mathfrak{L} \rightharpoonup \mathfrak{L}^* \times \mathfrak{B}$ modeling respectively the set of user-defined logic functions and the set of user-defined predicates. In practice, the assumptions made are guaranteed by Frama-C [1], which also computes the functions $\mathcal{F}, \mathfrak{F}$ and $\mathfrak{P}$. For any partial function f, $f\{x \backslash v\}$ is defined as $f\{x \backslash v\}(x) = v$ and $f\{x \backslash v\}(y) = f(y)$ for any $y \neq x$. It is also worth noting the following key remark about mini-ACSL.

Remark 1 (Accessibility of logic bindings). The only logic variables in $\mathfrak{L}$ bounded in a function or predicate body are its formal parameters, although global program variables in $\mathcal{V}$ may also be bounded.

3.3   Concrete Semantics

This section defines the concrete semantics of mini-C and mini-ACSL. Let m_{int} and M_{int} be respectively the smallest and biggest integer representable in the type `int` and $\mathbb{V} = \text{Int} \cup \mathbb{U}$ be the set of values that a mini-C expression may evaluate to, where Int is the set of possible values of a variable of type `int` and $\mathbb{U}$ is an infinite set of arbitrary undefined values representing the unitialized values. We have the following bijection for the representation of `int` values: $\overline{} : \text{Int} \simeq [m_{int}, M_{int}] : \underline{}^{int}$. The use of the set $\mathbb{U}$ and the explicit bijection between Int and $[m_{int}, M_{int}]$ are not necessary for the purpose of our analysis. This details could be omitted here, but we keep them to be consistent with the semantics of [3] since we prove here assumptions of this paper. We denote by $\mathbb{B} = \{T, F\}$ the set of truth values and by $\mathbb{Z}$ be the set of mathematical integers.

The semantics of our languages is evaluated in a *concrete environment* Ω, which is a pair of two partial functions $\Omega_V : V \to$ Int and $\Omega_{\mathcal{L}} : \mathcal{L} \to \mathbb{Z}$. For the sake of simplicity, we sometimes treat Ω as a single partial function, as determining which of the component is referred to is usually non ambiguous from the context. The semantics of a mini-C statement s is expressed by the judgment $\Omega \vDash s \Rightarrow \Omega'$, stating that evaluating s in the environment Ω yields the environment Ω'. Similarly, the semantics of a mini-C expression e is expressed by the judgment $\Omega \vDash e \Rightarrow v$, with $v \in V$, the semantics of a mini-ACSL predicate p is expressed by the judgment $\Omega \vDash p \Rightarrow b$ with $b \in \mathbb{B}$ and the semantics of a mini-ACSL term is expressed by the judgment $\Omega \vDash t \Rightarrow z$ with $z \in \mathbb{Z}$. Figure 3 presents the derivation rules for the semantics of mini-C. The result of a call to function f is transmitted from the callee to the caller through a distinguished variable res_f. The rest of this semantics is fairly standard and straightforward. Figure 4 presents the semantics of the mini-ACSL specification language. Again this semantics is quite standard, except that terms evaluate in the set of mathematical integers $\mathbb{Z}$ and not in the set of machine integers.

Semantics of declarations
$$\frac{x \notin \mathrm{dom}(\Omega_V) \qquad u \in U}{\Omega_V, \Omega_{\mathcal{L}} \vDash \mathtt{int}\ x \Rightarrow \Omega_V\{x \backslash u\}, \Omega_{\mathcal{L}}}$$

Semantics of statements

$$\frac{}{\Omega \vDash \mathtt{skip};\ \Rightarrow \Omega} \qquad \frac{\Omega_V(x) \in V \qquad \Omega_V, \Omega_{\mathcal{L}} \vDash e \Rightarrow z}{\Omega_V, \Omega_{\mathcal{L}} \vDash x\ =\ e \Rightarrow \Omega_V\{x \backslash z\}, \Omega_{\mathcal{L}}} \qquad \frac{\Omega \vDash s \Rightarrow \Omega' \qquad \Omega' \vDash s' \Rightarrow \Omega''}{\Omega \vDash s\ s' \Rightarrow \Omega''}$$

$$\frac{\Omega \vDash e \Rightarrow z \qquad z \neq 0^{\mathsf{int}} \qquad \Omega \vDash s \Rightarrow \Omega'}{\Omega \vDash \mathtt{if}(e)\ \mathtt{then}\ s\ \mathtt{else}\ s' \Rightarrow \Omega'} \qquad \frac{\Omega \vDash e \Rightarrow 0^{\mathsf{int}} \qquad \Omega \vDash s' \Rightarrow \Omega'}{\Omega \vDash \mathtt{if}(e)\ \mathtt{then}\ s\ \mathtt{else}\ s' \Rightarrow \Omega'}$$

$$\frac{\Omega \vDash \mathtt{if}(e)\ \mathtt{then}\ s;\ \mathtt{while}(e)\ s\ \mathtt{else}\ \mathtt{skip} \Rightarrow \Omega'}{\Omega \vDash \mathtt{while}(e)\ s \Rightarrow \Omega'}$$

$$\frac{\Omega \vDash e \Rightarrow z \qquad z \neq 0}{\Omega \vDash \mathtt{assert}(e) \Rightarrow \Omega} \qquad \frac{\Omega \vDash p \Rightarrow T}{\Omega \vDash \mathtt{/*@\ assert}\ p\ \mathtt{*/} \Rightarrow \Omega} \qquad \frac{\Omega_V, \Omega_{\mathcal{L}} \vDash e \Rightarrow z}{\Omega_V, \Omega_{\mathcal{L}} \vDash \mathtt{return}(e) \Rightarrow \Omega_V\{res_f \backslash z\}, \Omega_{\mathcal{L}}}$$

$$\frac{\mathcal{F}(f) = (x_1, \ldots, x_n; b)}{\Omega \vDash e_1 \Rightarrow z_1; \ldots; \Omega \vDash e_n \Rightarrow z_n \qquad \{x_1 \backslash z_1, \ldots, x_n \backslash z_n\}, \Omega_{\mathcal{L}} \vDash b \Rightarrow \Omega'_V, \Omega'_{\mathcal{L}} \qquad \Omega'_V(res_f) = z}{\Omega_V, \Omega_{\mathcal{L}} \vDash c\ =\ f(e_1, \ldots, e_n) \Rightarrow \Omega_V\{c \backslash z\}, \Omega_{\mathcal{L}}}$$

Semantics of expressions

$$\frac{\Omega_V(x) = z}{\Omega \vDash z_m \Rightarrow z_m} \qquad \frac{\Omega_V(x) = z}{\Omega \vDash x \Rightarrow z} \qquad \frac{\Omega \vDash e \Rightarrow z \qquad \Omega \vDash e' \Rightarrow z' \qquad \dot{z} \triangleleft \dot{z}'}{\Omega \vDash e \triangleleft_{\mathbf{C}}\ e' \Rightarrow 1^{\mathsf{int}}} \qquad \frac{\Omega \vDash e \Rightarrow z \qquad \Omega \vDash e' \Rightarrow z' \qquad \dot{z} \not\triangleleft \dot{z}'}{\Omega \vDash e \triangleleft_{\mathbf{C}}\ e' \Rightarrow 0^{\mathsf{int}}}$$

$$\frac{\Omega \vDash e \Rightarrow z \qquad \Omega \vDash e' \Rightarrow z' \qquad m_{\mathsf{int}} \leq \dot{z} \diamond \dot{z}' \leq M_{\mathsf{int}} \qquad \mathrm{not}(\diamond_{\mathbf{C}} = /\ \mathrm{and}\ \dot{z}' = 0)}{\Omega \vDash e \diamond_{\mathbf{C}}\ e' \Rightarrow (\dot{z} \diamond \dot{z}')^{\mathsf{int}}} \quad \begin{array}{l}(\triangleleft\ \text{models}\ \triangleleft_{\mathbf{C}};\\ \diamond\ \text{models}\ \diamond_{\mathbf{C}})\end{array}$$

Fig. 3. Semantics of the mini-C language.

The semantics presented here is blocking, that is only correct programs with correct annotations can be ascribed a semantics using these rules. In particular, terms and predicates calling logic definitions with ill-formed recursion schemes have no semantics, since as soon as a call is non-terminating, there is no finite derivation tree to ascribe a semantics to it. Constructs that would lead to runtime

Rules for terms

$$\frac{}{\Omega \vDash z \Rightarrow z} \qquad \frac{\Omega_{\mathcal{L}}(x) = z}{\Omega \vDash x \Rightarrow z} \qquad \frac{x \in \mathsf{Int} \quad \Omega_{\mathcal{V}}(v) = x}{\Omega \vDash v \Rightarrow \dot{x}}$$

$$\frac{\Omega \vDash t \Rightarrow z \quad \Omega \vDash t' \Rightarrow z' \quad \text{not } (\diamond = / \text{ and } z' = 0)}{\Omega \vDash t \diamond t' \Rightarrow z \diamond z'}$$

$$\frac{\Omega \vDash p \Rightarrow \mathrm{T} \quad \Omega \vDash t \Rightarrow z}{\Omega \vDash p\ ?\ t\ :\ t' \Rightarrow z} \qquad \frac{\Omega \vDash p \Rightarrow \mathrm{F} \quad \Omega \vDash t' \Rightarrow z'}{\Omega \vDash p\ ?\ t\ :\ t' \Rightarrow z'}$$

$$\frac{\mathfrak{F}(f) = (x_1, \ldots, x_n; b)}{\Omega_{\mathcal{V}}, \Omega_{\mathcal{L}} \vDash t_1 \Rightarrow z_1; \ldots; \Omega_{\mathcal{V}}, \Omega_{\mathcal{L}} \vDash t_n \Rightarrow z_n \quad \Omega_{\mathcal{V}}, \{x_1 \backslash z_1, \ldots, x_n \backslash z_n\} \vDash b \Rightarrow z}{\Omega_{\mathcal{V}}, \Omega_{\mathcal{L}} \vDash f(t_1, \ldots, t_n) \Rightarrow z}$$

Rules for predicates

$$\frac{}{\Omega \vDash \backslash\mathtt{true} \Rightarrow \mathrm{T}} \qquad \frac{}{\Omega \vDash \backslash\mathtt{false} \Rightarrow \mathrm{F}} \qquad \frac{\Omega \vDash p \Rightarrow \mathrm{F}}{\Omega \vDash\ !\ p \Rightarrow \mathrm{T}} \qquad \frac{\Omega \vDash p \Rightarrow \mathrm{T}}{\Omega \vDash\ !\ p \Rightarrow \mathrm{F}}$$

$$\frac{\Omega \vDash t \Rightarrow z \quad \Omega \vDash t' \Rightarrow z' \quad z \vartriangleleft z'}{\Omega \vDash t \vartriangleleft t' \Rightarrow \mathrm{T}} \qquad \frac{\Omega \vDash t \Rightarrow z \quad \Omega \vDash t' \Rightarrow z' \quad z \ntriangleleft z'}{\Omega \vDash t \vartriangleleft t' \Rightarrow \mathrm{F}}$$

$$\frac{\Omega \vDash p \Rightarrow \mathrm{T}}{\Omega \vDash p\ ||\ p' \Rightarrow \mathrm{T}} \qquad \frac{\Omega \vDash p \Rightarrow \mathrm{F} \quad \Omega \vDash p' \Rightarrow z}{\Omega \vDash p\ ||\ p' \Rightarrow z}$$

$$\frac{\mathfrak{P}(p) = (x_1, \ldots, x_n; b)}{\Omega_{\mathcal{V}}, \Omega_{\mathcal{L}} \vDash t_1 \Rightarrow z_1; \ldots; \Omega_{\mathcal{V}}, \Omega_{\mathcal{L}} \vDash t_n \Rightarrow z_n \quad \Omega_{\mathcal{V}}, \{x_1 \backslash z_1, \ldots, x_n \backslash z_n\} \vDash b \Rightarrow z}{\Omega_{\mathcal{V}}, \Omega_{\mathcal{L}} \vDash p(t_1, \ldots, t_n) \Rightarrow z}$$

Fig. 4. Semantics of the mini-ACSL language.

errors, which are restricted to division by zero in our arithmetic context, have also no semantics. In practice, E-ACSL embeds a mechanism that checks at runtime potential runtime errors such as divisions by zero in terms and predicates before executing them [9]. It allows E-ACSL to not add executable undefined behaviors in the generated code. This mechanism is not presented here.

3.4 Collecting Semantics

Our static analysis is based on abstract interpretation. Proving its correctness in Sect. 5 requires to show that its result includes the results from all concrete executions. A common way to proceed is to first define the *collecting semantics* that computes all these results at once. Since our analysis focuses on terms, we only define it for such constructs, not for the others. Let us denote $\varXi \in \mathcal{P}(\mathcal{L} \rightharpoonup \mathbb{Z})$ a collecting environment, i.e. a set of partial functions from binders to integers (otherwise said, a set of logic environments). The collecting semantics $\mathcal{C}(\varXi, t)$ of a term t in an environment $\varXi$ is then defined as follows:

$$\mathcal{C}(\varXi, t) \equiv \{z \mid \exists \Omega_{\mathcal{L}} \in \varXi, \exists \Omega_{\mathcal{V}} : \mathcal{V} \rightharpoonup [\mathrm{m_{int}}, \mathrm{M_{int}}], \Omega_{\mathcal{V}}, \Omega_{\mathcal{L}} \vDash t \Rightarrow z\}.$$

4   Abstract Interpretation Without Logic Functions

This section presents our static analysis based on abstract interpretation, assuming there is no logic definition: they will be added in Sect. 5. We only analyze mini-ACSL annotations: no static analysis is performed on the mini-C code. Our aim is to provide an interval associated to each term, so that a monitor generator can decide whether the term can be safely monitored with machine integers. If the interval contains integers that do not fit into machine integers, the monitor will perform the computation in arbitrary precision arithmetic for soundness. The monitor generator that uses the interval computed here is presented in [3].

4.1 Lattice of Intervals

Our analysis is only based on the integer interval domain, presented here. Indeed, while more evolved domains might provide more precise answers, it would be less efficient and could prevent E-ACSL to be as fast as optimizing compilers. The precision of the interval domain is enough in practice. Would a more precise domain be necessary in the future, our analysis could easily be adapted.

$\mathcal{I}$ denotes the set of (possibly empty) integer intervals with possibly infinite bounds. We denote by $\perp$ the empty interval and $\top$ the interval with infinite lower and upper bounds, which is $\mathbb{Z}$ itself. $\mathcal{I}$ and the set inclusion $\subseteq$ as partial order is a lattice. The join operator $\vee$ (resp. meet operator $\wedge$) is the set union $\cup$ (resp. set intersection $\cap$). We introduce the pair of maps $\mathcal{P}(\mathbb{Z}) \underset{\gamma}{\overset{\alpha}{\rightleftarrows}} \mathcal{I}$. with the map α being defined by $\alpha(X) = [\min X, \max X]$, assuming that $\max X = +\infty$ (resp. $\min X = -\infty$) if X has no upper (resp. lower) bound. For the empty set, we define $\alpha(\emptyset) = \perp$. α is named the abstraction map. γ, defined by $\gamma(I) = I$, is named the concretization map. This pair of maps is a Galois connection, i.e. for each $X \in \mathcal{P}(\mathbb{Z})$ and $I \in \mathcal{I}$, $X \subseteq \gamma(I)$ if and only if $\alpha(X) \subseteq I$. It allows us to convert data from the concrete world to the abstract world through α and conversely through γ, possibly by introducing approximations. Given an operator $\star$ on $\mathcal{P}(\mathbb{Z})$, we denote $\star^\sharp$ the corresponding operator on intervals, defined by $I \star^\sharp I' = \alpha(\gamma(I) \star \gamma(I'))$. This abstract operator allows us to lift operators $\diamond$ on concrete values to operators $\diamond^\sharp = \diamond^\sharp_{\text{set}}$ in the abstract world, where $\diamond_{\text{set}}$ is defined by $X \diamond_{\text{set}} Y = \{x \diamond y \mid x \in X, y \in Y\}$. We will also use *abstract environments* $\Gamma : \mathcal{L} \rightharpoonup I$ that abstract concrete environments by mapping logic variables to intervals. In order to ensure that the static analysis always terminates quickly, even in the presence of non-terminating functions, we will use a *widening* operator ∇, introduced in Sect. 6. For the time being, it is enough to know that it satisfies the two following properties, quite usual in abstract interpretation [8]:

(W1) For every pair of intervals I and I', we have $I \subseteq I \nabla I'$ and $I' \subseteq I \nabla I'$
(W2) For every increasing sequence (J_i), the sequence defined by $I_0 = J_0$ and $I_{n+1} = I_n \nabla J_{n+1}$ stabilizes.

4.2 Inference Rules

This section presents the inference rules for the derivation of interval judgments. We introduce an *environment of logic functions* $\Delta : \mathfrak{F} \rightarrow (\mathcal{L} \rightharpoonup \mathcal{I}) \times \mathcal{I}$. For each function f already encountered, it keeps track of the intervals inferred for each of f's parameters and the interval of the f's return value. This environment is useless right now in the absence of logic definitions: it will only be used in Sect. 5, but introducing it right now allows for rules of this section to remain unchanged.

In the absence of logic definition, our static analysis is a simple interval inference introduced by the judgment $\Gamma|\Delta \vdash t : I$ defined in Fig. 5. It means that the values of the mini-ACSL term t belong to the interval I.

$$\overline{\Gamma|\Delta \vdash z : [z, z]} \qquad \overline{\Gamma|\Delta \vdash x : \Gamma(x)} \qquad \overline{\Gamma|\Delta \vdash v : [\mathsf{m_{int}}, \mathsf{M_{int}}]}$$

$$\frac{\Gamma|\Delta \vdash t : I \qquad \Gamma|\Delta \vdash t' : I'}{\Gamma|\Delta \vdash t \diamond t' : I \diamond^{\sharp} I'} \qquad \frac{\Gamma|\Delta \vdash t : I \qquad \Gamma|\Delta \vdash t' : I'}{\Gamma|\Delta \vdash p\,?\,t : t' : I \cup^{\sharp} I'}$$

Fig. 5. Interval inference for the function-free core of the mini-ACSL language.

The rules are quite straightforward. The first rule associates to a constant the corresponding singleton interval. The second rule associates to a logic binder x, its interval stored in the environment Γ. The third rule associates to a C variable v the interval of integers representable in the type int. The fourth rule associates to an operation the result of its corresponding abstract operation. The last rule joins the results of both branches of a conditional. These rules are similar to the ones of [13], even if expressed here in another formalism.

4.3   Improving Precision for Conditionals

The rule for conditionals can be improved by taking into account that the condition is necessarily true in the positive branch and false in the negative one. When these properties can be encoded in the interval domain (e.g., when comparing a variable to a constant), it is possible to refine this rule to improve the precision of the analysis. Such an optimization is implemented in practice, even if the details are omitted here. For instance, when the condition is x >= 0, the rule can be refined to the following one:

$$\frac{\Gamma\{x \backslash \Gamma(x) \wedge [0, +\infty]\}|\Delta \vdash t : I \qquad \Gamma\{x \backslash \Gamma(x) \wedge [-\infty, -1]\}|\Delta \vdash t' : I'}{\Gamma|\Delta \vdash x\ {\tt >=}\ 0\,?\,t : t' : I \cup^{\sharp} I'}.$$

5   Abstract Interpretation with Logic Functions

We now extend our static analysis to handle recursive functions. We do not formalize the support for recursive predicates: it is very similar to recursive functions and even simpler since their body are Boolean values, which leads to a trivial finite lattice. Yet, they are handled in our evaluation, in Sect. 6. Throughout this section, we consider a function f such that $\mathfrak{F}(f) = (x_1, \ldots, x_n; b)$, meaning that its parameters are $x_1, \ldots x_n$ and its body is b.

5.1   Inference Rules

When encountering a function call, we need to extend the abstract environment in order to associate the interval of each argument to the corresponding function's parameter. We also need to update the abstract environment when encountering recursive calls up to reaching a fixpoint. Given an environment for logic functions Δ and a function f, we denote by $\Delta_{\mathrm{args}}(f)$ and $\Delta_{\mathrm{res}}(f)$ respectively the first and second component of $\Delta(f)$ in such a way that $\Delta(f) = (\Delta_{\mathrm{args}}(f), \Delta_{\mathrm{res}}(f))$. Given a list of intervals $I_1, \ldots, I_n$, we define $\Delta\langle f \nabla I_1, \ldots, I_n \rangle$ as follows:

$$\Delta\langle f \nabla I_1, \ldots, I_n \rangle \equiv \Delta\{f \backslash (\Gamma\{x_1 \backslash \Gamma(x_1) \nabla I_1, \ldots, x_n \backslash \Gamma(x_n) \nabla I_n\}, \Delta(f)_{\mathrm{res}})\}$$

$$\text{where } \Gamma = \Delta_{\mathrm{args}}(f).$$

This definition directly uses $\Delta_{\mathrm{args}}(f)$ in place of the abstract environment Γ, without taking care of any potential existing binding. Said otherwise, this definition does not depend on any abstract environment Γ'. This is possible since the only bounded logic variables in a function body are its formal parameters according to Remark 1, while the interval of any program variable is constant (directly derived from their types, which is necessarily int, as made explicit in Fig. 5), so we do not need to store them in the abstract environment.

Figure 6 presents the inference rules for the interval inference for logic functions. It depends on a second judgment, denoted $\Delta \vdash_f f : I$, which means that the result of the function f fits into the interval I in Δ. By convention, we consider that f not being in the domain of Δ, is equivalent to having $\Delta(f) = (\Gamma, \bot)$ with Γ the constant function equal to $\bot$. As such, this rule system is not deterministic since the premises of the rules (FUN) and (INIT) overlap, and so do those of the rules (BASE) and (IND). For determining the inference algorithm, we always apply (FUN) over (INIT) and (BASE) over (IND). The rules (BASE) and (IND) only depend on an environment of logic functions Δ and does not depend on any abstract environment Γ for the above-mentioned reason. Altogether, these rules compute two fixpoints: one over the inputs and one over the result of a function call. The rule (FUN) states that, when the fixpoint for the inputs is reached, the result of a function call is the interval computed for its body and stored in the environment Δ. The rule (INIT) initiates a fixpoint computation for the output of the function call, assuming widened intervals associated to each formal parameter before computing the function body. Such a computation also relies on a fixpoint: the rule (BASE) returns the interval computed for the body when the fixpoint is reached, while the rule (IND) is the recursive case that widens the previously computed interval for the body before computing it again.

$$\frac{\Gamma|\Delta \vdash t_1 : I_1 \quad \cdots \quad \Gamma|\Delta \vdash t_n : I_n \quad \forall i, I_i \subseteq \Delta_{\mathrm{args}}(f)(x_i)}{\Gamma|\Delta \vdash f(t_1,\ldots,t_n) : \Delta_{\mathrm{res}}(f)}(\mathrm{Fun})$$

$$\frac{\Gamma|\Delta \vdash t_1 : I_1 \quad \cdots \quad \Gamma|\Delta \vdash t_n : I_n \quad \Delta\langle f\nabla I_1,\ldots,I_n\rangle \vdash_f f : I}{\Gamma|\Delta \vdash f(t_1,\ldots,t_n) : I}(\mathrm{Init})$$

$$\frac{\Delta_{\mathrm{args}}(f)|\Delta \vdash b : I \quad I \subseteq \Delta_{\mathrm{res}}(f)}{\Delta \vdash_f f : \Delta_{\mathrm{res}}(f)}(\mathrm{Base})$$

$$\frac{\Delta_{\mathrm{args}}(f)|\Delta \vdash b : I' \quad \Delta\{f\backslash(\Delta_{\mathrm{args}}(f),\Delta_{\mathrm{res}}(f)\nabla I')\} \vdash_f f : J}{\Delta \vdash_f f : J}(\mathrm{Ind})$$

Fig. 6. Interval inference for recursive functions in mini-ACSL.

5.2   Example of Derivation

We illustrate our analysis by computing the derivation tree explicitly on a particular program. Figure 7 shows the derivation tree for the term (50) at line 6 in the example of Fig. 1, starting from an empty environment, and assuming that our widening operator satisfies the following equations

$$\bot\nabla[50,50] = [50,50] \qquad [50,50]\nabla[49,49] = [0,50] \qquad \bot\nabla[0,0] = \top.$$

These assumptions are not realistic for an actual choice of widening operator, but are taylor made for the example to converge quickly, so that we can construct a reasonably sized derivation tree. The derivation uses the following abstract environments and environments for logic functions:

$$\Gamma_1 = \{x : [50,50]\} \qquad \Delta_1 = \{f : (\Gamma_1, \bot)\} \qquad \Delta_2 = \{f : (\Gamma_1, [0,+\infty])\}$$
$$\Gamma_2 = \{x : [0,50]\} \qquad \Delta_3 = \{f : (\Gamma_2, \bot)\} \qquad \Delta_4 = \{f : (\Gamma_2, [0,+\infty])\}$$
$$\Gamma_3 = \{x : [1,50]\}.$$

For the sake of simplicity, c denotes the condition x <= 0, r denotes the recursive term f(x - 1) and b denotes the body of the function, in such a way that $b = c ? 0 : r + 1$. We also omit the environments in the abstract judgments for constants, and sometimes we also omit the whole judgment for constants, typically for most increment and decrement operations.

In this example, we can look at the environments Δ_i that appear in the derivation tree to understand how the fixpoints are computed both for the (unique) argument and the result of the function. The fixpoint for the argument is reached at the interval $[0,50]$, while the fixpoint for the result is $[0,+\infty]$. This allows us to have an argument of type int in the generated code, but is not precise enough to store the result in an int: a GMP integer is required. This observation generalizes: In practice, for recursive functions, it is much more common that our analysis gives useful information on the arguments of a function than on its output, and most of the time saved comes from performing internal computations with the arguments using machine integers. Indeed, in the presence of recursive functions, useful bounds for the results can unlikely be inferred.

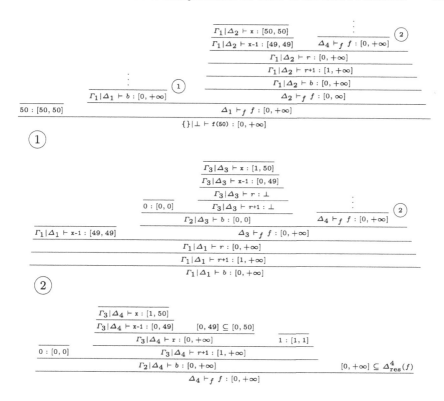

Fig. 7. Example of Interval Inference for a Recursive Function Call.

5.3   Termination of the Static Analysis

With the strategy of always chosing the rule (FUN) over (INIT) and (BASE) over (IND), our rule system is deterministic and defines an inference algorithm. This inference algorithm always terminates, as stated by the theorem below.

Theorem 1. *The rule system for intervals on mini-ACSL terms yields a terminating algorithm of interval inference.*

Proof (sketch). The proof is done by defining a well-founded order on the judgements, and showing that the judgements decrease for this order along any derivation tree. This order is defined as follows: first, we say that an environment Δ widens another one Δ' when, for every $f \in \text{dom}(\Delta)$ and x in $\text{dom}(\Delta_{\text{args}}(f))$, there is an interval $I_{f,x}$ such that $\Delta_{\text{args}}(f)(x) = \Delta'_{\text{args}}(f)(x)\nabla I_{f,x}$ and there exists an interval I_f such that $\Delta_{\text{res}}(f) = \Delta'_{\text{res}}(f)\nabla I_f$. The chosen order relation on judgments is the lexicographic order induced by this relation and the relation of being a structural subterm:

$$\Gamma|\Delta \vdash t : \_ \prec \Gamma'|\Delta' \vdash u : \_ \Leftrightarrow \begin{cases} \Delta \neq \Delta' \text{ and } \Delta \text{widens } \Delta' \\ \Delta = \Delta' \text{ and } t \text{ is a structural subterm of } u. \end{cases}$$

We also establish by convention that

$$\Gamma|\Delta \vdash t : \_ \prec \Delta' \vdash_f f : \_ \Leftrightarrow \Delta \, widens \, \Delta'$$
$$\Delta \vdash_f f : \_ \prec \Gamma|\Delta \vdash t : \_ \Leftrightarrow t \text{ is the body of } f \text{ or a structural subterm of it.}$$

This partial order $\prec$ is well-founded.

5.4 Interval Inference

Our rule system defines a deterministic inference algorithm that always terminates as stated in Theorem 1. Given an abstract environment Γ, we denote
$\mathcal{I}(\Gamma, t)$ the result of this inference on the term t in environment $\Gamma|\bot$. However,
we need to handle specifically the function's arguments that are widened. For
such an argument t of a function f appearing in a term u representing a function call, we infer the result of the function call by building the derivation of
$\Gamma|\bot \vdash f(t) : J$. In the corresponding derivation tree, consider the top-most
application of the rule (FUN) for term u. It has necessarily an hypothesis of the
form $\Gamma|\Delta \vdash t : I'$, where the interval I' is widened to the interval I associated
to t in the environment Δ_{args}. We define $\mathcal{I}(\Gamma, t)$ to be this interval I for such
function arguments. For instance, considering the term f(50) at line 6 of Fig. 1,
for which the derivation tree is shown in Fig. 7, we have $\mathcal{I}(\{\}|\bot, 50) = [0, 50]$.
Indeed, even though we first derive the interval $[50, 50]$ for its argument, it is
later widened to $[0, 50]$ in the derivation tree, as witnessed in Δ_4.

  As explained in the introduction, this paper extends the type system of [13]
(and changes its theoretical framework for relying on abstract interpretation)
in order to formalize the assumed static analysis of [3] and prove its assumptions, namely *type soundness* and *convergence*. The above-mentioned operator $\mathcal{I}$
matches the one of this latter paper. Theorem 1 ensures convergence, while
soundness is proved in the next section.

5.5 Soundness of the Static Analysis

We now prove that the static analysis is sound. Since both the inference and
the semantics require an environment, we first define a relation between such
environments. We say that an interval environment Γ *abstracts* an environment
for binders Ω, which is denoted $\Omega \triangleleft \Gamma$, if for every binder $x \in \mathrm{dom}\,(\Omega)$, we have
$x \in \mathrm{dom}\,(\Gamma)$ and $\Omega_{\mathcal{L}}(x) \in \Gamma(x)$. For a semantic environment $\Omega = (\Omega_{\mathcal{V}}, \Omega_{\mathcal{L}})$, we
define $\Omega \triangleleft \Gamma$ if and only if $\Omega_{\mathcal{L}} \triangleleft \Gamma$. For a collecting environment Ξ, we say that
Γ *abstracts* Ξ and we write $\Xi \blacktriangleleft \Gamma$ when $\Omega \triangleleft \Gamma$ for every $\Omega \in \Xi$.

Theorem 2. *For every mini-ACSL term t, every collecting environment Ξ, and
every abstract environment Γ such that $\Xi \blacktriangleleft \Gamma$, we have $\mathcal{C}(\Xi, t) \subseteq \mathcal{I}(\Gamma, t)$.*

Proof (Sketch). The proof is done by induction. It is trivial without recursive
definitions. With them, the main difficulty consists in finding the right invariants.
For this, we provides a rule system, denoted $\Xi \vDash_\Delta t \in X$ and defining the set X of
possible values for a term t in a collecting environment Ξ and an environment of

logic functions Δ. When $\Delta = \bot$, it over-approximates the collecting semantics defined in Sect. 3.4 (i. e. if the judgment $\Xi \vDash_\Delta t \in X$ is derivable, then X contains the collecting semantics) and allows us to perform a per-case reasoning. The following Lemma gives the right invariants, proved by mutual induction.

Lemma 1. *The judgments for the interval inference and fixpoint algorithm satisfy respectively each of the following property:*

1. *If the judgment $\Gamma|\Delta \vdash t : I$ is derivable in the abstract semantics, then for every collecting environment Ξ such that $\Xi \blacktriangleleft \Gamma$ and every derivation of the judgment $\Xi \vDash_\Delta t \in X$, we have $X \subseteq I$.*
2. *If the judgment $\Delta \vdash_f f : I$ is derivable in the abstract semantics, then denoting by b the body of the function, for every collecting environment Ξ such that $\Xi \blacktriangleleft \Delta_{\text{args}}$ and every derivation of the judgment $\Xi \vDash_{\Delta_{\text{res}}\{f\setminus I\}} b \in X$ in the collecting semantics augmented by $\Delta_{\text{res}}\{f\setminus I\}$, we have $X \subseteq I$.*

This theorem implies the soundness corollary below.

Corollary 1 (Interval Soundness). *For every mini-ACSL term t in an environment Ω such that there is a derivation of the semantics $\Omega \vDash t \Rightarrow z$, and for every abstract environment Γ such that $\Omega \vartriangleleft \Gamma$, we have $z \in \mathcal{I}(\Gamma, t)$.*

6   Experimental Evaluation

This section deals with the practical aspects of implementing our static analysis to analyse user-defined logic definitions and generate efficient monitors.

6.1   Practical Widening Operators

Our formal presentation is agnostic to the chosen widening operator, as long as it satisfies the properties mentioned in Sect. 4.1. However, in practice, the choice of this operator matters since it results in generating monitors with different efficiency. The choice is always a trade-off between efficiency and precision: depending on the widening operator, the fixpoint algorithm will converge in a small or large number of steps to a precise or unprecise interval. Our experimentation compares three different widening operators, presented below. The first two operators are extreme cases, which are only introduced for being compared against the third one, which is better and used by default in E-ACSL.

- The "naive widening", defined by the following formula

$$I_1 \nabla_{\text{naive}} I_2 = \begin{cases} I_2 & \text{if } I_1 = \bot \\ \top & \text{otherwise} \end{cases}$$

This widening strategy makes the fixpoint reached in at most two iterations. Yet, it is extremely imprecise. In fact, it often returns $\top$ for recursive functions: only non-recursive functions are handled precisely.

– The "precise widening", defined by the following formula

$$I_1 \nabla_{\text{precise}} I_2 = \begin{cases} I_1 \vee I_2 & \text{if } I_1 \vee I_2 \subseteq [\text{m}_{\text{int}}, \text{M}_{\text{int}}] \\ \top & \text{otherwise} \end{cases}$$

This widening strategy is quite opposite to the naive one: it converges extremely slowly, but is very precise. In practice, the convergence is too slow for any practical application, and the monitor generation even takes too much time on minimal examples.

– The "smart widening", defined by $I_1 \nabla_{\text{smart}} I_2 = [a, b]$ where

$$a = \begin{cases} \min I_1 & \text{if } \min I_2 \geq \min I_1 \\ \text{m}_{\text{int}} & \text{if } \text{m}_{\text{int}} \leq \min I_2 \leq \min I_1 \\ -\infty & \text{otherwise;} \end{cases} \quad b = \begin{cases} \max I_1 & \text{if } \max I_2 \leq \max I_1 \\ \text{M}_{\text{int}} & \text{if } \text{M}_{\text{int}} \geq \max I_2 \geq \max I_1 \\ +\infty & \text{otherwise} \end{cases}$$

When the function is not decreasing, this operator leaves the lower bound unchanged. Otherwise, it directly approximates it to m_{int} if the lower bounds of both operands are bigger and goes to $-\infty$ otherwise. The behavior is similar for the upper bound and an increasing function. In practice, E-ACSL generalises it to a family of C types, and not only one by jumping from the boundary of one type to the other (e.g., from int to long).

6.2   Evaluation and Comparison of Widening Choices

The static analysis formalized in this paper is implemented within E-ACSL [20], the runtime assertion checker of Frama-C [1]. It supports the three widening operators of Sect. 6.1. It is used to optimize the code of the generated monitor, as formalized on the same mini-C and mini-ACSL languages in [3]. It is worth noting that the language supported by E-ACSL is much larger than mini-C and mini-ACSL [19], and so is the implementation of our static analysis.

We have run a few different examples to evaluate our static analysis and the widening strategy. The precise strategy is quite unusable even in simple tests since the monitor generation is dramatically slow in that case. Hence we only present the results of the experimental evaluation of the smart widening against the naive one. We ran the test on 4 different annotated C files[2]: linear.c contains definitions of typical recursive logic functions, where $f(n)$ is an affine function of $f(n-1)$, fibonacci.c contains the definition and various calls to the Fibonacci function, mergesort.c contains a C implementation of merge sort as well as a few recursive predicates that assert that the resulting array contains the same elements as the original one and is sorted, and finally complex.c contains arbitrary recursive functions with complex recursion schemes. We ran the benchmark on a laptop equipped with a 16-core AMD Ryzen 7 processor and 32GB of RAM. For each file, we measured the time for generating the monitor

---

[2] Source files and scripts of at https://thibautbenjamin.github.io/software/ benchmarks-tap23.zip, the version of Frama-C/E-ACSL at https://thibautbenjamin. github.io/software/frama-c-tap23.zip.

and for running it, with both the naive and the smart widening strategies. Each measure was performed with the hyperfine[3] software and repeated 10 times. The results are displayed in Fig. 8, where the mean of the 10 runs is written along with the standard deviation (all the durations are given in seconds). They are also compared to runs (named GMP) for which the static analysis was not used, so that only GMP operations are used at runtime. For each test case, the column gen is the time for generating the code, while the column exe is the time for executing the generated monitor. The last two lines show the gain of the smart widening operator with respect to using GMP only, or using the naive strategy. Figure 9 graphically presents these results.

	linear.c		fibonacci.c		mergesort.c		complex.c	
	gen	exe	gen	exe	gen	exe	gen	exe
GMP	1.217 ± 0.008	96.034± 1.450	1.270 ± 0.007	75.617± 0.900	1.305 ± 0.009	71.196± 1.189	1.214 ± 0.006	Fails
naive	1.210 ± 0.007	95.866± 1.177	1.267 ± 0.005	75.454± 0.342	1.305 ± 0.007	62.170± 1.046	1.231 ± 0.010	52.453± 0.827
smart	1.207 ± 0.008	59.141± 0.363	1.294 ± 0.006	35.620± 0.366	1.300 ± 0.006	63.291± 0.552	1.217 ± 0.009	50.644± 0.217
vs. GMP	N/A	38%	N/A	53%	N/A	11%	N/A	Fails
vs. naive	N/A	38%	N/A	53%	N/A	N/A	N/A	N/A

Fig. 8. Experimental Evaluation With Different Widening Strategies.

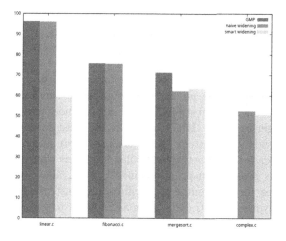

Fig. 9. Evaluation of Monitor Efficiency.

Overall, running the fixpoint algorithm with the smart widening as opposed to the naive one comes with no noticeable cost for the monitor generation. As

[3] https://github.com/sharkdp/hyperfine.

already mentioned, the cost of generating the monitor using the precise widening is prohibitive on all these examples, and therefore not displayed here. In terms of efficiency when running the generated monitor, the smart widening performs significantly better on every case than with no analysis at all. In particular, on the file `complex.c`, without analysis, the generated program sometimes fails to execute properly because it is too resource intensive and exceeds the memory limit. The widening strategy is also significant: on the files `linear.c` and `fibonacci.c`, the smart widening performs respectively 38% and 53% better than the naive widening, which does not perform better than the systematic use of GMP. On the contrary, for the `mergesort` and `complex` examples, the smart widening and the naive widening leads to similar efficiency, which is better than the systematic use of GMP. Indeed, the file `complex.c` contains complicated recursion schemes, on which the heuristics implemented in the smart widening fail, and the file `mergesort.c` contains mostly calls to functions whose arguments are C variables, whose intervals are already fixpoints of the function.

6.3   Further Improvements to Widening

As illustrated by our evaluation, the widening strategy is important in practice. It is also impactful for the efficiency of monitor generator. The current "smart" strategy is based on the intuition that, in practice, the boundary of C types are likely to be values of importance, where the function may change behavior, and thus are good candidates for looking for fixpoints. Few other heuristics might also be used, even if not yet experimented with nor implemented. First, one could also widen to the boundary of C types plus (or minus for the lower bound) a small offset, in order to take into account typical off-by-one. This case might be frequent enough that adding those values to the candidates might give good results. Another possible improvement for the widening strategy could be to run a small syntactic analysis to look for important constants, and add those to our widening steps. For this idea to be viable, the analysis has to be very lightweight in order to ensure that it does not induce a significant overhead on the monitor generation. In all of these suggestions, we are adding more widening steps, which makes the convergence slower. It is likely that the most satisfying solution is to keep our "smart" widening strategy as a default, and run other more precise ones only on a case by case basis for the particular functions where the default is not good enough. It is possible in practice since E-ACSL allows choosing different widening strategies for different logic definitions. Last, we could also benefit from existing analysis on the C code, such as EVA [5], to gain precision of the C program variables used in the logic definitions.

7   Conclusion and Further Work

This article has presented a static analysis based on abstract interpretation for infering intervals in logic definitions used in formal code annotations. We have proved its termination and soundness properties and evaluated its practical efficiency, which depends on a widening strategy that have been discussed.

It extends the work of [13] to logic definitions. This static analysis is used for generating efficient monitor for runtime assertion checking of arithmetic properties by allowing the code generator to soundly and efficiently choose between machine bounded integers and exact mathematical integers. How the monitors are generated based on our analysis is formalized in [3].

Three different widening strategies have been explored in this paper: investigating others strategies is left to future work, as well evaluating other abstract domains. Extending our formalization to rational numbers [13], memory properties [16], multi-state properties [12,18] or how to deal with undefined terms such as division by zero [9] is also left to future work. Our formalization effort would also greatly benefit from using a proof assistant, such as Coq [4]. Last, our static analysis might be complemented by a mechanism that would decide at runtime to use machine or mathematical integers. Such mechanisms already exist on top of exact arithmetic libraries, e.g., ZArith[4] for OCaml.

References

1. Baudin, P., et al.: The dogged pursuit of bug-free C programs: the frama-C software analysis platform. Commun. ACM (2021)
2. Baudin, P., Filliâtre, J.C., Marché, C., Monate, B., Moy, Y., Prevosto, V.: ACSL: ANSI/ISO C Specification Language. Tech. rep., CEA List and Inria. https://frama-c.com/download/acsl.pdf
3. Benjamin, T., Signoles, J.: Formalizing an efficient runtime assertion checker for an arithmetic language with functions and predicates. In: Symposium on Applied Computing (2023)
4. Bertot, Y., Castéran, P.: Interactive theorem proving and program development: Coq'Art: the calculus of inductive constructions. Springer Science & Business Media (2013)
5. Blazy, S., Bühler, D., Yakobowski, B.: Structuring abstract interpreters through state and value abstractions. In: International Conference on Verification, Model Checking, and Abstract Interpretation (VMCAI 2017) (2017)
6. Cheon, Y.: A runtime assertion checker for the Java Modeling Language. Ph.D. thesis, Iowa State University (2003)
7. Clarke, L.A., Rosenblum, D.S.: A historical perspective on runtime assertion checking in software development. SIGSOFT Softw. Eng. Notes (2006)
8. Cousot, P.: Principles of Abstract Interpretation. MIT Press (2022)
9. Delahaye, M., Kosmatov, N., Signoles, J.: Common specification language for static and dynamic analysis of C programs. In: Symposium on Applied Computing (SAC) (2013)
10. Falcone, Y., Havelund, K., Reger, G.: A tutorial on runtime verification. In: Engineering Dependable Software Systems (2013)
11. Filliâtre, J.C., Pascutto, C.: Ortac: runtime assertion checking for OCaml (tool paper). In: International Conference on Runtime Verification (RV) (2021)
12. Filliâtre, J.C., Pascutto, C.: Optimizing prestate copies in runtime verification of function postconditions. In: International Conference on Runtime Verification (RV) (2022)

---

[4] https://github.com/ocaml/Zarith/.

13. Kosmatov, N., Maurica, F., Signoles, J.: Efficient runtime assertion checking for properties over mathematical numbers. In: International Conference on Runtime Verification (RV) (2020)
14. Leavens, G.T., Baker, A.L., Ruby, C.: JML: A Notation for Detailed Design (1999)
15. Lehner, H.: A Formal Definition of JML in Coq and its Application to Runtime Assertion Checking. Ph.D. thesis, ETH Zurich (2011)
16. Ly, D., Kosmatov, N., Loulergue, F., Signoles, J.: Verified runtime assertion checking for memory properties. In: International Conference on Tests and Proofs (TAP) (2020)
17. Ly, D., Kosmatov, N., Loulergue, F., Signoles, J.: Soundness of a dataflow analysis for memory monitoring. In: Workshop on Languages and Tools for Ensuring Cyber-Resilience in Critical Software-Intensive Systems (HILT) (2018)
18. Signoles, J.: The E-ACSL perspective on runtime assertion checking. In: International Workshop on Verification and mOnitoring at Runtime EXecution (VOR-TEX) (2021)
19. Signoles, J.: E-ACSL Version 1.18. Implementation in Frama-C Plug-in E-ACSL 26.1 (2022). http://frama-c.com/download/e-acsl/e-acsl-implementation.pdf
20. Signoles, J., Kosmatov, N., Vorobyov, K.: E-ACSL, a runtime verification tool for safety and security of C programs tool paper. In: International Workshop on Competitions, Usability, Benchmarks, Evaluation, and Standardisation for Runtime Verification Tools (RV-CuBES) (2017)

Author Index

A
Antignac, Thibaud 68
Arias, Jaime 127
Arnaud, Mathilde 68

B
Benajmin, Thibaut 168
Bennani, Mohamed Taha 127
Boulmé, Sylvain 40

C
Cimini, Matteo 108
Clouet, Myriam 68

D
Desel, Jörg 127

E
Engel, Daniel 3

G
Gogolla, Martin 97
Gourdin, Léo 40

H
Hamann, Lars 97
Hurault, Aurélie 51

K
Klai, Kais 127

L
Lebeltel, Olivier 40

M
Marques-Silva, Joao 51
Mitsch, Stefan 149
Monniaux, David 40

N
Naus, Nico 21

O
Ochi, Hanen 127

R
Ravindran, Binoy 3, 21

S
Schoolderman, Marc 21
Signoles, Julien 68, 168
Strauss, Megan 149

V
Verbeek, Freek 3, 21

V. Prevosto and C. Seceleanu (Eds.): TAP 2023, LNCS 14066, p. 187, 2023.
https://doi.org/10.1007/978-3-031-38828-6

Printed in the United States
by Baker & Taylor Publisher Services